AF477932

Cousins in Love:

The Letters of
Lydia DuGard, 1665–1672

with a new edition of
The Marriages of Cousin Germans
by Samuel DuGard

MEDIEVAL AND RENAISSANCE TEXTS AND STUDIES

VOLUME 268

RENAISSANCE ENGLISH TEXT SOCIETY

SEVENTH SERIES
VOLUME XXVIII (FOR 2003)

Cousins in Love:

The Letters of Lydia DuGard, 1665–1672

with a new edition of
The Marriages of Cousin Germans
by Samuel DuGard

by

Nancy Taylor

Arizona Center for Medieval and Renaissance Studies
in conjunction with
Renaissance English Text Society
Tempe, Arizona
2003

Library of Congress Cataloging-in-Publication Data
Cousins in love : the letters of Lydia DuGard, 1665–1672 : with a new edition of
  The marriages of cousin Germans by Samuel DuGard / [edited] by Nancy
  Taylor.
        p. cm. — (Medieval & Renaissance texts & studies ; v. 268) (Renais-
    sance English Text Society ; 7th ser., v. 28)
    Includes bibliographical references and index.
    ISBN 0-86698-311-2 (acid-free paper)
        1. DuGard, Lydia, 1650–1675 — Correspondence. 2. Dugard, Samuel,
    1645?–1697 — Correspondence. 3. Women — England — Warwickshire —
    Correspondence. 4. Consanguinity — England — History — 17th century.
    I. DuGard, Lydia, 1650–1675. II. Dugard, Samuel, 1645?–1697. III. Dugard,
    Samuel, 1645?–1697. Marriages of cousin Germans. IV. Taylor, Nancy,
    1941– V. Arizona Center for Medieval and Renaissance Studies. VI. Title:
    Marriages of cousin Germans. VII. Medieval & Renaissance Texts &
    Studies (Series) ; v. 268. VIII. Renaissance English Text Society (Series) ;
    v. 28.
    CT788.D848A4 2003
    942.4'806'092—dc22   2003063732

To Fritz

Contents

Acknowledgments

This book has been a long time coming and could never have been completed without the generous help of so many. First of all, thanks to Laetitia Yeandle from the Folger Shakespeare Library, who introduced me to Lydia's letters. She and her colleagues at the Folger Library have supported the project enthusiastically and helped me at every turn. Certainly the Folger is a wonderful place to work. The Evergreen State College, where I have taught for thirty-four years, supported me financially through sabbatical leaves and sponsored research grants, allowing me to work in the British Library and at the Folger Library. Evergreen is a college devoted to teaching, but my colleagues continually inquired about Lydia and found ways to support my research and to use pieces of my work in programs they were teaching. Special thanks to Nancy Allen, Virginia Darney, Rudy Martin, Liza Rognas, Thad Curtz, Peter Elbow, and Cam Stivers. Susan Reynolds and Sara van den Berg read through the entire book at different stages and provided many helpful corrections and suggestions. Professional staff at numerous county record offices and libraries, especially the Warwickshire County Record Office, the Hereford and Worcestershire County Record Office, Queen's College Library, Oxford, and the Guildhall Library were willing to provide research assistance, even online, in the last stages. Over many cups of tea at the British Library, Al Braunmuller showed me how to do this editing work; he was incredibly patient and persistent, teaching me each step of the way. He, Arthur Kinney, and Carolyn Kent read through the entire book for MRTS. Thanks to Bill Gentrup, who shepherded me through the final editing; his careful reading certainly has made this a better book. And thanks to Nina Douglas for helping me with the layout of the family tree, and to Elspeth Pope for doing the index. I am most grateful to all. But most especially, I never could have conceived this project or completed it without the constant encouragement, support and help from my husband, Fritz Levy. He got to know Lydia as well as I did and was at my side throughout the whole project. He deserves special recognition and enormous thanks. I, of course, take responsibility for any errors.

List of Abbreviations

BL   British Library, London

Bodl.   Bodleian Library, Oxford

BPR   Barford Parish Register, Warwickshire County Record Office, Warwick

DNB   *Dictionary of National Biography*, ed. Leslie Stephen and Sidney Lee, 63 vols. (London: Smith, Elder, and Co., 1885–1900).

Errata   A reading from the errata list of the 1673 edition of *The Marriages of Cousin Germans*

Fasti   *Athenae Oxonienses, An exact history of all the writers and bishops who have had their education in the most ancient and famous University of Oxford, from . . . 1500 to the end of . . . 1690 . . . To which are added, the Fasti or Annals of the said university for the same time.* A new edition, with additions, and a continuation by Philip Bliss, 4 vols. (London: F. C. and J. Rivington, 1813–1820). The *Fasti* were issued in two parts. Part I is in volume 3; part II is in volume 4.

Folger   Folger Shakespeare Library, Washington, D. C.

Foster   *Alumni Oxonienses, 1500–1714*, ed. Joseph Foster, 4 vols. (Oxford and London: James Parker & Co., 1891– 1892).

FPR   Forton Parish Register, Staffordshire Record Office, Stafford

Guildhall   Guildhall Library, London

HWCRO   Herefordshire and Worcestershire County Record Office, Worcester

New Grove *The New Grove Dictionary of Music and Musicians*, 2nd ed., ed. Stanley Sadie, 29 vols. (London: Macmillan Publishers Limited, 2001).

OED   *The Oxford English Dictionary*, 2nd ed., ed. J. A. Simpson and E. S. C. Weiner, 20 vols. (New York: Oxford University Press, and Oxford: Clarendon Press, 1989).

Plomer (1907) Henry R. Plomer, *A Dictionary of the Booksellers and Printers Who Were at Work in England, Scotland and Ireland from 1641–1667* (London: Oxford University Press, 1907).

Plomer (1922)   Henry R. Plomer, *A Dictionary of the Printers and Booksellers Who Were at Work in England, Scotland and Ireland from 1668–1725* (London: Oxford University Press, 1922).

PRO   Public Record Office, Kew

SLPPR   St. Laurence Pountney Parish Register, Guildhall Library, London

STC   *A Short-Title Catalogue of Books Printed in England, Scotland, & Ireland, 1475–1640*, ed. A. W. Pollard and G. R. Redgrave, 3 vols. (London: The Bibliographical Society, 1991).

Tilley   Morris Palmer Tilley, *A Dictionary of the Proverbs in the Sixteenth and Seventeenth Centuries* (Ann Arbor: University of Michigan Press, 1950).

VCH   *The Victoria History of the County of Warwick.* General editor: L. F. Salzman; vol. 2, ed. William Page; vol. 6, ed. L. F. Salzman; vol. 8, ed. W. B. Stephens; 8 vols. (London: Oxford University Press, 1904–1969).

Venn   *Alumni Cantabrigienses*, ed. John Venn and J. A. Venn, 4 vols. (Cambridge: Cambridge University Press, 1922)

Visitations   *The Visitations of the County of Warwickshire, 1682–1683*, vol. 62 (London: Harleian Society, 1911).

WCRO   Warwickshire County Record Office, Warwick

William Dugard Will   The National Archives, PRO, PROB 11/309/quire 135, proved 14 December 1662. *Prerogative Court of Canterbury Wills (1661–1670)*, ed. J. H. Morrison (London: Morrison, 1935), 77–78.

Wing   Donald Wing, *Short-Title Catalogue of Books Printed in England . . . , 1641–1700*, rev. and ed. John J. Morrison et al., 3 vols. (New York: Modern Language Association of America, 1994).

Wood   Anthony à Wood, *Athenae Oxonienses, An exact history of all the writers and bishops who have had their education in the most ancient and famous University of Oxford, from . . . 1500 to the end of . . . 1690 . . . To which are added, the Fasti or Annals of the said university for the same time.* A new edition, with additions, and a continuation by Philip Bliss, 4 vols. (London: F. C. and J. Rivington, 1813–1820).

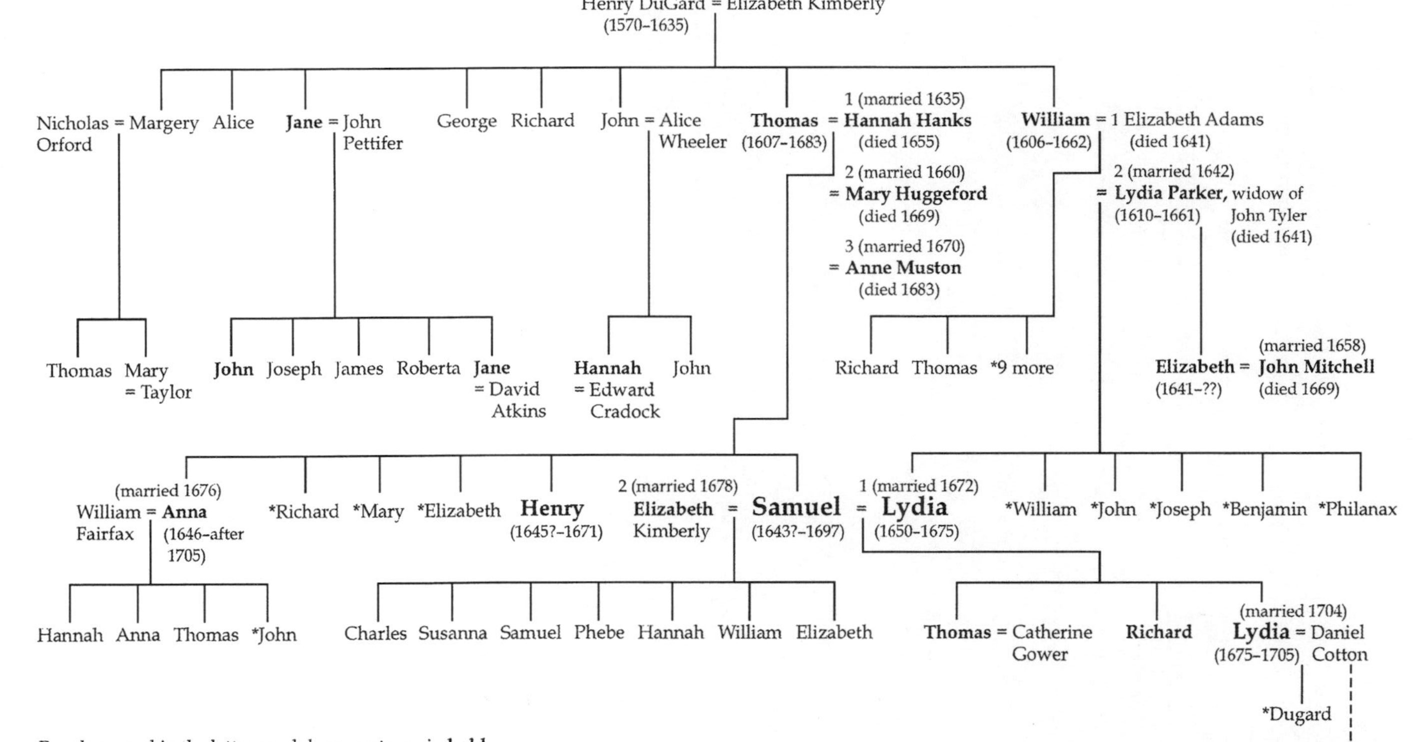

Henry DuGard = Elizabeth Kimberly
(1570–1635)

Nicholas = Margery   Alice   Jane = John   George   Richard   John = Alice   Thomas = Hannah Hanks   William = 1 Elizabeth Adams
Orford   Pettifer   Wheeler   (1607–1683)   1 (married 1635)   (1606–1662)   (died 1641)
                                                                                              (died 1655)
                                                                                  2 (married 1660)   2 (married 1642)
                                                                                  = Mary Huggeford   = Lydia Parker, widow of
                                                                                  (died 1669)   (1610–1661)   John Tyler
                                                                                                                  (died 1641)
                                                                                  3 (married 1670)
                                                                                  = Anne Muston
                                                                                  (died 1683)

Thomas   Mary   John   Joseph   James   Roberta   Jane   Hannah   John   Richard   Thomas   *9 more   Elizabeth = John Mitchell
= Taylor   = David   = Edward   (1641–??)   (died 1669)
                        Atkins   Cradock   (married 1658)

(married 1676)
William = Anna   *Richard   *Mary   *Elizabeth   Henry   Elizabeth = Samuel = Lydia   *William   *John   *Joseph   *Benjamin   *Philanax
Fairfax   (1646–after   (1645?–1671)   Kimberly   (1643?–1697)   (1650–1675)
            1705)   2 (married 1678)   1 (married 1672)

Hannah   Anna   Thomas   *John   Charles   Susanna   Samuel   Phebe   Hannah   William   Elizabeth   Thomas = Catherine   Richard   Lydia = Daniel
                                                                                                          Gower   (1675–1705)   Cotton
                                                                                                                                  (married 1704)

*Dugard

Jestin Homfray = Mary Anne
                        Cotton

People named in the letters and documents are in bold.
* Died in infancy

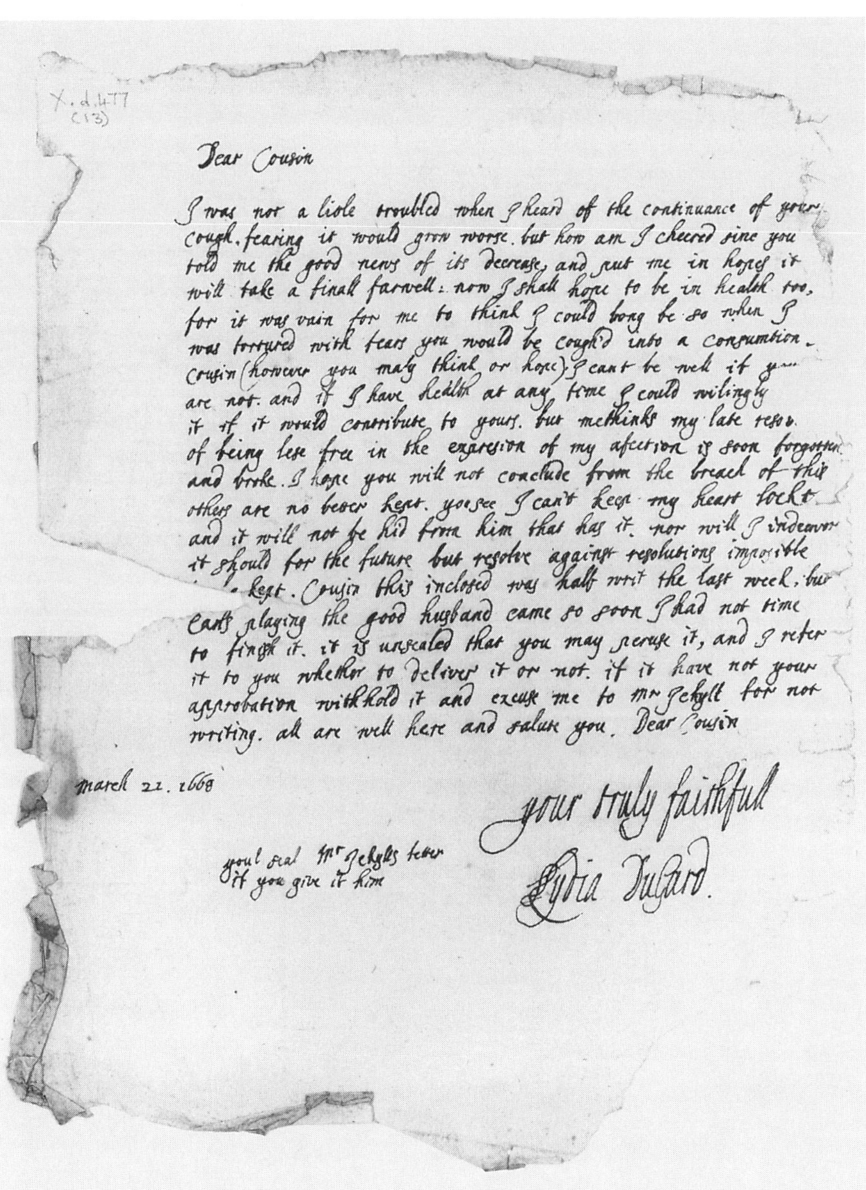

Dear Cousin

I was not a litle troubled when I heard of the continuance of your
cough. fearing it would grow worse. but how am I cheered since you
told me the good news of its decrease, and put me in hopes it
will take a finall farwell: now I shall hope to be in health too,
for it was vain for me to think I could bong be so when I
was tortured with fears you would be cough'd into a consumtion.
Cousin (however you may think or hope) I can't be well if you
are not. and if I have health at any time I could willingly
it if it would contribute to yours. but methinks my late reso.
of being lese free in the expresion of my afection is soon forgoten
and broke. I hope you will not conclude from the breach of this
others are no beter kept. yee see I can't keep my heart lockt
and it will not be hid from him that has it. nor will I indeavor
it should for the future but resolve against resolutions imposible
       kept. Cousin this inclosed was half writ the last week. but
Eastr playing the good husband came so soon I had not time
to finish it. it is unsealed that you may peruse it, and I refer
it to you whether to deliver it or not. if it have not your
approbation withhold it and excuse me to mr gekyll for not
writing. all are well here and salute you. Dear Cousin

march 22. 1668

youl seal mr gekyls teter
it you give it him

your truly faithful
Lydia Dugard.

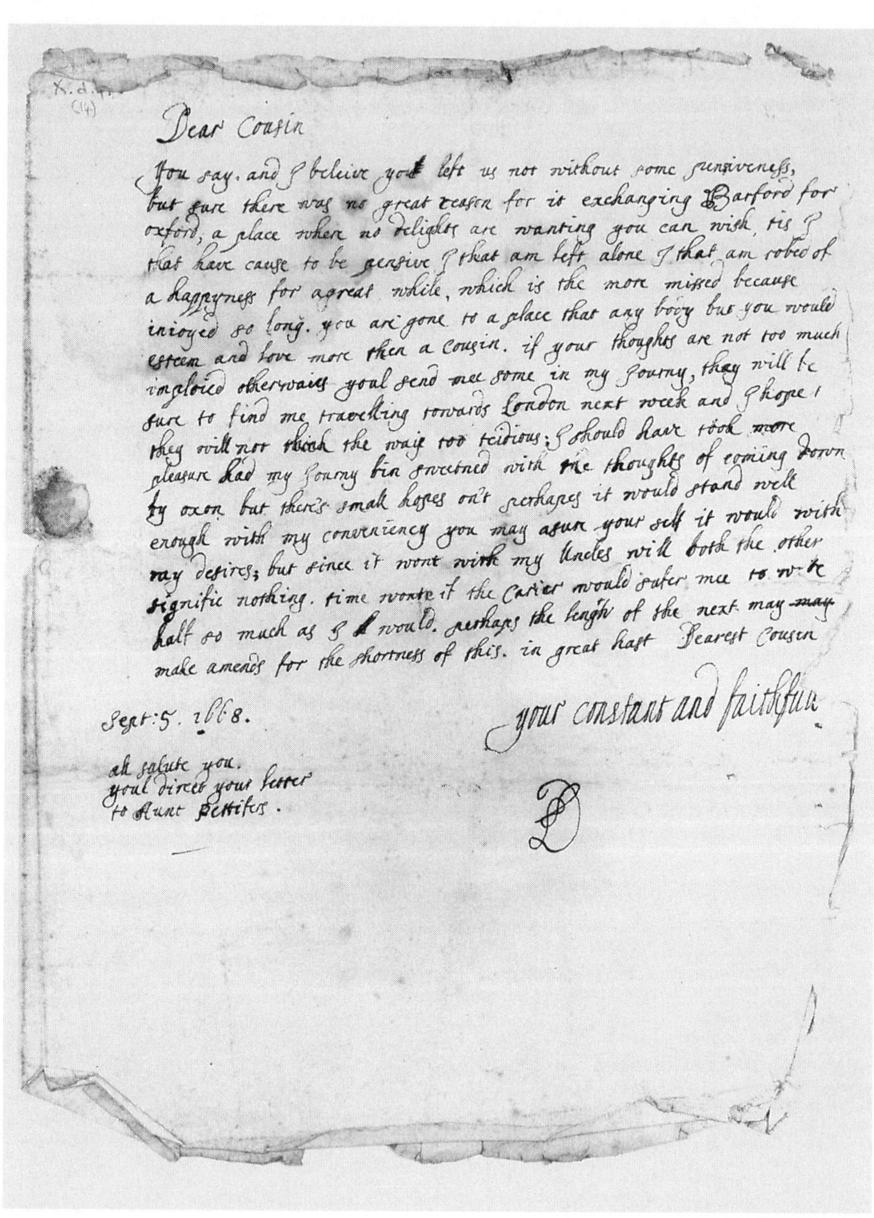

Dear Cousin

You say, and I beleive you left us not without some pensiveness,
but sure there was no great reason for it exchanging Barford for
oxford, a place where no delights are wanting you can wish, tis I
that have cause to be pensive I that am left alone I that am robed of
a happyness for agreat while, which is the more missed because
inioyed so long. you are gone to a place that any body but you would
esteem and love more then a Cousin. if your thoughts are not too much
imploied otherwaies youl send mee some in my Iourny, they will be
sure to find me travelling towards London next week and I hope
they will not think the waie too teidious; I should have took more
pleasure had my Iourny bin sweetned with the thoughts of coming down
by oxon but there's small hopes on't perhapes it would stand well
enough with my conveniency you may asure your self it would with
my desires; but since it wont with my Uncles will both the other
signifie nothing. time wonte it the Carier would sufer mee to write
half so much as I would. perhaps the length of the next may
make amends for the shortness of this. in great hast Dearest Cousin

Sept: 5. 1668.

all salute you.
youl direct your letter
to Aunt pettifer.

your constant and faithful

Introduction to the Letters

Lydia DuGard loved her cousin, Samuel, with all her heart. In 1665 at the age of fifteen she began a correspondence with him, which lasted until they got married in 1672. Her letters, which have been transcribed below, tell the story of this young woman's blossoming love and of her life in a small English village in Warwickshire. Her courtship with Samuel was complicated by their being first cousins. His response, clearly based on his own love for Lydia and his determination to marry her, was to write a treatise in support of first-cousin or cousin-german marriages. This treatise, entitled *The Marriages of Cousin Germans, Vindicated from the Censures of Unlawfullnesse, and Inexpediency,* has been included in this volume as well.

The thirty-two personal letters are especially unusual because of Lydia's social position. She belonged to the self-described "middling sort" of people. These people, defined in part by their occupations, were made up of clergy, schoolmasters, farmers, tradesmen, and minor gentry who were elevated to gentle status by virtue of their education, lifestyles, their civic responsibility, and their access to positions of authority.[1] In fact Lydia came from a family of clergyman and schoolmasters, the intellectual fringe of the "middling sort," people with significant education and responsibility but without significant wealth or land.[2] This singles her letters out since they allow a glimpse into the lives of women from a group not widely known. The letters tell a touching story in a woman's own voice, a story about courtship and love and about the daily life and thoughts of this young English woman living in the late seventeenth century.

The sheer quantity of Lydia's personal writings furthers the possibility of studying how a woman constructs a self within the context of that society. Primary to that construction is her relationship with Samuel. Lydia presents

---

[1] Keith Wrightson, "Estates, Degrees and Sorts: Changing Perceptions of Society in Tudor and Stuart England," in *Language, History, and Class,* ed. Penelope J. Corfield (Cambridge, Mass.: Basil Blackwell, 1991), 41.

[2] Margaret R. Hunt, *The Middling Sort: Commerce, Gender, and the Family in England, 1680–1780* (Berkeley: University of California Press, 1996), 20.

herself as the person she wants Samuel to know; her letters are meant for him alone. Because the act of writing necessarily involves selecting and interpreting, the content of the letters cannot be seen as a transparent account of Lydia's experiences. However, as Clifford Geertz has said, the self is constructed within a network of social values and relationships.[3] Reading Lydia's story involves uncovering at least three codes in this network: the codes of accepted women's behavior, of family and kin relationships, and of romantic love. Within these codes, and despite the way she foregrounds her relationship with Samuel, Lydia tells a story about herself.

Because Lydia was the child of a professional teacher and printer, a surprising amount of her early history can be retrieved. Lydia was born to William and Lydia DuGard in London in 1650;[4] she lived with her family in the city until 1662. Her father, William DuGard,[5] was headmaster of the Merchant Taylors' School and a member of the Stationers' Company. Although information is scant about Lydia's upbringing, her early life, centered around her father, appears to have been far from serene. DuGard was an active printer who got into trouble with the authorities for printing a royalist tract condemning the execution of Charles I;[6] he was dismissed from the school and his family put out of its housing. He spent a month in Newgate Prison just before Lydia was born. After being reinstated as headmaster he remained active in the Stationers' Company, printing the Greek and Latin textbooks[7] he had written, which had gained him

---

[3] Clifford Geertz, "Deep Play: Notes on a Balinese Cockfight," in his *The Interpretation of Cultures* (New York: Basic Books, 1973), 448.

[4] William DuGard married Lydia Tyler 22 March 1642 at All Hallows Stayning in London ("Allegations for Marriage Licences Issued by the Bishop of London," extracted by Joseph Chester and edited by G. J. Armytage, 2 vols. [Harleian Society 26, 1887], 2:264). This was the second marriage for both husband and wife. William's first wife, Elizabeth Adams, had died in 1641 leaving behind two sons, Richard and Thomas; Lydia's first husband, John Tyler, goldsmith, had died in 1641 leaving behind one daughter, Elizabeth. Lydia was baptized 30 September 1650 (SLPPR, Guildhall MS 7670).

[5] William DuGard (1606–1662), B.A. (1626); M.A. (1630); Sidney Sussex College, Cambridge. *DNB*, s.v. "DuGard, William"; Plomer (1907), 67–68; Wood, 3:366, 491.

[6] Plomer (1907), 67–68; Claudius Salmasius, *Defensio Regia Pro Carolo Primo* (London, 1650; Wing S737). In 1651 DuGard printed John Milton's *Pro Populo Anglicano Defensio* (Wing M2167), a rebuttal to Salmasius.

[7] DuGard's Greek grammar, *Græcæ Grammatices Rudimenta* (Wing D2466), first published in 1654, went through several editions and was widely used as a grammar school textbook. Among other books that he printed for use in his school were Lucian's

a good reputation among other schoolmasters, and serving as an inspector of grammar schools. Yet he continued to cause trouble for school authorities, printing controversial religious tracts and ignoring school statutes. By 1661 the school authorities had had enough and dismissed DuGard from his position, ostensibly because he had admitted more boys than the statutes allowed.[8] The more important, but unstated, violation was his failure to abide by the condition under which he was hired: "that he should not attend or follow anie other calling during his continuance of cheife schoole-master."[9]

Lydia's mother was totally occupied by the bearing of and caring for her children. In her first marriage she had given birth to a daughter, Elizabeth,[10] who was just one year old when her mother remarried. Elizabeth joined William's two sons, Richard and Thomas,[11] in family housing on Suffolk Lane provided by Merchant Taylors' School, where the family lived until 1661. There

---

Dialogues (1649), his own *Rhetorices Elementa* (1648; Wing D2468), and *Lexicon Græci Testimenti Alphabeticum* (1660; Wing D2467).

[8] The school statutes fixed the number of boys at 250, 100 to be children of poor parents, 50 to be children of a little higher economic status and 100 to be children of rich or middle-class parents. DuGard was dismissed for admitting 275 boys. *Merchant Taylors' School Register* (1562–1699), ed. Charles J. Robinson, 2 vols. (Lewes: Farncombe & Co., 1882–1883), 1:xiii.

[9] Cited in F. W. M. Draper, *Four Centuries of Merchant Taylors' School, 1561–1961* (London: Oxford University Press, 1962), 61.

[10] Elizabeth Tyler, daughter of Lydia and John Tyler, was baptised in London 16 September 1641, just two days after her father's death (All Hallows Lombard Street Parish Register, Guildhall MS 17613). She must have been born a year earlier, for she is mentioned in her father's will dated 6 November 1640 (Will of John Tyler, proved 14 September 1641, PRO, PROB 11/187 quire 99). She lived in the DuGard household until she married John Mitchell, 1 January 1658, and moved to Coventry (SLPPR; Guildhall MS 7670). Lydia lived with Elizabeth in Coventry after her father died (Folger MS X.d.477/2). This is the Folger Shakespeare Library reference in full. All future references to Lydia DuGard's letters are indicated simply by their number in boldface within the text. See commentary to Letter **2** here.

[11] Richard, born 25 June 1634 in Stamford, Lincolnshire, enrolled in Merchant Taylors' School, his father's school, in 1644 and matriculated at St. John's College, Oxford, in 1650. Thomas, born 29 November 1635, also in Stamford, enrolled in Merchant Taylors' School in 1644 as well; he was admitted Sizar of Sidney Sussex College, Cambridge, in 1649. Both died before 1662, unmarried, according to Thomas DuGard, Lydia's uncle. (*Merchant Taylors' School Register*, 1:157; Foster, 1:429; *Visitations*, 112.)

Lydia's mother gave birth to five sons between 1643 and 1649; three of these sons died before Lydia was born and two in 1650, the very year of her birth.[12] Since Richard and Thomas went to university in 1649, Elizabeth Tyler was the only sibling that Lydia would have known well. Elizabeth was nine years old when Lydia was born. Just after her father's second dismissal from the Merchant Taylors' School in 1661, when the family was living in Newington Butts, Lydia's mother died.[13] William moved to nearby Sion College in London, a society established in 1623 especially for the clergy.[14] Apparently, Lydia was sent off to Coventry to live with her now married half-sister, Elizabeth Mitchell. Just one year later, William himself died.[15] Out of the total of William's seventeen children, Lydia, the last born, was the only surviving child.[16] She was named sole heir of her father's estate and was entrusted to the care of a guardian, her

---

[12] They were William, born 1643, died 1643; John, born 1644, died 1647; Joseph, born 1645, died 1648; Benjamin, born 1648, died 1650; and Philanax, born 1649, died 1650 (St. Olave, Hart Street Parish Register, Guildhall MS 28868; SLPPR, Guildhall M s 7670). The death rate for children at this time was one in five before age ten; the highest death rate was in the first year. Clearly, the DuGard family suffered extraordinarily. See Roger Schofield and E. A. Wrigley, "Infant and Child Mortality in England in the Late Tudor and Early Stuart Period," in *Health, Medicine, and Mortality in the Sixteenth Century*, ed. Charles Webster (Cambridge: Cambridge University Press, 1979), 61–95. Also, Patricia Crawford and Laura Gowing, eds., *Women's World in Seventeenth-Century England* (London: Routledge, 2000), 187.

[13] On 27 August 1661, William DuGard paid 0/13/4 to have his wife, Lydia DuGard, buried in St. Laurence Pountney Parish Church (Churchwarden's Accounts, Guildhall MS 7670).

[14] Sion College was founded in 1623 under the will of Dr. Thomas White as a "college for . . . ministers, parsons, vicars, lectures and curates within London and also for a convenient almshouse for twenty persons, ten men and ten women." It was built in 1629 and a library was added in 1630. The building was on the south side of London Wall, west and south of St. Alphage Church. William Reading, *History of Sion College* (London, 1724), 8–15.

[15] "3 December 1662 Mr. Will DuGard, a schoolmaster" (SLPPR, Guildhall MS 7670).

[16] In a poem written on the occasion of William DuGard's death, Samuel DuGard, his nephew, explicitly states that sixteen sons and daughters had preceded their father in death (Bodl., Rawl. Poet., fols. 32–32v, 33–33v).

father's good friend Edward Waterhouse, the heraldic and legal writer, who also resided at Sion College in London.[17]

Lydia, then, grew up in London, in the midst of a well-established school run by her father, who defied authority and participated actively in public affairs, and in the midst of extraordinary family suffering. It is impossible to determine how she was educated. Because no girls were enrolled at the Merchant Taylors' School, either she was tutored by her father or mother, or else she attended a London dame school or one of the increasingly popular girls' boarding schools.[18] Certainly living in London among schoolboys and having brothers and cousins visiting from university must have made her mindful of education, even if opportunities for girls were limited. She would have learned to read first and then to write. Since her writing is really very proficient, her schooling must have been extensive, whether at home or not.

Sometime between 1662 and 1665 Lydia moved from her sister's house in Coventry to Barford, a small Warwickshire village of some twenty households, to live with her father's brother and his family in the old rectory. Thomas DuGard, who had been headmaster of Warwick Grammar School for fifteen years, had become rector of St. Peter's in 1648. His first wife, Hannah died in 1655, leaving three children: Samuel, Henry, and Anna.[19] Then in 1660 Thomas

---

[17] Lydia's cousin, Henry DuGard, was named beneficiary in the event that Lydia died before she was of age and able to inherit. Edward Waterhouse served as Lydia's guardian until his death on 30 May 1670 (William Dugard's Will).

[18] For a comprehensive description of education for girls in the seventeenth century, see Dorothy Gardiner, *English Girlhood at School* (London: Oxford University Press, 1929). Also see Hunt, *The Middling Sort*, 73–100; Anthony Fletcher, *Gender, Sex, and Subordination in England, 1500–1800* (New Haven: Yale University Press, 1995), 364–75; and Margaret J. M. Ezell, *The Patriarch's Wife* (Chapel Hill: University of North Carolina Press, 1987), 9–16.

[19] Samuel, Henry, and Anna were all born in St. Mary's parish in Warwick while Thomas was headmaster of Warwick School. However, exact birth dates cannot be ascertained since there is a gap in the parish register at the very time their births would have occurred. Letters written by Hannah DuGard to the Wyllys family in Connecticut indicated that Anna was born in May 1646. See Hannah DuGard in the Biographical Appendix and *The Wyllys Papers, 1590–1796*, in *Collections of the Connecticut Historical Society*, 21, ed. A. C. Bates (Hartford: Connecticut Historical Society, 1924), 90–91, 106–8. Samuel was most likely born in 1643 and Henry in 1645. Thomas DuGard recorded his wife's death in his parish register on 4 December 1655: "Death of Mrs. Hannah DuGard, the most vertuous and accomplish'd wife of Mr. Thomas DuGard, Rector" (BPR, DR48/3).

married Mary Huggeford of Henwood, near Solihull.[20] It was this second wife, Mary, who welcomed Lydia into her new home, and who provided her with motherly advice and help in her adolescent years. Mary died in October 1669, and sometime in 1670 Thomas married his third wife, Anne.[21] As will be seen in the letters, both stepmothers, Mary and Anne, played an important role as confidants to Lydia. Her cousin Anna, only four years older than she, lived with her in the rectory as a sister and provided continual companionship for her. Henry, the younger of the two brothers, lived in the household until 1664, when he left for Oxford to join his brother. Lydia may have moved to Barford before then. Samuel had gone off to Trinity College, Oxford, in 1661, so clearly she never lived with him growing up, but she must have gotten to know him over school holidays, and somehow they found time to fall in love.

The letters begin in 1665 when Lydia is just fifteen years old; one letter (1) is written to Henry; the others all go to Samuel in Oxford. Although the early writing is typically clear, but labored, as is common among young women's writing, Lydia already displays a keen sense of what she wants and the resolve to get it. Her character quickly emerges as one of determination and certainty. These letters are private; they do not show someone involved in political intrigue like Brilliana Harley or writing letters for publication like Dorothy Osborne.[22] Instead Lydia's letters portray a dutiful, young woman of strong feelings, writing ardent, intimate letters to the one she loves:

> for me to excuse my self were but to agravate the faughlt: and you would question the truth of it if I should say I wanted time to write to you: no Cousen I know no employment would be more pleasing if my

---

8

heade (which you know was never to pregnant) were as ready as my hand. (2)

These are Lydia's first words sent to Samuel at Trinity College. Lydia is not an advocate for change or someone protesting oppression, but she knows what she wants. She has very specific concerns: to overcome the barriers standing in the way of her marrying Samuel, the man she loves. Her words are remarkably strong, even at fifteen, and they get stronger. She does not define herself in terms of the tasks she performs or as a member of a family with obligations, although she accepts her role as a woman and "husswife" and welcomes her membership in a family (27). Instead, at least in these letters, she sees herself as the one in love with Samuel DuGard, and this provides the center of her identity. Every action she takes, every word she utters is made with Samuel's views in mind (2, 6, 21, 29). In her eyes her future depends totally upon him.

However, Lydia lives in a gendered world, whether she states it explicitly or not, and the letters are permeated with signs of the authority of men over women.[23] She submits unhappily to her uncle's dictating whether and when she can travel and the routes she has to take (14, 17). She fears his criticism for spending too much money while living in Worcester, even though this money is her own (21). In her relationship with Samuel she actually asks him to tell her what to do, refusing to make decisions for herself. She cannot even have a good time with her young relatives in Worcester without having second thoughts, saying that she would rather be alone than have fun when he is absent (24). In her mind Samuel gives her everything she wants: love, recognition, approval, support, praise, attention, advice, and security. Or so she tells the story. And she is happy to defer to him. Anything that gets in the way of her relationship with Samuel makes her unhappy, but it is in these situations that she shows her remarkable strength. For example, when her guardian attempts to match her with a gentleman from London, she scorns the attempt and persuades her uncle not to invite the young man to Barford (9). Yet outside the relationship with Samuel, Lydia fits a pattern typical of a seventeenth-century woman. She is loyal, sympathetic, protective, and motherly; she is sure of her feelings and unsure of her intellectual abilities. She wants to please, to be loved, to say and do the right things. She reflects the very common female traits of melancholy

---

[23] See Keith Wrightson, *English Society, 1580–1680* (London: Hutchinson, 1982), 90–92; Fletcher, *Gender, Sex, and Subordination*, 376–400.

and self-doubt; she is fearful of authority and of what people think of her. Still, she is far from timid, and she is certainly capable of asserting herself in writing. When she needs to act to protect herself from losing Samuel, she is perfectly capable of doing so.

What kind of a person was Samuel? In the absence of his letters to Lydia, there are two sources for his character: what Lydia reports him as saying in his letters to her and what he says in his own more official and public writings. Certainly Samuel had known Lydia as a child, for he was invited to visit his uncle, Lydia's father, in 1662, when she was twelve, and he wrote a poem on the occasion of William DuGard's death.[24] Judging by Lydia's responses to Samuel's letters, it appears that Samuel had as much affection for her as she did for him. Lydia indicates that he regularly sends letters to her expressing his love, including verses that he insists Lydia not show his father (17), and he sends little courtship presents. He worries about her if he does not receive a letter, and he says he dreams of her and has her constantly in his thoughts (3). This loving attention begins very early in the correspondence and never wanes. Samuel enjoys teasing Lydia about overstating her love, and he plays lighthearted jokes on her. (She is able to give back some of this teasing.) He praises Lydia for her writing skill and for her intelligence and states over and over again his respect for her (28). Exhibiting a strain of insecurity, he fears that Lydia would prefer staying in London or marrying a man with a greater fortune (22). He also goes through a period of melancholy, feeling confined in his fellowship at Oxford, fearing that he will not be able to provide well enough for Lydia and that she would be better off with someone else. Samuel does not want Lydia to suffer inconveniences and hardships on his account and asks her to try to be patient with him. Depression sets in when he is turned down by several parishes and, at this point, he begins to show signs of bitterness, believing that men less qualified are getting positions that he deserves (27). In terms of his relationships with his family, he clearly honors and loves his father but is intimidated by him. He has difficulties with his brother Henry, who constantly gets into trouble at Oxford, but he cares for him tenderly before his death (26). There are many

---

[24] William DuGard wrote to Samuel at Trinity College inviting him to come to London for a visit, 8 July 1662. On 16 July, William wrote again saying that he approved of Samuel's declining to visit London without having first obtained permission from his father (Bodl., Tanner MS 48, fols. 16, 22). Samuel's letter to his uncle is not extant, but see note 16 above for the location of the poem.

references to his ability to win people over by his generosity, to comfort them, to treat them kindly, whether they are relatives, pupils, or neighbors. So the picture that emerges is of a kind, sincere, conservative, and gentle man, constant in his views and concerned about Lydia and about his family. However, as the letters show, he also accepts, without questioning, the dominant role he is expected to play in his relationship to Lydia, and he acts accordingly.

Through Samuel's own more official and public documents comes a slightly different picture.[25] In these writings he emphasizes not his personal relationship with Lydia but his public identity at Oxford, within the church and within the neighborhood. He constructs a self that is comfortable in the world of men, one of strong patriarchal values, of scholarship, and of religious conviction. However, even through his public statements written during his courtship, his love for Lydia is evident. As the author of *The Marriages of Cousin Germans*, he shows himself to be dutiful to his father, fearful about what he and Lydia might be getting into, and intellectually more systematic than original. He earnestly wants to justify his actions, and he wants Lydia to feel confident in her marriage decision. In this public tract, Samuel alleges he was not a person involved in a cousin-german marriage, but this is transparently false.[26] Here he is a bit disingenuous. He is desperately in love with Lydia and equally desperate to gain his father's approval. He aims his words particularly at these two: "But, if I may make a wish more than Ordinary for this Paper, I would Choose one place peculiarly for its good acceptance, and that upon the account of two Persons, whose Credit and Interest is no less dear to me then mine own. . . ."[27] He is writing these words at the very same time Lydia speaks of their growing love and his efforts to find a living, so that he can leave his fellowship and get married (28). And by the time his treatise is published, he is indeed married, and he and Lydia have a young son.

The letters show Lydia and Samuel becoming more and more attracted to each another. Indications of the blossoming courtship are evident in the ex-

---

[25] Samuel DuGard published three books: *The Marriages of Cousin Germans Vindicated from the Censures of Unlawfullnesse and Inexpediency* (Oxford, 1673; Wing D2459); *A Discourse Concerning the Having Many Children* (London, 1695; Wing D2460); *The True Nature of Divine Law* (London, 1687; Wing D2461).

[26] See *Marriages of Cousin Germans*, below, 151.

[27] "The Epistle to the Reader," below, 151

change of gifts,[28] the time spent alone together, the rejection of other matches, and, finally, their pledges of love. Lydia keeps telling him she cannot love him any more than she already does, because she loves him as much as is possible. She tries to control her expressions of love, for fear she might make a fool of herself, but she admits that "I can't keep my heart lockd and it will not be hid from him that has it"(13). When her guardian, Mr. Waterhouse, attempted to match her with a London gentleman in November 1667, when she was just seventeen, she indicates her firm commitment to Samuel and reveals her growing self-confidence: "thus Cousin I have accquainted you with his [Waterhouse's] intent that you may see how I can scorn and despise all others with one thought of you and how firm and unshaken my afection is" (9). The first mention of marriage comes in January 1668; clearly from then on the two are in charge of their own destiny.[29] Lydia's joking about sending her ring in a copy of *The Mother's Blessing*[30] – "I could find never another book I could so well spare" – suggests their increased, but innocent, intimacy (**29**). The feeling is apparently mutual, for Samuel says if he cannot have her, he will marry no one. Lydia herself goes so far as to say that she has mean thoughts about men, but that Samuel is different; she would rather "venture leading Apes in hell" than marry anyone else (**23**). Samuel must have been proud of Lydia and pleased by his relationship with her, since he showed her letter to the president of his college (**28**). Lydia, though, shows herself to be much more idealistic about the marriage than Samuel. She has a positive frame of mind. He, on the other hand, is hesitant, not knowing how to act and wanting support at each step. He is certainly under much more external pressure. Yet when he does act, he does so

---

[28] The receiving and acceptance of gifts was seen as evidence of intentions in court cases, underscoring the significance of sending gifts. See Laura Gowing, *Domestic Dangers: Women, Words, and Sex in Early Modern London* (Oxford: Clarendon Press, 1996), 159–64.

[29] But they must wait until Lydia is twenty-one or else have the permission of her guardian, Edward Waterhouse. "The church canons of 1604 insisted that those marrying under the age of twenty-one should have their parents' or guardian's consent" according to Ralph A. Houlbrooke, *The English Family, 1450–1700* (London: Longman, 1984), 166–67.

[30] Dorothy Leigh, *The Mother's Blessing* (London, 1616; STC 15402). By 1670 there had been fourteen editions of this book. For a discussion of it, see Elaine Beilin, *Redeeming Eve* (Princeton: Princeton University Press, 1987), 275–80. It is available in full in *Women's Writing in Stuart England*, ed. Sylvia Brown (Stroud, Gloucestershire: Sutton Publishing, 1999), 3–87.

impulsively. Once he decides to do what he wants — that is, to marry Lydia — he does so in short order. As late as 25 March1672, Samuel had not made a decision, although he surely was talking about it. Just three weeks later, the two got married — Lydia in her "old Cloaths, and with an empty purss" (30).

Their words and actions demonstrate that the notion of romantic love was for them a familiar one and that individual initiative was an accepted factor in determining marriage partners. Marriage based on personal choice was not new in the late seventeenth century.[31] In fact, once men and women came of age,[32] the only essential ingredient to a legal marriage was the individual consent of the two people involved. Still, all kinds of factors could keep couples from exercising their legal rights to marry: financial arrangements, respect for family wishes, personal situations, prospects for employment, and the need to abide by church regulations. The normal pattern was to adhere to the wishes and suggestions of family and friends in making such an important decision. Samuel and Lydia, both quite dutiful by nature, want their family's blessings, so they carry out their courtship with sensitivity. They are fortunate in having a sympathetic family, which gradually come to accept their love. Moreover, they also have an advantage over other couples, for neither one is financially dependent on family money alone. Samuel would surely acquire a living eventually, and once Lydia reached the age of twenty-one she is legally entitled to her portion.

Other couples handled situations involving parental unease or displeasure differently. Dorothy Osborne and William Temple waited until their parents died before marrying in order not to go against their wishes.[33] In another less well-known case, Brilliana Mitchell married the man she loved, Richard Smith,

---

[31] Alan Macfarlane, *Marriage and Love in England, 1300–1840* (Oxford: Basil Blackwell, 1986), 124.

[32] The civil law and the common law state that females come of age at twelve and males at fourteen. However, as indicated above, church courts stated both men and women were supposed to have permission from parents or guardian to marry if they were under twenty-one. See note 29. "Children under the age of 21 were forbidden to marry without the consent of their parents of guardians, while marriage by licence required proof of parental consent irrespective of the age of the parties; but marriages made in contravention of these regulations were not declared invalid." Martin Ingram, *Church Courts, Sex, and Marriage, 1570–1640* (Cambridge: Cambridge University Press, 1987), 135–36.

[33] *Dorothy Osborne: Letters*, 4–6.

in spite of family objections, both religious and social. Mr. Smith was Roman Catholic and a glover, a station beneath the Harley family. Edward Harley, Brilliana's guardian, made every effort to annul her marriage, but he could not interfere in this personal choice to marry.[34] He did, however, make Brilliana suffer financially for acting without his approval, and she was only able to gain her portion by court order one year after her marriage and after a long, painful ordeal with her relatives.

In Samuel and Lydia's case, the objection was never very strong and appeared limited to Thomas DuGard, who was won over before the wedding took place, even though he refused to marry them himself (29). Something about the personality of the two can be seen, however, from their patience and concern not to offend their family and not to draw attention to themselves; the letters never even hint of an open confrontation.

However, there were three impediments to their marriage, all alluded to in the letters: the sensitivity over the controversy surrounding the marriage of first cousins; the need for Samuel to obtain a living, so that he could provide for Lydia and himself; and the settling of Lydia's portion. When Lydia mentions the "matter" or the "business," she is always referring to her hopes for marriage.

There was never any question about the legality of a marriage between Samuel and Lydia as cousins german. Such marriages had been legal in England since 1563. Still, some memory of the old prohibition must have lingered, and even in the 1670s people remained concerned about kinship marriages despite their evident legality.[35] Thomas DuGard was hesitant about giving Samuel and Lydia his unconditional approval (11), and there are frequent hints in the letters that friends and neighbors looked upon the relationship disapprovingly. Thus,

---

[34] Brilliana Mitchell married Richard Smith, glover of York, on 26 September 1685. She had been apprenticed in the Royal Exchange from 1682 and had two more years remaining when she married secretly. Edward Harley, her guardian, was in the midst of arranging a match for her at the time. She was under the age of twenty-one, which meant that in the eyes of the church she could not marry without her guardian's permission. Nevertheless, the marriage was legal since both partners had consented. Settling Brilliana's portion involved complicated legal maneuvers and endless agony for the Harleys. She was finally paid her portion by court order in 1686. The whole story can be found in the BL, Add. MS 70233, fols. 183–84, 267.

[35] Sir Bramston expressed great nervousness when his daughter married her first cousin. *The Autobiography of Sir John Bramston*, ed. Lord Braybrooke, Camden Society, o. s. 32 (London: John Bowyer Nichols and Sons, 1845), 105, 348.

both Lydia and Samuel felt cautious about announcing their desire to marry and tried to keep their plans secret (4).

Samuel's preoccupation with this issue of the marriage of first cousins is clear from *The Marriages of Cousin Germans, Vindicated from the Censures of Unlawfullnesse, and Inexpediency*, which he wrote in 1672 and eventually had published in 1673. Obviously, Samuel felt hostility from his own countrymen. As can be seen in the treatise, the people he wanted most to convince were his friends, his neighbors, and especially his father, for he referred to them directly, not to the academic or clerical community in Oxford. He ended his treatise "Sir, if you will please to think well of this *Paper*, and will give me that share in your *Love*, which I have had hitherto beyond my Deserts it shall the less matter what others think of it, or me."[36] Lydia's letters are more understandable if read with this very sensitive issue in mind.

The second impediment to the marriage was Samuel's inability to contribute his share to the marriage contract. He had become a fellow of Trinity College in June 1667 (7). Soon after, he had received his M.A. and was ordained.[37] Under the college's rules he would lose this fellowship (22) if he married, so he needed to obtain a living in order to provide for his future wife and family.[38] There are numerous references in the letters to his attempts to secure a position, but by 1672 he had not yet been successful (20, 22, 27). He was considered for a preferment in October 1670 in Baginton, near Coventry; however, the salary was very low — sixty pounds a year — and even though Sir William Bromley, patron of the living, was a friend of the family, Samuel decided against the position (20).[39] He was also hoping to become the rector of St. Nicholas, Warwick, but lost to Samuel Jemmatt in 1672;[40] he had asked Walter Blandford, the Bishop of

---

[36] See *Marriages of Cousin Germans*, below, 190.

[37] H. E. D. Blakiston, *Trinity College* (London: F. E. Robinson, 1898), 59.

[38] The statutes of Trinity College held that fellows would lose their claims in the case of "marriage, heresy, misconduct, absenteeism, or a benefice or an inheritance worth a hundred shillings a year." C. E. Mallet, *A History of the University of Oxford*, 3 vols. (1924–27; reprint, New York: Barnes and Noble, Inc., 1968), 2:158.

[39] As a comparison, Ralph Josselin was paid eighty pounds a year from 1641–1683 for his living in Earls Colne, Essex. Alan Macfarlane, *The Family Life of Ralph Josselin* (London: Cambridge University Press, 1970), 17.

[40] There is no clear indication that the man appointed was less qualified than Samuel. Samuel Jemmatt, son of the puritan divine William Jemmatt, became vicar of St. Nicholas, Warwick, 8 February 1672, and served in this capacity until his death, 3 May

Worcester, to write a letter supporting his candidacy for this position. After he was rejected, Samuel wrote to Blandford again, complaining that he had lost to a less qualified man and asking for aid in securing another position.[41] At this time he was obviously depressed about his situation, and Lydia tried to cheer him up, assuring him that she would not love him half so much if he held a large estate (**22, 27**). By 1672 Samuel was getting desperate, for he believed he could not marry without a living: seldom in seventeenth-century households did sons marry without a means of support, remaining in their parents' household.[42] To return to a father's household after establishing independence was even more rare. However, Samuel turned out to be the exception, for in February 1672 Lydia wrote that even her aunt and uncle expected the wedding and that she and Samuel would live with the senior DuGards (**29**). Samuel, in fact, did not acquire his living until a year and a half after his marriage.

Lydia had a difficult time providing her share of the contract, too. The bride was expected to bring furnishings, capital, and skills to the marriage.[43] While her father had made provision for her portion in his will, there were complications in getting the money (**30, 31**), even though she had reached her twenty-first birthday in September 1671. It is impossible to estimate the value of Lydia's inheritance; in addition to lands in Grafton Flyford, Worcestershire, and a house in Newington Butts, she might well have inherited a part of her father's printing operation that had been taken over by Henry Lloyd (**31**).[44] Still, she implied that her estate was not large (**22**). The issue of her jointure was not a problem. Apparently, Thomas DuGard was willing to agree to the wedding by March 1672, for Lydia says, "as for Joynture, Ile leave it wholly to my Uncle. for I am confident heel deal handsomely by me" (**29**).

1713. He got his B.A. (1655) from Corpus Christi and his M.A. (1658) from Magdalen Hall, Oxford (*Fasti*, pt. 2:214, 248; Foster, 2:806). He also served as Master of Lord Leicester's Hospital in Warwick for forty-one years. One of his services was to hold a school in the hospital (*VCH*, ed. William Page [1908], 2:310, and *VCH*, ed. W. B. Stephens [1969], 8:532, 549).

[41] Samuel DuGard to Walter Blandford, Bishop of Worcester, 26 January 1672 (Bodl., Tanner MS 44, fol. 282).

[42] Macfarlane, *Marriage and Love*, 28, 91, 94–95; Houlbrooke, *The English Family*, 20.

[43] Macfarlane, *Marriage and Love*, 278.

[44] Plomer (1907), 119; Plomer (1922), 191. Henry Lloyd is listed as a printer in London, 1662–1675. Lloyd took over William DuGard's press in 1662 when DuGard died.

But one more problem stood in the couple's way. Samuel wanted to keep his marriage secret so that he could retain his fellowship as long as possible. Therefore, he wished to avoid the public calling of banns and to marry outside his own parish. To do this he needed to obtain a special license from the proper ecclesiastical authority. Lydia mentioned the problem on 25 March 1672 (31). The conditions for getting a license were listed in canon law: there must be no impediment of pre-contract, consanguinity, affinity or other lawful cause; there must be no pending suit touching marriage of the couple; the couple must have the consent of parent or guardian if under the age of twenty-one; and the marriage would then still have to be celebrated publicly in the parish church or chapel where one of the two lived, between eight in the morning and noon unless the license specified otherwise.[45] Getting married by license was becoming more popular in the seventeenth century.[46] These licenses had become a status symbol, since they were affordable only by the middle and upper classes. For Samuel and Lydia to be married by license, then, was not particularly unusual. However, getting the license was an additional hurdle, possibly delaying their wedding day. Samuel's insistence on one indicated his willingness to do something a bit suspect; he wanted to hide his marriage in order to keep drawing his salary.

By 20 March 1672, Lydia was certain that she and Samuel would manage to marry quite soon despite all the impediments (31). Within a few days Samuel came home to Barford, license in hand, and they got married on 18 April 1672, not in his father's church but in the neighboring parish of Wasperton.[47] After the marriage, in order to protect Samuel's fellowship, Lydia did not mention the wedding in her letters, for she feared that someone might read them and she didn't want to be personally responsibly for his losing his fellowship (32). The news, however, did reach Oxford quickly, and in June 1672 Samuel lost his position at Trinity. Finally, Lydia could sign her letters "your most afectionate

---

[45] Edmund Gibson, *Codex Juris Ecclesiastici Anglicani*, 2nd ed., 2 vols. (Oxford, Clarendon Press, 1761), 1:428.

[46] Ronald A. Marchant, *The Church under the Law, 1560–1640* (London: Cambridge University Press, 1969), 20.

[47] The license was signed by John Rogers and Samuel DuGard; it explicitly stated that the marriage between Samuel and Lydia could take place in Barford or Wasperton, a village just south of Barford. John Rogers was a friend of Thomas DuGard and his wife, and rector of Hampton Lucy, a neighboring village; he was authorized by the Bishop of Worcester to issue marriage licenses (HWCRO, Ref. No. 797, 3A 2035/9 no. 3736).

and faithfull Wife" (33). With this closing the letters come to an end. Lydia and Samuel were happily married, and Samuel had returned home to live with his wife.

Apparently, she and Samuel lived with Samuel's family at least until August 1673 since Samuel was still corresponding with Thomas Barlow, Provost of Queen's College, using the Barford rectory as his return address.[48] And on 1 April 1673, Lydia gave birth to her first child, Thomas, who was baptized by his grandfather. In August 1673 Samuel finally was called to be rector of the church of All Saints in Forton, Staffordshire. Everyone must have been blissfully happy. He was ordained in his new church in October 1673, and a year later Lydia gave birth to a second son, Richard, who was baptized on 29 September 1674 at All Saints by his own father.[49] Just less than a year later, on 20 August 1675, Lydia died in childbirth.[50] The child, a daughter, survived and was named Lydia after her mother and grandmother. So sadly, after all the waiting and planning, Lydia and Samuel had only three married years together; she left Samuel with three small children, Thomas, age two, Richard, age one and the newborn Lydia.

A few more details complete Lydia's story. Gregory King in his Notebook in 1679 reported that Samuel had a "neat oval marble stone fixt to the South wall of the Chancel"[51] in memory of his wife. Three years after Lydia's death Samuel married Elizabeth Kimberley, his second cousin. This is the same Elizabeth Kimberly whose company Lydia enjoyed so much when she lived with the

---

[48] Samuel wrote to Thomas Barlow at Queen's College, Oxford, from Barford in August 1673, thanking him for his long letter (Queen's College, Oxford, MS 275, fol. 36).

[49] Richard DuGard, son of Samuel and Lydia DuGard, was baptised 29 September 1674 (FPR, D4049/1/1).

[50] Lydia DuGard, wife of Samuel DuGard, died 20 August 1675. Lydia DuGard, daughter of Samuel and Lydia DuGard, was baptised 20 August 1675 (FPR, D4049/1/1). Audrey Eccles estimates that maternal mortality was about twenty-five per one thousand births: Audrey Eccles, *Obstetrics and Gynecology in Tudor and Stuart England* (London: Croom Helm, 1982), 125. Roger Schofield concluded that maternal mortality was 15.7 per thousand — as high as 23.5 per thousand in London — during the reign of Charles II: Roger Schofield, "Did the Mothers Really Die? Three Centuries of Maternal Mortality in 'The World We Have Lost,' " in *The World We Have Gained: Histories of Population and Social Structure*, ed. Lloyd Bonfield, Richard M. Smith, and Keith Wrightson (Oxford: Blackwell, 1986), 232–33.

[51] "Gregory King's Staffordshire Notebook," ed. Gerald P. Mander, in *Collections for a History of Staffordshire*, William Salt Archeological Society, 3rd series, (London, 1920), 24.

Ashbys in Worcester in 1671 (**8, 17, 24**). Samuel and Elizabeth had seven children,[52] and Samuel was inspired to write another short treatise entitled *A Discourse Concerning the Having Many Children* (1695).[53] Once again he defended his private actions in a public way. And one more piece of Samuel's personality fits into place. He loved the idea of having many children. From his will dated 6 June 1696, it is clear that he looked after his children fairly and expected a great deal from them. When he died on 10 April 1697, he left behind ten children: Lydia's three and Elizabeth's seven. In his will he was careful to make provision for all of them, making sure that Lydia's children inherited the things that he and Lydia had prized.[54] In fact Thomas, Lydia's oldest son, inherited the Grafton Flyford lands in Worchestershire, which Lydia had inherited from her father, and was living there with his wife Catherine Gower in 1698 (**34**). Richard, the second son, disappeared from the records. Lydia's daughter, Lydia, married Daniel Cotton, iron master, of the Cotton family of Holmes Chapel, Cheshire, on 13 May 1704 in Tong, Shropshire. She was his second wife and for a very short while she was mother to his two small children, Sarah and Thomas. However, on 26 February 1705, she wrote her will (**35**), most likely because she knew the risks of her own pregnancy. As fate would have it, within a few days she gave birth to a son who was named, Dugard Cotton, and sadly both mother and infant died on 3 March 1705.[55]

These letters of Lydia, written over a short period of time, tell just one woman's story. Nevertheless, her passing comments about the people she knew (mostly family and neighbors), about education and pastimes, about health, and about travel and communication as well as her passionate feelings toward Samuel give insights into the lives of other women in similar social positions.

There has been considerable discussion among social historians about

---

[52] Elizabeth, 18 February 1679; William, 5 October 1680; Hannah, 20 September 1682; Phebe, 21 May 1684; Samuel, 18 April 1686; Susanna, 14 March 1688; and Charles, 28 February 1691 (FPR, 4049/1/1).

[53] Samuel DuGard, *Polupaidia, or A Discourse Concerning the Having Many Children* (London, 1695; Wing D2460).

[54] The will of Samuel DuGard, dated 6 June 1696, proved 29 April 1698, with an inventory of his goods dated 6 May 1697 (Litchfield, Litchfield Record Office, B/C/11).

[55] J. P. Earwaker, *History of Sandbach* (Manchester: E. J. Morten, 1972; first published 1890), 194–95.

relations among kin in seventeenth-century England.[56] Clearly family was central to Lydia's life. In family, she included not only her substitute nuclear family, where her primary loyalty lay, but also her extended family, composed of aunts and uncles, cousins and more distant kin. From her letters (and from other contemporary letters written by women)[57] it is easy to see that women played an essential role in "kinkeeping."[58] That is, very often the duty and obligation of maintaining kin contact fell to women. They did this not only out of obligation, but also because they were the most likely ones to benefit from keeping up such ties. For women, social contacts were much more restricted than for men. Their friends were drawn from neighbors and kin almost exclusively, while men's circles of friends more often came from their schooling, their profession, their travel, and their much wider business associations. Lydia exemplified this restricted social life, although she was probably more adventuresome than most since she had the wherewithall to travel and relocate as she pleased. She saw kin as providing a wonderful advantage, not a restriction, for they gave hospitality when she traveled, housing when she was in need or wanted to go somewhere to study, companionship, entertainment, emotional support, and security. In fact, most of the people with whom she interacted were

---

[56] Alan Macfarlane, *Family Life of Ralph Josselin*, 127–39, 154–58; Keith Wrightson, *English Society*, 44–51; Lawrence Stone, "Family History in the 1980s: Past Achievements and Future Trends," *Journal of Interdisciplinary History* 12 (1980): 51–87 and idem, *Family, Sex, and Marriage in England, 1500–1800* (New York, 1977), 123–32; Rosemary O'Day, *Family and Family Relationships, 1500–1900* (Basingstoke: Macmillan, 1994); Houlbrooke, *English Family*, 39–58; David Cressy, "Kinship and Kin Interaction in Early Modern England," *Past and Present* 113 (1986): 38–69; Miranda Chaytor, "Household and Kinship: Ryton in the Late Sixteenth and Early Seventeenth Centuries," *History Workshop Journal* 10 (1980): 25–60.

[57] For example, see Margaret Verney in Frances Parthenope Verney, ed., *The Memoirs of the Verney Family*, 4 vols. (New York: Barnes and Noble, 1970); Dorothy Gardiner,ed. *The Oxinden Letters, 1607–1642*, (London: Constable & Co., 1933); D'Ewes Correspondence, BL MSS. Harl. fols. 382.67e, 384; Harley Correspondence, BL, Add. MS 70233, and *Tixall Letters*, ed. Arthur Clifford, 2 vols. (London: Longman & Co., 1815). There are many collections of unpublished women's letters in county record offices that illustrate this point. For example, see Surrey Record Office, Guildford Muniment Room, Loseley MSS, Correspondence/1083; Cumbria Record Office, Lonsdale Collection, D/Lons/L1.

[58] David Cressy confirms that women were often the main "kinkeepers" through their letters; that is, they had a central role in maintaining contact among relations. See his "Kinship and Kin Interaction."

relatives. They felt obligations for one another. Her uncle came to her rescue when her parents died; other more distant relatives such as the Pettifers and the Kimberleys were interested in her welfare as well. She made continual efforts to maintain kinship ties with her DuGard relatives in London and elsewhere through letters and visits (2, 6, 8, 14, 17, 24). Ironically, Lydia's close ties with family gave her freedom. As a young, orphaned woman she was able to move from relative to relative, withdrawing from under the pressure of her uncle's household in Barford when necessary, but still feeling family loyalty and security. She was even able to move to Worcester to follow her passion for music because her relatives, the Ashbys, were willing to house her (19–25). And her Kimberley relatives from Whitford, near Bromsgrove in Worchestershire, provided her great joy and companionship (8, 17, 24, 32, 35) during the sad time when her Aunt Mary died. Certainly for Lydia no other people were as important to her well-being as kin.

But Samuel shared his friends with Lydia as well, so she wasn't totally limited in her exposure to society. She specifically mentions four Trinity College colleagues who came to Barford to visit and whose company she enjoyed very much. John Cudworth, Thomas Twithy, Thomas Jekyll, and John Willes all joked with Lydia and knew about her relationship with Samuel (9, 13, 23, 27, 29, 31, 32). She wrote to them and was included in college life through their friendship.

Clearly, Lydia lived among educated women as well as men. In the course of her letters, she mentions nine women, relatives, and neighbors: all of these women were literate. Her aunt, her sister, her cousins, in London, Coventry, Worcester, and Barford, her neighborhood friends, both young and old, all wrote letters routinely. It is widely accepted that people learned to write after learning to read, so these women were almost certainly readers, too.[59] Was the widespread literacy among these women unusual? Or was literacy a common feature of the wives and daughters of schoolmasters and clergy, the group to which most of these women belonged? Limited educational records suggest that daughters of the clergy were often sent off to school along with the daughters of the gentry, which might account for this situation, since so many of Lydia's

---

[59] Keith Thomas, "The Meaning of Literacy in Early Modern England," in *The Written Word: Literacy in Transition*, ed. Gerd Baumann (Oxford: Clarendon Press, 1986), 99.

relatives were members of the clergy.[60] Literacy rates for women in the seventeenth century are difficult to ascertain. Scholars today assume the literacy rate of women to be quite low, especially in the provinces and outside the gentry.[61] However, Lydia's letters give anecdotal evidence for a more widespread literacy even in the provinces. In the DuGard family in the 1660s all the women regarded letter-writing as a normal, expected skill. To judge from Lydia's own letters, women's letters were not simply painfully chiseled notes but could rise to wit and eloquence.

Numerous handbooks published during Lydia's lifetime were aimed especially at women, instructing them on how to construct letters and address people of various ranks.[62] Historians have assumed that these manuals, such as Henry Care's *The Female Secretary*, were necessary because education levels were so low that model letters were needed. This may be true, but Lydia's letters point in the opposite direction. She at least felt free to express herself in her own voice. Her spelling, punctuation, and use of upper and lower case might be idiosyncratic, but that reflected emerging conventions rather than lack of

---

[60] In a letter dated 1 April 1647, Stanley Gower, vicar, wrote to his son about taking in his granddaughter to learn reading, writing, and cookery, and possibly sewing and starching, saying they are great assets in marriage (Folger X.d.428/199). Ralph Josselin, vicar in Earls Colne, Essex, sent his daughters off to various boarding schools in Bury St. Edmunds, Colchester, and Hackney, London, from the time they were ten to fourteen to learn to read and write (Macfarlane, *Family Life of Ralph Josselin*, 49, 93, 112). Martha Mayhew, niece and adopted daughter of Reverend Giles Moore, a Sussex parson, was sent in 1667 "to learne to write of Mr John Breukes of Rotherfield," then in 1669 and 1670 she was sent to Mrs. Chaloner's school in London. See *The Journal of Giles Moore*, ed. Ruth Bird (Lewes: Sussex Record Society, 1971), 72–74, 76.

[61] David Cressy puts literacy rates for women at 11 percent in general but at 22 percent in London in the 1670s, while J. Paul Hunter surmises that they are greater than that, possibly 30 percent. David Cressy, *Literacy and Social Order: Reading and Writing in Tudor and Stuart England* (Cambridge: Cambridge University Press, 1980), 147; J. Paul Hunter, *Before Novels: The Cultural Contexts of Eighteenth-Century English Fiction* (New York, W. W. Norton, 1990), 73. For general discussions of literacy, see Cressy, *Literacy and Social Order*; Liza Picard, *Restoration London* (London: Weidenfeld & Nicolson, 1997), 184–90; and Peter Earle, "The Female Labour Market," *Economic History Review* 42 (1989): 328–53.

[62] Henry Care, *The Female Secretary* (London, 1671; Wing C519); Hannah Woolley, *The Gentlewoman's Companion* (London, 1675; Wing W3277); John Hill, *The Young Secretary's Guide* (London, 1687; Wing H1992).

knowledge. Her later letters are as sophisticated and flow as smoothly as letters written by men of the same social station. Her self-confidence and individuality are evident in the way she differed from the models in the handbooks. She did not need them any more than the "Ladies of Noble Birth" whom Henry Care addressed.[63]

Lydia did, of course, follow some standard conventions. She always addressed her letters "Dear Cousin" or "Dearest Cousin" and signs most of her letters "your faithfull" or "your afectionate and faithfull." She adhered to the convention of making the ending "seem naturally emergent from the precedent matter."[64] Henry Care had a great deal of fun with his letters. Although there is no evidence that Lydia read Care's handbook, its utility for her would in any case have been slight. She chose her own words, expressing herself naturally by making the "style match the substance and suit the audience."[65] Lydia wrote a great deal; in fact she stated that expressing herself in writing came easier than in spoken words (28). Writing for Lydia was a passion, not an ordeal. And she used her own writing to think through what she believed and who she was.

In the midst of Lydia's words of love and support are comments about what she did each day. One of her greatest enjoyments was music. Both Samuel and Lydia were fond of playing the viol and singing. Lydia mentioned learning to sing and to play the viol early in the letters (2). She also attended concerts, for she mentioned one musician, Peter Young, and recommended that Samuel travel to London to hear him play at court (25). Girls of her background going to boarding school learned to sing and to play various instruments as a regular part of their curriculum. She might have had this experience.[66] She deliberately

---

[63] Jean Robertson, *The Art of Letter Writing: An Essay on the Handbooks Published in England During the Sixteenth and Seventeenth Centuries* (London: University Press of Liverpool, 1943), 60.

[64] Care, *Female Secretary*, 146.

[65] For examples of Care's style see *Female Secretary*, 15–16.

[66] Music was an important part of the curriculum in all the girls' boarding schools in London and in the provincial towns, and even girls that were tutored at home often had music masters come to their houses. John Evelyn records when his daughter, Mary, began to learn music (*The Diary of John Evelyn*, ed. E. S. DeBeer, 6 vols. [Oxford: Clarendon Press, 1955], 4:271). Susanna Perwich taught music at her mother's school (John Batchilier, *The Virgin's Pattern* [London, 1661; Wing B1076], 2.) The five daughters of Anthony Walker, rector, had a singing master teach them in their house at fit seasons (Anthony Walker, *The Holy Life of Mrs. Elizabeth Walker* [London, 1690; Wing W305], 18.

went to Worcester to live with her relatives, the Ashbys, so that she could take viol lessons from Mr. Wright, a music master. She practiced conscientiously; in fact, keeping up her lessons was one of her main reasons for staying in Worcester. She hoped that by the time she returned to Barford, in about nine months, she would be able to play well enough to please Samuel (21). Lydia found great comfort in playing music that Samuel himself played:

> I sit as contentedly in my chamber as can be: and have as good company as in your absence I can wish for, tis your letters and my viol, whilst I read the former I fancy you present, and talking to mee. and when I play upon the latter I fancy, (especialy and I play some of your things,) that I hear you play. (22)

But she made a point of saying that she could not play nearly so well as he. Apparently she was playing divisions, for Samuel asked for his division book to be sent to him at Oxford (33). Playing divisions was a particularly popular discipline in the mid-seventeenth century. It is not easy, requiring improvisational ability on the part of the performer. Lydia took her viol playing seriously and got great pleasure from it.

Inquiring after and reporting on the illnesses[67] and deaths of relatives and friends is a regular feature of personal letters, then and now. Women and men in the seventeenth century did this with an almost formulaic frequency. For Lydia to ask about and be worried about health matters is expected. But her dwelling on Samuel's conditions and her agonizing over his illnesses is best explained by her close identification with him. Lydia's attitude is made even clearer by Roy Porter's comment that "Conditions of the body, registering the ups and downs of health and sickness, meshed with wider ideas of identity and destiny, or social, moral and spiritual well being."[68] Talk of health was one of the many ways that Lydia expressed her love: ". . . if I have not had perfect health of late twas to simpathise with you for I heard you were ile. now you are well I shall be better," and "you need not ask how I doe you may know by your self sinc I am as you are. if you are sick I cant be well if you are in health I am so

---

[67] A detailed description of illness and people's experience of it can be found in Lucinda McCray Beier, *Sufferers & Healers* (London: Routledge & Kegan Paul, 1987).

[68] Roy Porter, *Disease, Medicine, and Society in England, 1550–1860* (Basingstoke: Macmillan Education, 1987), 24.

too" (10). She made the same kind of comment again when Samuel suffered from a cough, which she feared would turn into consumption: "I cant be well if you are not. and if I have health at any time I could wilingly [forsake] it if it would contribute to yours" (13). Lydia was troubled by Samuel's scurvy and wanted to send him Goody Hawkes's water, since it had helped her in the spring (16). She was aware of her exaggerated concern, though, for she said in February 1669 that she knew she feared the worst when others thought there were few grounds for fear, but she knew that Samuel would understand her overconcern for his welfare (17). Lydia chastised Samuel for not reporting immediately to her on his health, as country folk normally did, and for her having to get the news from others that he was not well. Other than this mention of Goody Hawkes's remedy and a reference to a nurse for Mrs. Dodd, Lydia mentioned no medical practitioners, confirming the notion that people depended upon neighbors, friends, and relatives — oftentimes, women — more than on professionals to help them deal with their maladies. Her attitude toward health and medicine exemplifies that described by Roy Porter:

> Illness was seen as a life event, integral to the sufferer's whole being. Sickness meant that the body was out of balance rather than the modern notion of the body being attacked by external bugs (e.g., flu) or broken (e.g., heart failure). Sickness was seen as personal and internal. Treatment consisted of restoring lost equilibrium. Health then was a personal responsibility, not a doctor's.[69]

In Lydia's case Samuel's health was her responsibility as well as his.

Lydia's frequent travels indicate that she was not a homebound young woman.[70] Over the course of the five years covered by her letters, she traveled to London, Coventry, Oxford, Worcester, and Bromsgrove. She also made shorter journeys to neighboring places like Lighthorn and Warwick. She did not take traveling lightly, always planning her trips with care. She traveled by

---

[69] Porter, *Disease*, 24.

[70] Books and maps covering travel conditions in the seventeenth century are too general to cover Lydia's travels in any detail. However, Virginia LaMar's small pamphlet *Travel and Roads in England* (Washington, D.C.: Folger Library, 1960) and Joan Parkes's *Travel in England in the Seventeenth Century* (London: Humphrey Milford, 1925) are helpful in giving general conditions.

horseback, never alone, and always with a specific purpose. She never traveled on Sundays;[71] neither did Samuel (18, 31). She never traveled without being granted permission from her uncle (6, 8, 14, 17, 18). Lydia was fully aware of the dangers of travel—often expressing thanks for safe arrival (11, 15, 27, 29, 32)—but did not allow these conditions to stop her from doing what she needed to do. After talking for over a year about going to London to see family and friends and her guardian, Lydia finally made that journey with her Uncle Thomas in September 1668 (14, 15). The distance from Barford to London was about eighty-five miles. To average five miles an hour in winter or seven miles an hour in summer on fairly decent roads was good going, so it would have taken two days minimum. She stayed with her Aunt Pettifer in St. Giles without Cripplegate for about three weeks. During the summer of 1668 and again in 1669, she went with Samuel and her uncle to look over family lands in Worcestershire. Her bravest trip was to Oxford to see Samuel in July 1669 (18). This trip she instigated herself, arranging to travel with her sister and the local schoolmaster, asking for Samuel's advice at each stage of planning. She only stayed two or three nights in Oxford, probably at an inn. It was certainly possible to cover the thirty-two miles from Barford to Oxford in a single hard day. In addition it was also quite common for women to travel short distances to take care of sick people or to visit family and friends. When Lydia returned from Worcester to live in Barford, she went six miles over to Lighthorn, staying there for several weeks in March 1672, to care for old Mrs. Dodds (29). Aunt Mary went to Warwick to stay with her sister, Cousin Spooner (17). These letters indicate that travel for women, while uncomfortable and difficult, was not infrequent.

---

[71] Proclamations restricting Sunday travel were frequently issued between 1627 and 1663. The royal proclamation for observation of the Lord's Day of 22 August 1663 further stated that this proclamation "must be read once a month for six months to every congregation." See *Calendar of State Papers, Domestic Series, of the Reign of Charles II, 1663–1664*, ed. M.A.E. Green (London: Longman & Co., 1862) 249–50. There was not another proclamation until 1677. The DuGard family was still observing the restrictions in 1672. Samuel Pepys says on 20 September 1663, "got my Lord's warrant for travailyng today there being a proclamation read yesterday against it at Huntingon, at which I am very glad, I took leave. . .": *The Diary of Samuel Pepys*, ed. Robert Latham and William Matthews, 11 vols. (Berkeley: University of California Press, 1970), 4:313. John Evelyn reports on 17 September 1665, "I was forc'd to travel all Sunday": *Diary of John Evelyn*, 3:418.

Introduction to the Letters

Lydia's letters make her come alive. Lydia has spark, intelligence, a sense of humor, compassion and most interestingly, a remarkable, individual voice. She has a sense of agency, revealing that women as well as men seek their own happiness. Her words demonstrate that it was possible for a woman in the late seventeenth century to be strong and assertive while living within the norms of her society. Unfortunately, many, many of her letters were not preserved, and I can't help but crave information that she does not provide. But these letters that have been passed down help us experience a young woman's life, what she is thinking about, and what she does. They are indeed a very special treasure.

Editorial Procedures

The letters have been transcribed from the original manuscripts preserved unbound in the Folger Shakespeare Library in Washington, D. C. They are in surprisingly good condition; only in a few places is the ink faded or the paper torn. Lydia wrote in the modified Italic hand typical of women of her day. While she did not crowd the words on the page, she did write along the margins, so that the paper is often completely filled with words. The handwriting gets more and more fluent as the years go by. The addresses are complete and intact in sixteen of the letters; four are simply addressed to Mr. Samuel DuGard, and the rest either are unaddressed or are missing their address leaf. Ten of the thirty-two letters are undated, but they can be put in sequence quite reliably from internal evidence. All of them are signed or initialed by Lydia, sometimes with very elaborate designs made up of Samuel's initials intertwined with her own. It is impossible to state for certain that these letters are the ones actually sent to Samuel. There is a great deal of talk in the letters themselves about copying letters and sending letters written to other people to each other for perusal. She asks Samuel, "will you doe so much as send me this letter again tis call'd for, and so I cant have time to transcribe it" (22). Typically, Lydia made copies of her own letters (22), but it is my impression, as well as that of Laetitia Yeandle of the Folger Library, that most of the Folger letters must be the ones actually sent. All have the usual fold marks of sent letters; eighteen have pink seal marks; another five have holes where a seal would have been and another five are missing the address leaf, so that no address or seal is shown at all. They could have been sent to Samuel in a bundle along with other letters from the family. There are four letters that include an address leaf with no seal marks. Of special interest are letters **28** and **29**, which appear to be very carefully written first drafts, and since they have no seal marks on them, Lydia could have made copies of these and sent copies to Samuel. There are large gaps in the correspondence. Lydia talked about expecting a letter every week from Samuel while she was living in Worcester, so clearly not all the letters that Lydia wrote to Samuel over the five years were preserved.

Since Lydia's daughter, Lydia Cotton, died shortly after she wrote her will in 1705 and had no surviving children, it is hard to determine how the letters were preserved. Samuel may have kept them during his lifetime, but he died in 1697. They must have gone to Lydia Cotton and stayed in the Cotton family. The letters passed on to a Mary Anne Cotton, (three generations later) who married Reverend Jestin Homfray in the mid-eighteenth century, and then through the Homfray family. In 1968 the Folger Shakespeare Library purchased them from Miss Winifred Myers, a book and manuscript seller of Martin Fields, London. Although originally kept in a roll, they had been flattened and repaired by the owners. The letters came in an envelope addressed to Wm. Homfray, Broad-waters House, Kidderminster, Worcestershire from Mrs. Addenbrooke, 421 So. Pine Ave., Austin, Illinois, dating from 1922. In a note attached to the letters Mrs. Addenbrooke states that these letters were "part of a parcel of letters" belonging to her family and that Mrs. Alfred Homfray of Stratton, North Cornwall, had the other part. Unfortunately, the Folger staff was unable to trace these people in 1968, and I have also been unsuccessful in locating them.

In transcribing the letters, the original spelling, punctuation, and capitalization have been reproduced as accurately as possible. However, distinguishing lower case from upper case, especially with the letters C, L, M, N, O, S, T, U, and W, where size is the only indicator, is difficult. Oftentimes, too, the line between commas and periods is hard to draw. I have made judgments in these cases. Lydia uses a capital I in all cases where the modern J would be used today. I have followed Lydia's pattern. F and ff have been reproduced as written. Lydia is not consistent in capitalization, sometimes capitalizing place names and proper names, sometimes not, sometimes beginning sentences with upper case and sometimes not. I have left these inconsistencies alone. She frequently abbreviates names by the use of a colon, i.e. Hen:, and she often uses two lines "=" to divide a word at the end of a line. I have followed Lydia's pattern in both cases, even when the "=" does not come at the end of my line. Square brackets [Barford] indicate words I have supplied in explanation or ellipses [. . .] where the paper is torn. Angle brackets <. . .> indicate where the ink is blotched or the handwriting is indecipherable, and angle brackets with a line through the letter or words <~~such as~~> indicate phrases that Lydia crossed out, but that are still legible. Pluses + + indicate words inserted by Lydia above the line.

The letters are catalogued under the title Folger MS X.d.477/1–33; however, in this introduction I have used only the letter number to this edition for reference. In fact, there are just thirty-two letters by Lydia, since letter **25** is a postscript to letter **24**. The order established by the Folger Library catalogue has been maintained. The DuGard collection also includes a short note (**34**) from

Thomas DuGard, Lydia's eldest son, to his sister, as well as the will (35) of Lydia Cotton, Lydia's daughter. These have been transcribed as well.

Other manuscript sources closely linked to Lydia DuGard include the will of William DuGard, the will and inventory of Thomas DuGard, and the will and inventory of Samuel DuGard. Besides the two treatises already mentioned, Samuel DuGard published *The True Nature of Divine Law* (1687). Other documents written by him include the poem written on William DuGard's death, four sermons, and the letter to Walter Blandford, Bishop of Worcester, all in the Bodleian Library at Oxford, and two letters written in Latin to Thomas Barlow, Provost of Queen's College, preserved at Queens College, Oxford. Two letters written 7 May 1646 and 10 April 1648 by Hannah DuGard, Samuel's mother, to her cousin Mrs. Mary Wyllys in Connecticut are also extant. Parish registers from Barford (Warwickshire), Wasperton (Warwickshire), Forton (Staffordshire.), St. Olave, Hart Street (London), and St. Laurence Pountney (London) provided most of the genealogical data. A family tree and a Biographical Appendix listing Lydia and Samuel's relatives, friends, and neighbors are also provided.

The

Letters

of

Lydia DuGard

1–1

[Folger MS X.d.477/1]   [Barford, September, 1666]

Dear Cousen

We heard of Londons sad flames as soon as you and were as much
aflict+e+d with it, I wich we could be more for no doubt but we as well as
5   others had a hand in drawing doune these Iudments. and therefore tis fit
wee should bewail the cause and repent in scakcloth when such a part of
the kingdome lyes in ashes, heaven grant we may come as gold out of the
fire, purifi'd, but I feare some <. . .> took more care to preserve there gold
from the fire then to come out themselfs like it: Cousen I need not tell you
10   we ought not to reioyce at the fall of an enemie, much les of one that at
least pretends frendship as M^r waterhouse to you. I'm afrade the flames of
his house drounded your sorow for the loses of the whole city, though it
semes thay are not only felt by sympathy, but Cousen +if+ others had no
greater loses then you have I think thay would be allmost as litle bewaild
15   as my Gaurdians are, but perhaps you'l be angrey if I say any more: in hast

your loving Cousen
Lydia DuGard.

[vertically in left margin] remember me to Cousen

[addressed on verso:]   for Mr Henrey DuGard in
20   trin: Coll:
                                                these
                                        oxon

1–2

1   **[Barford, September 1666]:** This letter is catalogued as number **1** by the Folger Shakespeare Library. Chronologically, I believe it is number **3**, since it mentions the London fire of 2 September 1666, which occurred after the biggest plague scares mentioned in number **2**. It was certainly sent from Barford, Warwickshire, and is the only letter in this collection sent to Lydia's cousin, Henry, who was five years older than Lydia. Henry was a student at St. Paul's School in London from 1663–64 and may have gotten to know Lydia in London before she moved to Barford. Henry matriculated at Trinity College, Oxford, in May 1664.

3   **as soon as you:** News about the London fire arrived in Lydia's small village of Barford just as quickly as it arrived in Oxford.

6   **repent in scakcloth:** Matthew 11:21; Luke 10:13. Clearly, at age 16, biblical sayings were a part of Lydia's common language.

7–8   **heaven grant . . . purifi'd:** Job 23:10; Zechariah 13:9; 1 Peter 1:7.

8   **< . . . >:** One letter is indecipherable.

10   **reioyce . . . enemie:** Job 31:29-30 and Proverbs 24:17.

10   **enemie:** The second "e" has been written over an "i" or vice versa.

11   **M^r waterhouse:** Edward Waterhouse, heraldic writer and author, was a friend of William DuGard and was named Lydia's guardian in her father's will. Henry DuGard was named beneficiary in this will in the event of Lydia's death before marriage, but this inheritance hinged on his being a "good scholler." Since Henry was at school in London, he most certainly would have met Mr. Waterhouse. Apparently, neither Lydia nor Henry were fond of Mr. Waterhouse, calling him their "enemie." There are many references to Lydia's struggles with her guardian throughout the letters. See the *DNB* for Waterhouse's career.

12   **house:** Waterhouse lived in Sion College, where Lydia's father had lived during his last years. Sion College was badly damaged in the London fire of 1666. Only the library and some of the gate remained. Waterhouse reported that "he lost manuscripts fitted for the press, together with the general collections of the study of my life." See his *A Short Narrative of the late Dreadful Fire in London* (London, 1667; Wing) 87. This small book, written in October, 1666, was addressed to the Speaker of the House of Commons; it chronicled Waterhouse's losses at Sion and called for rebuilding it, for relieving merchants of their debts, and for providing housing for the poor and for learned clergy. Merchant Taylors' School, the school where Lydia's father had served as Headmaster, when she was born, was also burned down in the fire.

18   **Cousen:** Lydia is referring to Samuel DuGard, Henry DuGard's older brother by two years and the recipient of all the rest of Lydia's letters.

2–1

[Folger MS X.d 477/2]   [Coventry, summer 1665]

Dear Cousen

for me to excuse my self were but to agravate the faughlt: and you would
question the truth of it if I should say I wanted time to write +to you+: no
5   Cousen I know no employment would be +more+ pleasing if my he+a+de
(which you know was never to pregnant) were as ready as my hand, but
such as it is if you pleas dont disdain it, shall pleas me as well as if +you+
had as much cause to aprove of it as I have to admire you in every thing,
fortune that has smild upon you has not frownd upon Cousen, nor Lydia.
10   I fear worse, if people are look't upon acording to mirete it can't be
otherwise: Cousen my Uncle tells me he [was] with you twice but not at
London, the plaug [. . .] he was fearfull: I heard lat+e+ly from cousen pa
[. . .] are all well and Aunt Petefir but I cant hear [. . .] such strangness
should not rest in the bosome of fren[ds] [. . .] Cousen I hope you'l som-
15   tims give your self the trou[ble] [to send] a line or two. Cousen Anna tells
me you writ you [hope] to be thear with your viol: but I cant expect [. . .]
with hearing it: I am Iust learning to sing I [know not] whether to any
purpose: he teaches [me] the viol [. . .] fear not to well: one of my aquain-
tanc has an[. . .] good viol and maks litle use of it: <. . .> if I can have it I
20   shall not be un willing to learn: but your advice shall rule Cousen

                                        your oblidged Cousen

my servis to Cousen henrey

                                        Lydia DuGard

[addressed on verso:]   These
25   for Mr Samuell DuGard
                         in trin: Coll:
                  oxon

2–2

1   **[Coventry, summer, 1665?]:** This dating is derived from the comment about the London plague and Lydia's tone, which is more tentative than in Letter **3**; most likely the letter was sent from Coventry where she was staying with her sister, Elizabeth Mitchell. See Letters **17**, **18**, and **33**. The right-hand margin is torn in the middle third of the page. Missing words, when apparent, are supplied within brackets [   ]; when not apparent, they are indicated with ellipses [. . .].

11   **Uncle:** Thomas DuGard was Samuel's father.

12   **plaug:** One of the worst plagues in London's history came in the summer of 1665. Clearly, Thomas DuGard did not travel to London for fear of this plague.

13   **Petefir:** Jane Pettifer was the sister of Thomas and William DuGard. She lived in St. Giles Cripplegate , London, one of the parishes hardest hit by the plague of 1665.

15   **Anna:** Anna DuGard was Samuel's sister. She was nineteen years old at this time.

16   **you:** Lydia has written "y" (yoy) and changed it to a "u" (you).

16   **viol:** Viol was the generic name for the viola da gamba. It is a bowed, string instrument with frets, usually played held downwards on the lap or between the legs. Most viols have six strings. The viol which Lydia refers to was most likely a division viol, an English form of bass viola da gamba, smaller in size than a consort bass viol, but larger than a lyra viol. The division viol reached its height in popularity in England in the mid-seventeenth century. Lydia apparently got this viol and began learning to play at the age of fifteen; her viol provided continual pleasure for her, as evidenced throughout the letters. See *New Grove*, s.v. "division viol," and "viol."

19   **<. . .>:** One letter is crossed out and indecipherable.

23   **Lydia DuGard:** Lydia has woven an S into her DuGard signature. This sentimental practice became quite common for Lydia, and her decorative signature got more elaborate.

3–1

[Folger MS X.d.477/3]   [Barford, March 8, 1666]

I never in the least question'd my Cousin's fidelity and Constancy: nor
have I reson when he gives me such proofs of it, if one apearing with so
many, nay all manner of advantages over me (and that may ese+i+ly be,
for you love meerly becose you will love. and I have wondred many times
what could ever move you to it) isay if one having all advantages could
not prevail with you to forget your mean L Cousin. I can take as much
sat+i+sfaction in the remembrance of it as if it had bin real. for dreams for
the most part are agreeable to our waking thoughts, and I hope Cousin
you wont disesteem and think the wors of me, seeing me come short of
your imaginary Heiress: I am glad to hear the heavens are so propitious to
you. but methinks thay should ether give greater favors or you not
acknowlidg um to be <t> there gift. but to come by chance. we are all prety
well. Aunt and Cousin remember um to you. Cassandra lies still this cold
wether. and all we can do will hardly keep us from it: in hast and allmost
frose. Dear Cousin

                                    your oblidg'd and faithfull
march 8 1666   Lydia DuGard

[addressed on verso:]   These
                             for her very loving Brother
                             M<r> Samuel DuGuard at
                             Trinity Colledge in
                             Oxoford

3–2

1	There is no saluation on this letter; it begins mid thought, so presumably the first part is missing.
7	**L:** Lydia starts to write an "L" and then writes "Cousin."
14	**Aunt:** Mary DuGard was Thomas DuGard's second wife; they were married in 1660, so she acted as Lydia's mother when Lydia moved to Barford.
14	**Cousin:** Anna DuGard, Samuel's younger sister, about nineteen years old.
14	**Cassandra:** I have been unable to identify Cassandra.
20	**Brother:** This is the only occasion in the letters in which Lydia calls Samuel her brother.

4–1

[Folger MS X.d.477/4]   [Barford, November 17, 1666]

Deare Cousin

I told you I should want those opertunites +of writing+ I inloyed at
Coventry and I find I cant have the same privacy I had there, and besids
5   here are those that do as good as tel me +they+ suspect the truth, so I can
not be to warey, nor give um to litle ground for there suspicion therefore
Dear Cousin you wont say I am so composed and unconserned as to rest
pleased with a seldomer convers, you will know it is a forsed silence sinc
you had ofter visits els where. and you wroung me Cousin if you think
10   you are not more in my thoughts then ever. thay say the absenc of frends
couls the afections. but it is not, nor cant posibly be so here; I thought I had
sayd enufe from time to time to let you know I nurish more then half a
respect for you and that you have more then half a heart. I am sorey my
Dear Cousen you so much question my fidelity: let it sat+i+sfie that you
15   have as large a rome in my esteme as you can in reson desire: I think the
time of my Aunts going to tadmarton is unsertan as yet. but it semes you
intend to give her that one day you promised me, and spin out the time to
the length of a cruell twelve mounth: I must confes, you will give your self
the les trouble but me les satisfaction: thanks for your verses I can take
20   most of them prety well. but +want+ the oughter to explain your Londons
fall: my Dearest Cousen

nov: 17 1666   your faithfull
                    Lydia DuGard

[addressed on verso:] for Mr Samuel DuGard

4–2

4   **Coventry:** Lydia had been living in Barford for over a year; she last wrote to Samuel from Coventry in the summer of 1665. See Letter **2**. Clearly, she was more confined living in the rectory with her aunt and uncle than in Coventry with her sister.

5   **suspect the truth:** This refers to Lydia and Samuel's being in love.

8–9   **sinc you had ofter visits els where:** Later when Lydia is living in Worcester, she writes to Samuel as often as once per week and expects the same from him. She may have been writing as often from Coventry, but she is worried about writing so frequently from Barford. Unfortunately, many, many of her letters have not survived.

16   **tadmarton:** Tadmarton was a small village half way between Barford and Oxford. The DuGard's former housekeeper, Mary Kemp, lived there with her husband, Creswith Whately, the vicar. Samuel might be planning to meet his step-mother at Mary Kemp's rather than make a trip to Barford, where he would see Lydia.

19   **verses:** Sending verses of poetry was a very common part of courtship in the later seventeenth century.

20   **oughter:** author

5–1

[Folger MS X.d.477/5]   [Barford, Good Friday, April 5, 1667]

Dear Cousin

If I thought I could add any thing to the contentment you<r> are pleased
+always+ to expres. and if I did not think you knew me well enough not
5   to doubt of an affection the greatness of which you can not better imagin
then in comparing it with your own. I should strive to testifi it more by
oftner telling you my thoughts – which are still the same thay ever have
bin. and can't posibly admit of any change or alter=ation. and if you had
bin commendable in nothing but your affection, you would not have bin
10   lov'd b+e+fore twas made known. there is difrence t'wixt those that love
meerly because they are belov'd – and those whose love is an efect of the
deserts of the person beloved. so that my knowlidg of your affection was
so farr from being the cause of mine. that it could add but litil to my
formor esteme of you after all this Dear Cousin you cannot think a sel-
15   dome writing to prosede from a disrespect: but tis natural to mee not to
delight in that which I know may with more +reason+ cause laughter then
esteme. but if it do – it shant displeas me. knowing it deserves no other:
Dearest Cousen

   April 5 1667.   your faithfull
20   Aunt and Cousin remember um to you   Lydia DuGard.

5–2

3   **you<r>:** Lydia has written "your" and then crossed out the "r."
8   **alter=ation:** Lydia uses "=" to divide a word, if it does not fit on a line. I have maintained her practice even when the word does not need to be divided.

6-1

[Folger MS X.d.477/6]   [Barford, May 28, 1667]

Dearest Cousin

A growing health is the more gratfull to me since you are so much consern'd in it as to have made it the subject of your desires. and I should
5   abuse your tendernes if I did not strive what in me lies to <increas>
continue it and if heretofore I have bin somthing mine own enimie in too
sedentary a life. now the pleasantness of the season will invite one to walk
forth and view the new beauties of the feilds where one <mak> m+i+ght
take uninterupted delights. and it would be hard to say whether it would
10   contribute more to ones health or pleasure. if I had not the thoughts of a
long absence to turn it rather into solitariness. I thought I should have bin
at London before this time. but since I can not so conveiniently go. I must
be content <with> with my old Gaurdian another year. for t'was upon his
acount I should have gone. we heard from Aunt Petefer the other day. she
15   is well and remembers her to you and Cousen Harey, ah Cousin what sad
newes do you send conserning him. so unexpected that it dous a great
deale the more trouble us. but God is able to bring good out of ev+i+le.
and wee'l hope it may be so here. Cousin Anna rem+em+bers her to you
Dear Cousin

20   your faithfull
May 28 1667:   Ly: DuGard

[addressed on verso:]   for Mr Samuel DuGard in
                            Trinite Colledg in oxford
                            these

6–2

7   **pleasantness:** This word is written on top of "new."
7–8   **walk forth . . . fields:** Barford is situated in a beautiful part of Warwickshire; the rolling hills and cultivated fields would have made for a very pleasant springtime walk.
8   **feilds:** "Feelds" has been changed to "feilds" or vice versa.
9   **would:** "Will" has been changed to read "would" or vice versa.
13   **my old Guardian:** Lydia's relationship with her guardian, Edward Waterhouse, was never good. She must have had hopes of going to London and arranging for another one. Thomas DuGard even mentioned that he would be willing to serve as her guardian, but a change was highly unlikely. As guardian Waterhouse was obligated to find a suitable match for Lydia and oversee her inheritance. She wanted to be left alone to find her own match in Samuel.
17   **God is able to bring good out of ev+i+le:** Genesis 50:20; Romans 8:28.

7-1

[Folger MS X.d.477/7]   [Barford, June 8, 1667]

June 8. 1667.

Dear Cousin

I hear of your good fortune, though you your self are are silent: and do as
5   much reiose in it as one who desires anothers wellfare more earnestly then ·
their own. <del>would had thay their desires granted;</del> and indeed one need
not question your haveing preferments. you that winn hearts may well
obtain what others would be denied. Dear Cousin I will not fear (though
I should from any other) your new dignity will make +you+ abate any
10 thing of that Love and afection you are wont to expres, nor cause you to
repent of what is past: +and+ though I lose the good opinion of others, I'le
hope this wont make any Impresion upon you to my disad=vantage, and
then I shall acount my self much hapier then if I had every bodies esteme
and wanted yours: <del>you</del> Cousin you need not fear my speaking any
15 thing to my Uncle conserning Cousen Henrey. I should be loath to aflict
him so much, as I fear, the relation of his misdemeanor would. indeed tis
hard for me to keep it from Aunt, and Cousen Ann. but you <del>wont</del> will
not fear them. my Dear Cousin, are your desires of so visiting Barford
quite extinguished, or will not your imploiments give you leave: Will: put
20 us in hopes, not long sinc, but now he sa<y>+i+s you [vertically in left
margin] intend not to come this summer. I confes it will be but to draw
you from farr greater delights. but where ever you go. you will never find
+a+ heartier wellcome then at barford, and espechaly from my Dear
Cousin

25   your constant and faithfull
                                              Lydia DuGard.

Cousin Ann remembers her to you.

[addressed on verso:]   for Mr Samuel DuGard
                             Fellow of Trinity Coll:
30   in oxon

7–2

4	**good fortune:** Samuel had just become a fellow at Trinity College.
4	**are are:** Lydia repeats herself here.
12	**this:** The word "this" is written on the top of the word "that" or vice versa.
15	**Cousen Henrey:** Henry had gotten into some kind of trouble in Oxford; it is difficult to say what this misdemeanor was. Stephen Porter mentions gambling, drunken-ness, whoring and mixing with unsavory campanions as the most likely serious sins of Oxford students. There was plenty of opportunity to go astray for there were 370 ale houses in Oxford by 1680. Stephen Porter, "University and Society" in *The History of the University of Oxford,* ed. Nicholas Tyacke (Oxford: Oxford University Press, 1997), 71–72.
19	**Will:** Lydia uses the colon to abbreviate names and places. I have retained her usage. William was the carrier who came regularly to the rectory.
22	**where:** Originally this was written "when."
22	**ever:** "eaver" has been changed to "ever."
23	**+a+:** The tail on this "a" was written too long, so it has been deliberately crossed out.

8–1

[Folger MS X.d.477/8]   [Barford, 1667]

My Dear Cousin

Can you entertain so harsh a thought of your faithfull Lydia, as this, that
she was weary of her happyness, that she was glad when it was gone, and
that the thoughts of a long absence can be pleasing to her. if it be thus t'is
I that have committed faults to great for punishment, and faults which I
hope you think me not only a stranger to but incapable of unles you count
me a great desembler. but that I am sure you cannot. what can it be then
makes you speak so much against your knowlidg. for though I can't tell
you how much I love. yet you know so much that you may asure your self
of the continuanc and growth of it, and that you have a heart that is and
ever will be lwholey [*sic*] yours. Dear Cousin how cruel are you in puting
so un=charitable a construction upon a short silence. as if so great a love
when you were present, could pass to such a coldness and indifrence
when absent, no Cousin I am the same I was, and so shall be till I shall
sease to live. I began to blame you alitle when I saw not your wish'd for
letter, till t'was opened. it seemes I must have it but at second hand, but it
could not come into better then it was directed to. I hear nothing of my
going to London. my Uncle writ to M^r waterhouse, but no answer yet. it
may be heell take another half year to be even with him. Cousin Kimberley
his wife and eldest son was here a fortnight sinc. who remember um to
you and Cousen Hen: they wo[ul]d have bin glad to have seen you both
here. I think Cousin [. . .] had not come had it bin in hopes of that [th . . .
but ...] [vertically in left margin] them then and will's not calling the last
weeke I had sooner given you thanks for my knife. I hope tis not to late
now: Aunt and cousin remember them to you. My Dearest Cousin

                    your constant and faithfull
                    Lydia DuGard

8–2

[addressed on verso:] 30	for Mr Samuel DuGard felow of trinite Coledg in oxford

---

1   **[Barford, 1667]:** This letter must have been written in the fall of 1667, just after Samuel had returned to Oxford, having spent the summer at Barford.

17   **second hand:** Samuel's letters to Lydia were often included in packets of letters sent to his other members of the family. Likewise, Lydia's letters were also sometimes sent together with other letters going to Samuel without an external address. See Letter **10**.

19   **my Uncle . . . yet:** Lydia and Thomas were planning to go to London to meet with Edward Waterhouse. See Letter **6**. Thomas DuGard apparently was negotiating with Mr. Waterhouse to become Lydia's guardian. She did not actually go to London until the fall of 1668. See Letters **14** and **15**.

20   **to be even with him:** That is, it could take another half year for Thomas to meet up with him.

20   **Cousin Kimberley:** This was probably William Kimberley and his wife, Elizabeth, with their son, Samuel, from Whitford, Worcestershire.

23   **[. . .]:** The bottom right corner is torn off this letter, so one word is missing. The word is likely Samuel, the eldest Kimberley son.

23–24   **[th . . .but . . .]:** Because the corner is torn, about four words are missing; only these letters can be read.

24   **will:** Lydia expected the carrier, William, to come every week to take her letters to Samuel.

25   **knife:** Samuel sent Lydia many small presents, all part of his expression of love for her.

26   Several words running vertically are crossed out in the bottom left corner of the letter. None can be read.

9–1

[Folger MS X.d.477/9]   [Barford, October 19, 1667]

My Dearest Cousin

Can you think a letter coming from M^r Du: can be reseved with more Love
and respect then if it came from S'r. that would be to love him for a
5   deggre, but that can not make him <mast> Master of my affections more
then he is allready. degrees in love are taken every day, nay every thought
breeds more esteem then other: +with+ what contempt and scorn could I
look upon one of Mr Waterhouses Cre+a+tures: indeed Cousin I am very
much oblidg'd to the man for the great care he takes for my well being. (as
10   he calles it) he wrote to my uncle. and signifie[d] a willingness to be freed
from his troublesome Gaurdianship. I was +glad+ to hear what I had more
re+a+son to desire then he, but it was not to my Uncle he would resign up
his charge but the better to cover his base unfaithfullness. he motion'd me
to a frende of his in london a pious, rich, genteel young man. he doubted
15   not but it would be a very conveinient and comfortable mache for me. he
was so forward that he would have come down into the Country and have
brought him with him. my Uncle accquainted me presently with <th> his
design but as he did not perswade, so he would not disswade me +from
it+ least it might be thought self intrest. I told him I needed no deswsion
20   from that or any other mache, for were the man every way accomplished
and had a vast estate I could never be <l> moved from my resolutions. he
wondred I was so avers, and so discontented at My Gaurdians letter I told
him I had divers waightey reasons that made me speak as I did. My uncle
sent <M> him (contrary to his expectations) for he made no doubt <but>
25   of his consent to all) a negative answer. I beleve he was vex'd to see his
design come to nothing. but in his last did not signifi much displeasure
thus Cousin I have accquainted you with his intent that you may see how
I can scorn and despise all others with one thought of you and how firm
<and> and unshaken my afection is. no My Cousin you need not fear any
30   takeing the place I have given you in my heart. you'l give me a litle in
youres, and if you can think of nothing in me to deserv it yet think me

9–2

4   **S'r:** Beginning in the seventeenth century it became customary in some colleges to address students who had gotten their degree with the title, Sir. *OED*, s.v. "sir," 5.

5   **deggre:** Samuel got his M.A. 31 October 1667.

8   **Cre+a+tures:** These were potential suitors presented by Lydia's guardian.

11   **Gaurdianship:** Since Lydia was under twenty-one years old, she had to have her guardian's permission to marry and to gain access to her inheritance. Her uncle, Thomas DuGard, was at this time trying to negotiate with Mr. Waterhouse to transfer her guardianship to him. Waterhouse himself wanted to be free of it. Maybe, as Lydia suggested, he realized he was not being faithful to her. But instead of resigning his charge, Mr. Waterhouse tried to match Lydia with a gentleman from London. Lydia clearly was not interested in his offer and was not bound by it.

13   **better:** Lydia has written a "p" and then a "b".

17–19   **my Uncle ... self intrest:** Thomas DuGard did not want to be seen as interfering with the match that Waterhouse was trying to make, for fear that he would be accused of self-interest.

23   **uncle:** Lydia has written a "y" and then a "u."

31   **youres:** Here Lydia has written the cursive downward loop to abbreviate "es." I have expanded it.

9-3

faithful. Cousin I am overIoy'd at the good newes Cousen Hen: tells of
himself, a while since I had small hopes < . . . > [vertically in left margin]
of so sudin a change. I dont fear but heel keep his good resolutions you'l
35 remember me to him. I think my Aunt writ to him and so would I if I had
time. <she> Cousen <my k . . . would I desire you to . . .> Mrs Warner
expects the key Mr Ieckell and you borrowed should be returned. you'l
pardon my scribling and [bla.. ..us] of time which makes me sooner than
I would say Dear Cousen,
40   your faithfull
    oct. 19 1667   L D

    [addressed on verso:]   for Mr Samuel DuGard ffellow
                               of Trinity Colledg
                               in oxon

9–4

32   **Cousen Hen:** Lydia talked about Henry's bad behavior on 28 May 1667 and on 8 June 1667; Apparently, he is doing better now. What his "bad behavior" was was never stated. See Letters **6** and **7**.

33   < . . . >: One word is crossed out and is indecipherable.

36   <my k . . . would desire you to . . . >: These words are all crossed out and two are indecipherable.

36   M^rs. **Warner:** I have been unable to identify Mrs. Warner. She must have lived in the village of Barford, and Thomas Jekyll and Samuel must have borrowed a key from her when they were in Barford during the summer of 1667.

37   **Mr Ieckell:** Thomas Jekyll was a student at Trinity College at the same time as Samuel. He got his B.A. in 1667. He came from London and was a student at the Merchant Taylors' School in 1652, when Lydia's father was headmaster there. Lydia met him when he visited Barford with Samuel during the summer of 1667. See Biographical Appendix.

38   [bla . . . us]: The letter is torn at this point, so a couple of words can not be read.

10–1

[Folger MS X.d.477/10]   [Barford, Tuesday, November 26, 1667]

My Dearest Cousin

To tel you a degree can not add to my este+e+me of you, and that I loved
you not less when you was without it,. [*sic*] were but a needles repeition
5   of my last; but I may say I am pleased with it to, not that you may seem
more meet for my afection, but because tis your honer and advantage. how
glad I am to hear of my cousins health you may esely gues. and how did
I fear the contrary til I heard from your own mouth. if I have not had
perfect health of late twas to simpathise with you for I heard you were ile.
10   now you are well I shall be better. distanc can not hinder me from hearing
bad newes though you are somthing unwiling to tel it. you are not like
countr+e+y people that give there frends the satisfaction to tel um there in
good health at the first word, you need not ask how I doe you may know
by your self sinc I am as you are. if you are sick I cant be well if you are in
15   health I am so too. I am sorie to hear Cousin Hen: has so soon broken his
resolutions that he has no more regard to his credit, if no other consideration could work upon him he told my Aunt the name of the DuGards
should not begin to fall in him, and that his crimes were come to the
height. but I am afraid thay were not and I +wish+ a relaps prov not the
20   most daingerous. Cousin I think it will not be the safest way to inclose
your letters in my uncles least thay be opened for me. +though+ he does
not seem to be displeased nor to take the least notis of any thing. <~~~~at
~~least nothing his memory knows not~~> only askes me what newes my
cousin writes <~~me~~> and what he saies of Cousin Hen:. what his thoughts
25   are I know not but if he saw more letteres I am afraid I should know to
soon Cousin Anna remberes her to you. Dear Cousin
novem: 26 l667.

your constant and faithfull
Ly: DuGard.

10–2

30   [addressed on verso:]   for Mr Samuel DuGard ffellow
                             of Trinite Coledg
                                 these.

                    oxon

---

15   **Cousin Hen:** Henry's good behavior obviously did not last long, for here just a month after he said he would change, he broke his resolution. Lydia spoke of his crimes, but other than their being recurrent, it is not possible to determine what they were.

21–22 **he does not seem to be displeased:** Lydia worried constantly about her uncle's view of her relationship with Samuel. She feared that if Samuel included his letters to her in packets of letters to his father, he might open them. She was also worried about her uncle's noticing that she was writing too often to Samuel, so she asked him not to blame her for writing less.

22–23 **<~~. . . at least nothing his memory knows not~~>:** Eight words are crossed out. The first one cannot be reliably read.

25   **letteres:** Here Lydia uses the cursive downward loop to abbreviate "es."

11–1

[Folger MS X.d.477/11]   [Barford, January 28, 1668]

My Dear Cousin

My satisfaction would be as great as yours were I assured of my Uncles
approbation; but how can I when my Aunt puts me in fears and tells me
5   he likes it not? it may be she does it to keep me in suspense, that I may not
have a full contentment. that I may not think my self too happy, if it be so
she is cruel to me, if she speak realy, there is cause enough of sorrow, you
say he saies he will not be against it. not that he aproves of it so much but
because tis gone so farr that he thinks he cannot hinder it without injuring
10   a son that he loves so well. and therfore will not crose him though perhaps
he would wish things otherwise, thus I am kept in suspense and know not
what to think, and yet he does not frown. he looks upon me with the same
eye, and speaks as kindly to me as ever. my care shall be (and indeed
always has bin) to observe and pleas him. and if heretofore I have dis-
15   pleas'd him my sorrow afterward has bin greater then his anger. te+l+l me
how I shal pleas him more, tel me any thing that he dislikes in me and Ile
strive to mend it. I am glad you got safe to oxford but we began to fear
when we saw not Thomas til ten aclock. I keept you constant company in
Your iourny, and not lese now. methinks I see you in your study, som-
20   times hear you play. chearfull, nothing to disturb your pleasures and
contentments. Cousin I am almost afraid to write; <. . .> my Aunt reseved
a le+t+r from Cousin Hen: open how it came so I belive we shant know;
Carl knowes how to excuse it with a lye, but if he be not more carfull, my
Uncle will return to his old carier again. Cousin Hen: hopes yet for his
25   <del>degre</del> degree, I hope when he has it heel be better. youl remember me
to him as all here doe to you. Dearest Cousin

                                       your faithfull
Ian: 28 1668   LSD

[addressed on verso:]   for Mʳ Samuel DuGard
30   these

11–2

3   **yours:** Lydia has appreviated "es" with the standard cursive downward loop.

3–4   **Uncles approbation:** Lydia was still worrying about her uncle's approval; Samuel must have just assured her that his father would not stand against their getting married. See Letter **10**.

7–8   **you . . . it:** Apparently, Samuel had told Lydia that his father would not be against their marriage.

17   **oxford:** Samuel came home to Barford for the Christmas holidays, returning to Oxford in late January.

18   **Thomas:** Thomas Eliot was a servant of the DuGards.

21   **< . . . >:** A letter is written here and crossed out; it is indecipherable.

23   **Carl:** A new carrier named Carl was now serving the DuGards.

24   **old carier:** The old carrier was William. See Letters **7** and **8**.

24–25 **Cousin Hen: hopes yet for his <degre> degree:** Lydia clearly hoped that once Henry got his degree his bad behavior would stop. In fact, Henry had just gotten his B.A. on 22 January 1668, and his troubles continued. Foster, 1:429

28   **Ian 28:** The "8" is clearly written over a "7."

28   **LSD:** Lydia entwined an "S" in the "L" of her signature.

12-1

[Folger MS X.d.477/12]   [Barford, early 1668]

Dear Cousin

My Uncle counterfeits an ignorance as much as ever, and never takes the
least notis of any thing, but so long as I think (and indeed I have reason to
think so in some regards) that it is not an angry silence, a silence that
speaks dislike and discontent, I am very well pleas'd with it. I neither
expect nor desire he should tell me what he knowes I know allready. I
wish he may be silent <still> longer and so I need not fear but he will. at
least till he sees that discretion and consideration which you flateringly say
have bin ripe in me so long, but you wroung mee and speak against your
self in saying I have shewed so little in my choise. I confese I was to blame
I did not ask your Counsel and desire you to chuse for me, no doubt but
you would have made a better choise, and then I should not have bin
taxed with indiscretion, because I took your advice. doe but consider how
much prudence you have shew'd in chuseing for your self and then tell me
if you can find [fa]ult with mine. but am I indiscrete in my love too, 'tis
sertain that that cannot be to large, but the expresion of it may, and
insteead of indearing, may beget a slighting and a disesteem. if you thinke
I have bin to free and shew'd to great a fondness, (I confese I can't return
to my first coldness but) I can if you would have it so, keep [my] most
pasionat thoughts within my heart, and then though you have [. . .] Cousin
we have had a melancholy house

[addressed on verso:]   for Mr Samuel DuGard Fello[w]
                              of trinity Colledg in
                                   oxon

12–2

8   **but he:** Lydia has written "we" and then changed it to "he."
21   **[. . .]:** The paper is torn, so the first half of the line is missing.
22   **melancholy house:** I can not determine why the house is melancholy.
22   The bottom third of this letter is torn off.

13–1

[Folger MS X.d.477/13]   [Barford, March 21, 1668]

Dear Cousin

I was not a litle troubled when I heard of the continuance of your cough,
fearing it would grow worse. but how am I cheered sinc you told me the
5   good news of its decrease, and put me in hopes it will take a finall farwell:
now I shall hope to be in health too, for it was vain for me to think I could
long be so when I was tortured with fears you would be cough'd into a
consumtion. Cousin (however you may think or hope), I cant be well if
you are not. and if I have health at any time I could wilingly [forsake] it if
10   it would contribute to yours. but methinks my late reso[lve] of being lese
free in the expresion of my afection is soon forgotten and broke. I hope
you will not conclude from the breach of this others are no better kept. you
see I can't keep my heart lockt and it will not be hid from him that has it.
nor will I indeavor it should for the future but resolve against resolutions
15   imposible [to be] kept. Cousin this inclosed was half writ the last week; but
Carls playing the good husband came so soon I had not time to finish it.
it is unsealed that you may peruse it, and I refer it to you whether to
deliver it or not. if it have not your approbation withhold it and excuse me
to Mr Iekyll for not writing. all are well here and salute you. Dear Cousin

20   March 21. 1668   your truly faithfull
                                             LSydia DuGard.

youl seal Mr Iekylls letter
if you give it him

13–2

8   **Consumtion:** Consumption was a general term for a wasting of the body; it did not refer to a specific disease. Lydia was concerned that Samuel's cough would turn in to a consumption of the lungs. *OED*, s.v. "consumption," 4.a.

16   **Carls playing the good husband:** that is, he husbands his time well.

19   **Mr Jekyll:** Lydia had written to Samuel's friend and colleague, Thomas Jekyll, who had come with Samuel to visit Barford in October, 1667. She wanted Samuel to read her letter and approve of it before sending it on to Mr. Jekyll. See Letter **9**.

21   Lydia has now established the custom of intertwining an "S" into the "L" of her name.

14–1

[Folger MS X.d.477/14]   [Barford September 5, 1668]

Dear Cousin

You say, and I beleive you<l> left us not without some pensiveness, but
sure there was no great reason for it exchanging Barford for oxford, a place
5   where no delights are wanting you can wish, tis I that have cause to be
pensive I that am left alone I that am robed of a happyness for agreat
while, which is the more missed because inioyed so long. you are gone to
a place that any body but you would esteem and love more then a Cousin.
if your thoughts are not too much imploied otherwaies youl send mee
10   some in my Iourny, they will be sure to find me travelling towards London
next week and I hope t they will not think the way too teidious; I should
have took more pleasure had my Iourny bin sweetned with the thoughts
of coming down by oxon but there's small hopes on't perhapes it would
stand well enough with my conveniency you may asure your self it would
15   with my desires; but since it wont with my Uncles will both the other
signifie nothing. time wonte if the Carier would sufer mee to write half so
much as I <sh> would. perhaps the leng+t+h of the next may <may> make
amends for the shortness of this. in great hast Dearest Cousin

Sept: 5. 1668.   your constant and faithfull
20   LSD
all salute you.
youl direct your letter
to Aunt Pettifers.

[addressed on verso:]   For Mr Samuel DuGard
25   Fellow of trin Coll:
                                        these
                         oxon

14–2

7   **inioyed so long:** Samuel had obviously spent time in Barford during his summer vacation.

10   **they:** The "e" is written on the top of an "a".

10   **travelling towards London:** Lydia was planning to travel with her uncle to visit her relatives in London and possibly to meet with her guardian, Mr. Waterhouse.

11   **t:** There is not sufficient room to finish the word, so Lydia moves to the next and begins again.

11   **think:** There are letters underneath this word, but I can not read them.

11   **way:** Lydia has written "y" on top of "ie."

15–16   **but since . . . signifie nothing:** Since it isn't her uncle's will to go to London by way of Oxford, it signifies nothing that Lydia thinks it both convenient and desireable to go that way.

20   **LSD:** This signature provides a particularly artful example of intertwining initials.

23   **Aunt Pettifers:** This was Jane Pettifer, Lydia's father's and Samuel's father's sister. Lydia and her uncle were obviously planning to stay with the Pettifers in St. Giles Cripplegate.

15–1

[Folger MS X.d.477/15]   [Barford, October 3, 1668]

My Dear Cousin.

I thank God my Uncle and I came safe home and found all here in health.
I confese it was not without some reluctance I left London so soon but
5   since I was forsed to it I strove to be contented. Barford is not lese pleasant
to mee +now+ then +was+ before you know how I stand afected to a
country <life> retired life how much content I take in it and that I love it
the more because you seem to be taken with it. you have heard me say I
could not live at London but perhaps you might think I spoke so because
10   it was so long since I had bin there that I had forgoten the place. and so
might fancy it to be lese pleasant then I should find it. but I say so still. I
saw nothing there to be taken with; nothing that could make mee desire
to stay longer then to salute and take leave of all friends. I was with you
often in thoughts even when I was in the company of renew'd aquaintance
15   and freinds whome I was glad to see, it troubled me to hear you say you
took physick and I could not but be consern'd for the want of a health
more dear to mee then my own which I thought ocationed it. ah Cousin
how much am I aflicted at the bad newes of your headach. it is cruel to
mee now and tortures me as much as if I realy felt it you told me a great
20   while since you were advised to an Issue sinc it was conseavd proper for
you methinks you are alittle to blam[e] you are still without one I should
be glad with all my heart it would prove your cure. Cousin Anna
rem<b>emberes her to you and gives you many thanks for her token. Dear
Cousin

25   oct: 3 l668.   your ffaithfull
                                                                       Lydia DuGard.

[vertically in left margin] Nan presents her humble service to you and will
needs present with a token. my Aunt will expect [her] napkin.

15–2

[addressed on verso:]   for Mr Samuel DuGard
30   These

---

3   **home:** Lydia had just returned home to Barford from London where she had
        stayed with the Pettifers for about three weeks. See Letter **14**.
13   **friends:** Lydia moved from London when she was twelve years old. Clearly, she
        knew relatives there and she had kept track of some friends, but she did not want
        to return there to live.
20   **Issue:** An issue was an artificial sore kept open for the purpose of counter
        irritation or for the discharge of pus in order to relieve congestion in or pressure
        on a part. *OED*, s.v. "issue," n. 4.med.b.
27   **Nan:** Nan must have been a servant in the DuGard household; she is mentioned
        just this once.
28   **napkin:** A napkin could have been a pocket handkerchief at this time. *OED*, s.v.
        "napkin," n.2.a.

16–1

[Folger MS X.d.477/16]   [Barford, November 13, 1668]

novemb. 13 1668

Dear Cousin

Would my occationes have permited I had told you how I did last week
5   but I was so much employ'd that I could not doe more then think a letter
and wish you the satisfaction (for I have cause to belive it is so) to hear of
my health but I thought I should not need to excuse it suposeing you
would not expect to hear from mee sooner: I can say with you I am not
allwaies silent when I dont pen my thoughts nor have I lese afectionat ones
10   when you dont read them, I am sorry you are troubled with my distemper
the scurvy and <need goody Hawkes medicine> could +wish+ goody
Hawkses water had so much vertue in it now as in the spring. but since
you have a mind to try it you shall have a bottle the next week. Cousin I
thank you for your ttoken. a token which for +the senders and+ its own
15   sake finds a better wellcome and is much more accseptable then if it were
one of those vanity's you mention. I am not of the humore of those who
would be courted by presents and esteme their lovers no longer then they
are feeding them with costly toyes. let those whose estates easeed there
parts make mony there spoksman and purchas there good or bad fortune
20   at to dere a rate. give me a man that needs not be beholding to his purs to
testifie <testif> his affection, whose parts and vertues exites the greatest
love. the paper you inclos'd in your last after my uncle had read it I lay'd
up safe. looking upon it before I had read your letter I went presantly and
gave it my uncle, not thinking since it was lattin it was to be keept by mee.
25   Aunt Smith is not lese aflicted with her ague then heretofore. Cousin Mary
is come home. Iohn I saw at London who presented his service to you. I
fear some bad newes from or of Aunt +Pettifer+ since we can't hear from
her. bambury is not yet return'd. he writes to his wife. takes care for the
payment of his rent and promises to send her some mony shortly. but he
30   <went> run +like a knave+ away without her knowlidg, and +tels her+

16–2

11   **scurvy:** The symptoms of scurvy were pains in the limbs, foul breath, and skin eruptions. *OED*, s.v. "scurvy," n.1.a.

11–12   **goody Hawkses water:** Goody Hawkes was a neighbor in Barford known for her medical treatments. The "water" was most likely an herbal medicine. See Beier, 'The Character of a Good Woman: Women and Illness" in *Sufferers and Healers*, 211–41.

24   **lattin:** It is difficult to understand why Samuel would send Lydia something written in Latin. A few women early in the century learned Latin, such as Brilliana Harley or Nancy Verney, but by 1660, girls of Lydia's social station were usually only taught reading, writing, some accounts, religion, French, music, and embroidery. There is no indication that Lydia has studied Latin. See Gardiner, *English Girlhood at School*; Ezell, *The Patriarch's Wife*, 9–12.

25   **Aunt Smith:** Mary Smith of Birmingham was the sister of Hannah DuGard, Samuel's mother. She was mentioned in the letters Hannah DuGard wrote to Mary Wyllys in Connecticut in 1646 and 1648.

25   **ague:** This is a general term for an attack of "shaking and shivering" or chills and fever. *OED*, s.v. "ague," n. 3.

25   **Cousin Mary:** Mary Orford was Lydia and Samuel's first cousin, the daughter of their uncle and aunt, Nicholas and Margery Orford. She lived in London.

26   **come:** Lydia has written "at" over "come" or vice versa.

26   **Iohn:** This was either John DuGard, the son of Uncle John and Aunt Alice DuGard, or John Pettifer, the son of Uncle John and Aunt Jane Pettifer. In either case, he would be a first cousin of Lydia and Samuel.

28   **bambury:** Bambury was a tenant farmer on DuGard lands.

16-3

neither where he is, what employment he has, nor when heel come home. my Aunt would have you write to him and lay law and gospel before him those are hir words. hee lives in greens ally in westminster.

[vertically in left margin] I am sorry Cousin Hen: still slights and despises
35   admonition. hee sent a peevish discontented letter to my Aunt. he signified a great desire to leave oxford and retire somwhere from a chamber ffellow that hated him. he wondred you should make him the mark of his spleen who was never yet hated by any in oxford except you and your slaves. he sais it is reported the viol <you> he gave you makes you <sowr> and
40   fretfull and that it was not in the nature of Davids musick for insted of curing others you possesed your self with a melancholy male contented spirit. affter this strang rate he went on. and earnestly beg'd my Uncles and Aunts consent to his departure. I am heartily sorry for him and ernestly desire his reformation. all salute you Deare Cousin your faithfull

45   LD

[addressed on verso:]   [Mʳ Sa]muel DuGard
Trin+i+ty Colledg
[Ox]ford

16–4

34–36 Cousin Hen . . . leave oxford: Henry was still living in Oxford, even though he received his degree in January. He was up to his old antics, whatever they were. He was clearly unhappy and asked permission from his father and mother to leave Oxford.

36–38 a chamber ffellow . . . slaves: Clearly, he and Samuel had had a falling out, for Henry referred to Samuel as the chamber fellow that hated him.

40 Davids musick: 1 Samuel 16:14–23.

39–41 [Mr Sa] . . . [Ox]ford: The address leaf is torn so the first part of the address is missing.

17–1

[Folger MS X.d.477/17]   [Barford, February 6, 1669]

Feb: 6. 1669.

Dear Cousin

How glad I am to hear of your better health you may easily guise, when
5   I shall tell you how much tis wish't for and desired by mee, how like you
I grow when I am told the contrary, and how apt I am to fear the worst
when <there> to others thinking there is so litle ground of fears that
should some know perhaps they'd smile and say my thoughts were too
much taken up, and it was <to be> +needles+ to be so much consern'd for
10   another's wellfare. but sure you won't be one of those, won't blame me for
that which your self is the cause of. till the cause be removed the effects
will continue, and till you sease to bee what you are (which I beleive will
never be) I cant allter or grow weary of Loving one whose deserts call for
the greatest respect and whose affection I should be ungratfull too did I
15   not answer with the like, but I begin to chek my self for writing so freely,
and taking such a liberty as will cost me a blush when I think you are
reading it. it is a fault (for some would call it so, if you dont,) I <am> often
run in to, which I somtimes blame my self for, but which I the lese unwill-
ingly allow my self in because (if I have not forgot) I speak with lese
20   confidence and more feare by word of mouth then in paper. if you dislike
it, tell me, and Ile promise to be guilty of it no more. I did not think such
reports would have bin spread abroad from our Whitford Iourny. a year
or two since it would have troubled me much, but now since I am so used
to hear people talk of you and mee I matter +it+ but litle and can hear all
25   they say. a Genteelwoman at london hearing my Uncle had two sons said
she beleived one of them would not allwayes call me cousin. she told me
she wish'd me very well and bid me be well advised, and not rashly
dispose of my self. with abundance more of good counsell. she urged me
so much and beg'd me so earnestly to tell her the truth, that at last, <being
30   tired with her importunity. . .> since she was my Mother's great freind,

17-2

21   **promise:** Lydia has written "promise" on top of "be."

22   **Whitford Iourny:** Lydia first wrote "B," then a "W," presumably thinking automatically of Barford. Samuel and Lydia probably visited the Kimberleys in Whitford near Bromsgrove, in Worcestershire during the summer of 1668. Worcestershire was the ancestral home of both the DuGards and the Kimberleys.

30   ~~importunity ...~~>: The last word in this string of crossed out words cannot be read.

30   **Mother's:** This was Lydia Parker DuGard, who had died in London in 1661.

17–3

since she lov'd me almost from my cradle, since I realy beleivd sheed be
faithfull, and sinc I was tired with her importunity I confes'd some of the
truth. I am not sorry I did so. if I had bin silent she would have thought (it
may be) I was inveagld, and should undervalue my self. but when I told
35   her what you was. she changed her advice and cautions into approbation
and said she liked it a great deal better then if I had lov'd some young
gallant though he had a good estate. sure that report +you spoke of+ will
be fresh again at easter when we go a secund time into worsester shire. My
Uncle intends you shall acompany him to graffton, and spend some of that
40   litle time you have left in seeing what we should have seen in the summer.
all wish to see and hear you and expect a sermon when you come. I thank
you for that which you have presented mee with. it realy deserves thanks
as well for its own as the <senders> +aughthers+ sake. it is such a one as
might be expected from you, and such a one as cant but take with all. My
45   Uncle would fain have seen it but I neither shew'd it him nor told him
what it was. I should have done both had not you forbid me. <all> cousin
Anna saluts you but, is half angry at your long silenc. her distemper God
be thanked <be> wears away a pace and she is returning to her former
mirth and livlyness. Aunt is still at warwick with Cousin spooner who is
50   very weak and in a consumption. My Sister presents her service to you.
she sent me latly the most pasionat sorrowfull letter that ever I reseaved
from her. wherin she tels me her dear M^r I has bin at deaths dore, and
though beyond expectation he is recoverd yet she fears her troubles are of
the same length with her life. she and I have a great desire to +see+ each
55   other. sheed fain impart her greifs to me at large that I might simpathise
with her and comfort her. I intreated my Uncle to let me goe to Coventry
but he as +he+ constantly does denig'd me so that I must contentt my self
(but with much ado) with writing to her, if it wo+u+ld +not+ be <no>
trouble I would request you to give her aline or too, and enclose it in your
60   next to mee. Sheel take it exeeding kindly, and youl at once oblidg her and
(Dear Cousin)   your ffaithfull

LSydia DuGard.

17–4

65   I should have writen to Mrs Milbourn as you desired me but that her son came hither and spared me the labor. M^r frankland told her that which you wrote conserning him. I supose she would gladly have him at that Coledg but he is so weakly that he is all=together unfit for a scoller in that regard.

---

37   **report +you spoke of+:** Obviously, the relatives were spreading the word that Samuel and Lydia were in love.

38   **we go . . . worsester shire:** Lydia, Samuel, and Thomas DuGard were planning a trip to visit family lands at Eastertime.

39   **graffton:** Grafton Flyford (Worcestershire). William and Thomas DuGard were both born in Grafton Flyford, and Lydia inherited some land there from her father.

41   **sermon:** Four of Samuel's sermons have been preserved. The texts for the sermons were (1) and (2) Hebrews 4:14, (3) Ecclesiastes 7:2, and (4) Psalms 3:8. Bodl., Rawl. E 69, "Four Sermons by Samuel DuGard."

42   **that . . . with:** Verses.

45   **aughthers:** author's

46–47   **cousin Anna:** Samuel's sister.

49   **Cousin spooner:** Margaret Huggeford Spooner was the sister of Mary DuGard. She was married to William Spooner of Henwood Hall, Solihull. She died in 1674.

50   **Sister:** This "sister" was Elizabeth Tyler Mitchell, Lydia's half-sister, who was approximately twenty-eight years old at this time. Elizabeth's husband, John Mitchell, was very sick. He must have died soon after this letter was written, for Elizabeth was free to travel with Lydia to Oxford in June. See Letter **18**.

52   **M^r I:** John Mitchell, Elizabeth's husband.

58   **<~~no~~>:** Lydia has written "to," then "no" and crossed both out.

63   **Mrs Milbourn:** Mrs. Milbourn was a Barford neighbor and friend of the DuGards. She had a daughter, Betty, about Lydia's age and also a son. Mrs. Milbourn asked for advice about her son's going to Coventry Grammar School, but apparently Lydia believed he was unfit to be a scholar.

64   **M^r frankland:** Rev. Samuel Frankland was Headmaster of Coventry Grammar School and a friend of Thomas DuGard.

18–1

[Folger MS X.d.477/18]　　　　　　　　　　　[Barford, June 30, 1669]
　　　　　　　　　　　　　　　　　　　　　　　Iune. 30 l669.

Dear Cousin

It has not alitle troubled me that I could not sooner send to you, and thank
5　　you for my book and string, which I +(did not)+ receavd (as youl see in the
inclosed) till <the> Iune the 23. Carl is so neg[li]=gent and careles that one
can put no trust in him. 3 dayes this letter has bin sent affter him and still
return'd. all this morning I have bin contriving how to send, and before
your messinger came to mee I heard of Mr Atherly's Iourny to Oxford and
10　　intended to trouble him with a letter. at last Cousin I am fully resolv'd to
break th+o+row all dificultys and come to Oxford, with my sister, whos
company I am very desierous of. she would gladly bear me company but
she beleivs you won't think it conveinient, and would needs have me ask
your councell which I have done in my last I am very glad to hear you
15　　speak of [Elizabeth's] +her+ coming. I confes I should not very willingly
come without her, nor indeed doe I think it +will b[e]+ so handsom to be
without a companion. but Cousin I doubt we shall be trouble'd for a man.
Mr hamersly whom I have spoken too would willingly wait upon us but
that he can't be absent from his scollars thursdays and saterdays. so that
20　　if we have him we can't be at oxford before munday come sennight, and
must be at home again a wedensday. pray Cousin If you can contrive no
other way for us will you doe so much as write 2 or 3 words to him. I
beleive you may prevail with him to doe what you'd have him. I know not
whither I had best let Mrs Milbourn and Betty know that I goe any fu+r+th-
25　　er then to Mr Dods, but they will hear on't some how or other and perhaps
speak more on't if it be done slyly then if I aquaint them with my purpose.
I am very sorry Cousin Harry demeans him=self no better yet, and that he
had so soon broken his promises to mee I am not pleas'd to think of his
being with you since I know heel be your trouble and vexation. sister and
30　　Betty Millbourn present their service to you. Dearest Cousin

　　　　　　　　your affectionat and faithfull
　　　　　　　　　　LS.D.

18–2

5   **string:** This most likely was a string for her viol. Note the range of gifts Samuel sent Lydia: gloves, a knife, books, string, verses, and other tokens.

6   **Carl:** Carl was still the carrier being used by the DuGard family, but he was obviously not held in high regard. See Letters **11** and **13**.

9   **Mʳ Atherly's Iourny:** I have not been able to identify Mr. Atherly, but clearly he was travelling to Oxford, and Lydia was happy to take advantage of anybody going to Oxford to deliver her letters to Samuel.

11   **come to Oxford:** This trip to Oxford was the only one that Lydia arranged herself. Her sister, Elizabeth, was to accompany her, and Mr Hamersly, a tutor or schoolmaster, had agreed to "wait" on them. They traveled by horseback and could get to Oxford in one day. They left on Monday morning and returned to Barford on Wednesday evening.

11   **sister:** This was Lydia's sister, Elizabeth, from Coventry. See Letter **17**. Presumably, her husband, Mr I, had died, but I have been unable verify his death.

17   **we:** This can be read as "we" or "I." Lydia has written both and it is impossible to tell which one she wrote first.

17   **a:** Lydia first wrote "Mʳ" and then in dark ink wrote "a" on top of this.

20   **munday:** All members of the DuGard family observed restrictions on Sunday travel, so she could not leave until Monday.

21   **If:** Lydia has written both an upper case and a lower case "I" in the word, "if."

24   **Mʳˢ Milbourn and Betty:** Here is evidence that the neighbors were indeed talking about Lydia's relationship with Samuel as she had feared.

25   **Mʳ Dods:** John Dodds was the vicar of the church in nearby Lighthorn.

26   **slyly:** This can be read "slyly" or "slily."

27   **Cousin Harry:** Cousin Henry's misdemeanors went on. Lydia was called in to try to get him to reform, but she was not successful.

18–3

[vertically in left margin] cousin youl be sure to write to me as soon as posible and tel me how long a stay we must make at Oxford that I may
35   know what to do for horses. I would not wilingly exced too or three nights at most. I would not have seal'd this letter if there had bin anything in it worth your reading but you shal know the conte[nts of] it when I see you.

[addressed on verso:]   For Mr Samuel DuGard ffellow
        of trin: Coll: these
40   present
    Oxon.

18–4

34   **make:** This word can be read as "make" or "take" since Lydia wrote one on top of the other.

35   **to:** Lydia has written a "d" and then changed it to a "t" in the word, "to."

36–37 **I would not . . . I see you:** Apparently, Lydia had enclosed a sealed letter to someone else in the packet. Normally, she left such letters unsealed, allowing Samuel to read them before he sealed and sent them.

37   **conte[nts of]:** The paper is torn at this point.

19–1

[Folger MS X.d.477/19]   [Worcester, September 5, 1670]

Dearest Cousin.

I am sorry you were put to such fears for me last week, and though I had
rather be troubld my self then you should be soe yet (as you said once) I
5   am well enough pleas'd with it, and can't but take it kindly, and must
needs conclude, (if I had no greater asurance of your love) that you who
can be so much concern'd at the delays of the Carier or porter love me as
much as you say you doe. I think I was almost as restles and troubld as
you +that when my dresing box came+ <about a fortnight agoe> when I
10   saw not your letter till saterday morning. though Kuman not com+m+ing
to town before I had no reason to fear but there was one for me. <I> if you
should fail to write one week you would put me to a great de<a>l of
torture, and I should have a thousand fears. and Cousin so long as I am at
Worcter, if you dont reseave a letter from me every week you may con-
15   clude tis either lost, or I+'m+ not able to hold a pen. meathinks tis hardly
to be credited that my Uncle would have me write to his son Harry. for my
part I don't see to what end I should; let there be never so many discontents amongst them, I am sure I can't make um less, <and> I have often
endeavor'd it, and have found it to so litle purpose that I am resolv'd Ile
20   try no more. if I should write to Harry it would be so far from loveingly
that it would be much after the rate you write to Smith. but I dont intend
to trouble my self with him. 2 or 3 letters agoe Cousin I remember you told
me twould not be ill taken if I would write to my uncle so my Aunt wrote
me word upon his reception of my last. I thought that was very small
25   encouragement to write agen, and twas taken so little notice of that I have
no mind to venture any more, unles youl lend me your pen, that will make
it so good that my uncle must needs be pleas'd with it and votsafe me an
answer too. your letter to smith is exelent good, and I could wish he had
it, but could rather wish you had held your resolution of never writing to
30   him again. you need not care for his thretnings, and I thought you would

19–2

1   **[Worcester, Sept. 5, 1670]:** Lydia sent this letter from Worcester to Samuel, who was in Barford at the time. There are no letters in this Folger collection between 30 June 1669 and 5 September 1670. Mary DuGard, wife of Thomas, died 4 October 1669. Lydia moved to Worcester in August 1670, and she was living there with her relatives, the Ashbys. Lydia's hand has become more fluent and sloppier over the fourteen months. Her guardian, Edward Waterhouse, died 30 May 1670. Lydia was still under age, so she was not free to marry without permission. I can only assume that Thomas DuGard had become her guardian after Waterhouse died.

10   **Kuman:** Presumably this was the carrier between Warwick and Worcester.

12   **de<a>l:** It looks like Lydia wrote an "l" and then wrote over this "l" to make the word "deal."

21   **Smith:** There was a Smith living in Barford who was regularly in trouble with the authorities over land disputes. Maybe Samuel was referring to this man. Lydia clearly did not want to be associated with him. He might even have been trying to make a match with her. Certainly, Samuel had written a harsh letter to him. See lines 28–30. Lydia did not want to send Samuel's letter to Smith directly for fear it would appear as a love letter from her. See lines 34–35.

23   **my Aunt:.** Thomas married Anne, daughter of Hugh Muston of Tibbols, Kinsbury (Warwickshire), sometime in 1670. Lydia already appeared to have cultivated a good relationship with Thomas's new wife, Anne.

28   **Your letter:** Samuel sent Lydia the letter he had written to Smith (line 21) for her perusal. This was common practice, for Lydia had sent letters to Samuel for his review earlier. See Letter **13**.

19–3

not have daind to take notice of them though in such a way as you have.
if you would have me send it I will though I can't con=veniently. I think
my best way will be to enclose it in one, either to Mrs Ann Ioans, or
Thomas Milner. otherwise I am afraid some will think tis a love letter of
35   mine to him. I thought Cousin I should have troubld you at oxon by this
time. a while since my Cousin Ashby was in a mind to give her London
Daughter the meeting there, and would needs have me a long with her,
but bad ways or one thing or other have made +her think+ it best to stay
at home, and to speak truth I am not sorry she has alter'd her mind. pray
40   cousin let me know whither Cousin Ann be come home yet. M^r hunt was
in <wo> +town+ tother day and told Cousin Ned: Ashby there was a
match proposd for her, I wish I knew who twas. she is so melancholy that
you had need cheer her up, and pray wish her to write to me, but not to
say a word of her mony this 2 mounths. for if she does her letters won't be
45   wellcome. best Duty to Uncle, service and love to whom you pleas, in
great hast, (for I han't playd a stroke this morning) my Dearest Cousin

> your constant and faithfull
> LSydia DuGard.

Sept. 5. 1670

50   Cousin Ashbys respects to you. if you intend an old shirt for Abigail pray
Cousin send to me that I may cut it for her.

[addressed on verso:]   For Mr Samuel DuGard
these

19-4

33   **M[rs] Ann Ioans, or Thomas Milner:** I have not been able to identify these two people although they must have lived in Barford and been trustworthy acquaintances of Lydia.

36   **Ashby:** Anne Ashby, who had married Edward Ashby, was a distant cousin of Lydia. He had died in 1660; she had remarried George Bagnall in 1665 in Worcester. Lydia paid her Aunt Ashby to live with her in Worcester.

36–37 **London Daughter:** Presumably, this was a daughter or daughter-in-law of Anne and Edward Ashby.

40   **M[r] hunt:** Henry Hunt, Gentleman, of Barford was High Constable in Kineton Hundred, Warwickshire, in 1670. (*Warwick County Records: Orders Made at Quarter Sessions, Easter 1665 to Epiphany 1674*, ed. R. C. Ratcliff and H. C. Johnson [Warwick: L. Edgar Stephens, 1939], 5:141.)

41   **Cousin Ned: Ashby:** Edward Ashby, son of Anne and Edward Ashby, was an apothecary in Worcester.

42   **match:** Lydia's cousin, Anna, was now twenty-four years old and unmarried. Clearly, she was troubled by this. In fact, she didn't marry until 1676, when she was thirty, which would have been quite unusual for that time.

42   **I:** This can be read either "I" or "we," since Lydia wrote one on top of the other.

43–45 **but . . .welcome:** Samuel's sister, Anna, could count on a larger portion from her father than Lydia had inherited from hers. In fact, when Anna did marry, she received a portion of 300 pounds.

46   **Playd a stroke:** Lydia came to Worcester to learn to play the viol. She took her lessons very seriously and referred to her viol and to practicing frequently in her letters.

50   **old shirt for Abigail:** It was likely that Lydia offered to make something for her friend, Abigail Cross, or her expected baby, using one of Samuel's old shirts. Abigail was about seven months pregnant at this time.

20–1

[Folger MS X.d. 477/20]   [Worcester, October 24, 1670]

Dear Cousin.

sure you think I am strangly melancholy, that you had ra+t+her have me
love you less then <not> be uncheerfull. I am chearfull enough, and as
5   cheerfull as I am like to be. but if in this regard or in any other I am not as
you could wish me, I heartily wish I could alter my self that +I+ might
pleas you the more. I did not think S^r william Bromly would have desir'd
you for Baginton since it is but 60^# a year. I was speaking on't to Cousin
Ashby, and she thinks since you have such good hopes from other gentle-
10   men you wont doe ill in accept+ing+ this at present. and that tis probable
since sr william so earnestly desires you, hee'l be a good freind, these are
her thoughts. for my own part I have little to say; for I don't question but
what you doe will be for the best. if you accept of it you shall not hear me
complain, if you refuse, I shall be contented, and shall rest satisfied in this
15   that you will act for your own and my good and advantage. freinds salute
you, and Cousin Bagnall either does or will thank you for her Bottle of
watter. my dear Cousin,

oct: 24.
1670.   your most afectionate and faithfull
20   LSydia DuGard.

pray Cousin when you send more then a single letter enclose them in a
loose paper, for I don't love to have um half worn out. if it wont be to great
a trouble to you I <shoul> I should be glad to see a coppy of your letter to
S^r william, for I am sure it will be a very good one

20–2

7   **S^r william Bromly:** Sir William Bromley was lord of the manor of Baginton (Warwickshire) and patron of the living. He was also justice of the peace *(Warwick County Records,* 5:150; *VCH,* 6:23; Wood, *Athenae,* 4:664; Foster, 1:87).

8   **60*:** Lydia used the symbol (#) normally used for weights to indicate pounds. Samuel had been offered sixty pounds a year for a post in Baginton. In contrast, Samuel's father had obtained the wealthy living of Barford at 250 pounds per annum in 1648. Samuel decided to turn the Baginton post down.

10   **gentlemen:** Samuel was being considered for a position at St. Nicholas, Warwick, which he thought was preferable to the Baginton post. See Letter **22**.

16   **Cousin Bagnall:** Elizabeth Bagnall, daughter of Anne and Edward Ashby, married Nicholas, son of George Bagnall (25 May 1668).

17   **Bottle of watter:** Samuel showed his generosity again by sending a present to Elizabeth Bagnall. This was most likely orange flower water or rose water, both very popular gifts for women (Picard, *Restoration London,* 125).

21–1

[Folger MS. X.d.477/21]   [Worcester, December 1670]

My Dearest Cousin.

I am very sorry to hear my cousin Ann continues so unhealthy and if upon
her account or any other you think better of my being at Barford then here
5   Ile remove thither. you tell me my company will doe her good, but I doubt
it; for I am the worst in the world to drive away melancholy (and +that+
I know she is somtimes to much given too) and in stead of makeing her
chearfull, +Im afraid+ I shall grow like her. you tell me too that if I were
at Barford you could see me oftener. if I thought you would doe so it
10   would be no small inducement. I dont know what I had best to doe and
yet as I said before if it were not for hindering my practice I would to
Barford once more. I intend to learn <to> till Xtmas. and iust a mounth
after I shall have bin here 3 quarters of a year, by that time tis to be hoped
I shall begin to play and so shall part with worcsester somthing more
15   willingly then before. I wish cousin you could perswade my uncle to mend
that cold chamber or els it will doe me harm comming out of <su..> one so
close and warm. you may tell my uncle, Chandler has brought me some
mony. november yᵉ 12 I reseavd 9 pounds which being due to cousin
Ashby I payd +to+ her the same day. 5 pounds for half a years board, and
20   4 I borrowd of her. there is 3 pound more due +to me+ which chandler
cant help me +to+ till Xtmas. I m afraid my Uncle thinks I have layd out
a great deal of mony since I came hither but +I+ beleive heel find this years
ac+c+ounts wont rise to near so much as the last. I am sorry for Mʳ Tribles
lose, and very glad Abigail is lik+e+ly to recover. duty and love to all at
25   Barford. my dearest Cousin

your loveing & faithfull
L D.

[vertically in left margin] frends salute you and expect you hear at Xtmas.
pray Cousin let me know whats become of my Cousin Harry; I can't but

21–2

30   conceit his sick or dead, or gon further off that you tell me I need not fear
his troubling me at Barford.

[addressed on verso:]   For Mr Samuel DuGard
Fellow of Trin: Coll:
these.
35   oxon.

---

3   **cousin Ann:** Samuel's sister, Anna, was clearly unhealthy and distraught.

4–5   **my being . . . thither:** Lydia was independent enough and financially able to stay
in Worcester to continue her viol lessons or to move back to Barford.

11   **practice:** One of Lydia's main reasons for staying in Worcester was to learn to
play the viol.

12–13   **I intend . . . of a year:** Based on this information Lydia must have gone to
Worcester to live in May, 1670.

16   **<su͞:>:** One word beginning with "su" is crossed out.

17   **Chandler:** Thomas Chandler was a tenant of William DuGard, living on his lands
in Grafton Flyford (Worcestershire) in 1662. After Lydia's father's death, Chandler continued living there and sent his rent to Lydia as stipulated in DuGard's
will.

19   **5 pounds:** See Introduction to the Letters, note 60.

22   **hither:** Lydia has inserted another "I" after the "h."

23   **Mr Tribles:** Presumably, Mr. Tribles lived in Barford, but I have been unable to
identify him further.

24   **Abigail:** Abigail Cross, Lydia's friend in Barford, was most likely suffering from
the difficulties of childbirth. She had given birth to a daughter, Elizabeth, on 17
November 1670. This daughter had lived only twelve days.

29   **Cousin Harry:** Samuel's brother, Henry, might have left Trinity College after his
plea to his parents in September, 1670, but based on Lydia's comment, he was not
living in Barford at the time of this writing. Lydia appeared worried about him
but not eager to see him. Clearly, there was a falling out between them. See Letter
19.

22–1

[Folger MS X.d.477/22]   [Worcester, January 16, 1671]

Ian 16 1671

My Dearest Cousin

It's a sad thing you should loose your Mistrises <afte> one after another
thus: but I must confess I dont pity you much and need not ask you
whither you are sorry or not to let pass so many good fortunes and acom-
plish'd Ladys <ł> for I am confident, and dare be bold to say, my Cousin
loves his +honest+ Lydia so much; (whether he has good reason or no)
that he would not part with her to gain a Beauty or a fortune. you tell me
you think, that had you not a Cousin alive, you should be either in love
with solitariness, or els out of love with every thing: and I doubt not but
<your would think you should> if I should be now taken from you,
you<ł> would think you had lost a faithfull freind and lover, and, soe
could not presantly forget me. but I hope, my Cousin, my death would not
work such a strange alteration in you as to make you delight in nothing
but retirements and solitude: your reason +and piety+ would in a short
time conquer your grief, by shewing you the fruitlessness of it. and since
you are (as I know you are) so much disposed, and desierous to advan=
tage others; you would soon be <a> weary +of+ a life which would be
displeasing to God and unprofitable to man. and you that can bring such
good arguments to alay the greiffs of others sure could not so much for get
them or be soe much your own enemy as not to <. . .sho . . .ied> endeavour to moderate your own by them. but I am so apt to run into melancholy
and dismall thoughts my self, that I don't wonder at you for it. but yet cant
but think my self uery much loved by you that the very thoughts and
aprehendtions of my death can be so grevious to you. I thank you for the
many and great expresions of your love, and though a mean capacity or
want of art denighs me the privilidg of expresing my most advan=tagious
thoughts of you, yet you may be and I hope are confident my afection is
as great as if it were better exprest. that you are soe well pleas'd and doe
count your self so happy in your Lydia, I can't but thank you; but that the

22-2

1   **[Worcester, January 16, 1671]:** This letter was sent to Samuel in Barford, after his return there from visiting Lydia in Worcester over the Christmas holidays.

14   **my death:** "my" is written on top of "you."

22   **enemy:** This word is written first as "enimy;" an "e" is then written over the "i."

22   **< ...sho...ied>:** Four words are crossed out; only these few letters can be read.

26   **aprehendtions:** "tious" is written on top of "ious" or vice versa.

22–3

thoughts of her should add to your fears and cares, I can't but be concern'd. if by being melancholy, by being troubld at your fortune, and by
quarr=iling with your confinement, you could advantage either your self
35   or mee; you were not to be blam'd; but since you can not, to what end
should you trouble and perplex your self +and+ be concern'd at things
which you cannot help: which, I think, is to disquiet your self in vain. first
you say you are sometimes mel=ancholy that, though you love me much,
yet you can shew it only in words; that you may see I am not soe, I must
40   tell you (and you may beleive me) that so long as those words are real and
hearty; I shall rest very well satisfied and contented; and did you not
express your love as you doe I should slight and condem all other signifi-
cations of it though great ones, and such as take with the most. 2ly you are
apt to be troubl'd at your fortune and to find fault with your mean estate;
45   but are not you to blame to think it not good, and to find fault with that
which gives you not only ordinary comforts, but delights? but I know this
trouble too is partly upon my acount, and that you would have your
fortune such as that I might be a sharer in it; and soe I dont doubt but it
will be one time or other. but as to the present: you are not at all mistaken
50   if you think that had you bin born to a great estate I could not have lov'd
you with so much delight as I doe. for had you bin soe; I am not certain
that you would have bin so good in every respect as now you are and tis
probable you would not have daignd to cast your thoughts upon me; or
if you had. you would not have bin so constant and afectionate as now. so
55   that (my Cousin) had you bin great in the world, I should have love'd you
partly for your self, and partly for your estate, but I realy think I could not
have lov'd you as I doe now purely for your self. lastly you quarri[l] with
your Confinement in a Colledg. as to this I think you know my thoughts
allready: and as I have often told you, so I tell you again I would not have
60   you hasten from thence, upon my acount. though I love you as much as
any one in the world can love anoth[er] yet I am not so maddly, and
childishly desierous of your company as to be impatient when I know I
can not have more on't no, my Dearest, I love you seriously; and <it> +my
love+ has nothing in it of that rash and ugly fondness <in it> which some

22–4

34   **confinement:** This referred to Samuel's confinement as a fellow.
43   **such as take with the most:** although these are the words Lydia wrote, I can not decipher their meaning.
53   **probable:** The first "b" in this word is written over a "p."

22–5

65   have shew'd. I have no reason to be discontented at your staying at oxforde for first I know tis your nesesity not your Choice that keeps you <hear> there, and then I am confident you don't more desire to be settled <again> els where upon your own account then<e> mine. and soe long for my part I have noe reason to be dissatisfied; and why should you? after all

70   this that I have said, I hope you won't be concernd upon my account. and I must confess till now I did not think you had upon your own; that you had bin so weary of an oxford life as to soe much wish your self els where. mee-thinks you have as much reason to be <contented> pleas'd as I. you indeed have more business then I, but you have more pleasures and

75   delights too. have good company, credit and esteem, and all that you can wish for in oxfor+d+ I sit as contentedly in my chamber as can be: and have as good company as in your absence I can wish for, tis your letters and my viol, whilst I read the former I fancy you present, and talking to mee. and when I play upon the latter I fancy, (especialy and I play some

80   of your things,) that I hear you play. though I must confess there is a vast diference: and it is not to be expected I should yet (if I shall ever) play like you. and I'm afraid you will not find me soe much improved as you expect; though I long to see you, and shall think it a great while to Easter, yet I am the better contented with your long absence. because I have some

85   <h> things which Im sure will pleas you when they are got perfict (as I hope by that time they will) which should you hear now they would but torture you. I have almost run my self out of breath, and I think it is high time to leave off. but it is one of my greatest pleasures (in my Cousins absence) to write to him. and I hope he wont think my letters too long. My

90   Dearest Cousin

                          your most faithfull   L.D

[vertically in left margin] Cousin Ashby presents her best respects to you. pray Cousin will you doe so much as send me this letter again tis call'd for, and so I cant have time to transcribe it. I know it is not worth it but I'm

95   loath to break an old custome. dont fail to send it. duty and love to all at Barford

[addressed on verso:]   for her dearest

22–6

65–68 I have . . . mine: Samuel had apparently turned down the offer from Sir William Bromley at Baginton.

68 <again>: One word is crossed out; it may be "again."

84–85 I have . . . perfict: Lydia was practicing some divisions on her viol which she wanted to perfect before playing them for Samuel.

93–95 pray Cousin . . . old custome: It was customary to keep copies of letters that were sent. Normally, Lydia followed the custom, but she was unable to transcribe this long letter before the carrier arrived, so she asked Samuel to return it to her.

23-1

[Folger MS. X.d.477/23]   [Worcester, late January, 1671]

My Dearest Cousin.

I was much concern'd for 2 or 3 days about my last, fearing you would
either take some things ill er els laugh at them; that I hope you have not
5   done; this I don't see how you can forbear, if you can I m sure I cant now
I read it a gain to see first <and> second, and thirdly in it, and to see how
gravely I take upon me to satisfie you. if you were here now +I+ should
laugh heartily at it and would tell you more of my mind when my mirth
was over, well I am resolv'd, Ile never give you any more arguments, since
10   you make no better use of these; I intended them for your contentment and
instead of working that it seems they whett your desires and give you new
ones. but to speak truth I am so far from being angry that I am very well
pleas'd with your answer. because you desire it, I have sent you back your
letter. otherwise I think <you> I should not. not that the sight of that or
15   any other of my own letters is pleasant to me; for I was never yet so self
conceited <of> as to think them better then ordinary; and in the best of
them I can find some fault or other <in them>, which yet I have not witt
or skill enough to mend. if I had not frequently heard your praises and
was not well aquainted with my own writeing, I should grow proud of it.
20   but <since> I am so much used to the one, and doe so well know the other,
that cōmendations can doe me no harm. the women are very much
beholden to you for your good thoughts of them. they shant choous you
for a spokesman, by my consent; and if some of them did but know what
you say of them, I beleive they would be reveng'd on you if they could by
25   inflicting some kind of punishment or other upon you. but for my part I
like you the better: can laugh at them as much as you. and doe think them
as very fooles as you doe. as for men, you and I know them so well, that
I neither +need+ tell nor be told what they are and <I +should+ . . . for your
self I should> I have <though> such mean thoughts of them; that but for
30   you, who are worth them all I'de venture leading Apes in hell. I have one

23–2

1   **[Worcester, late January, 1671]:** This letter was written to Samuel in Barford after the letter of January 16, 1671 and before the death of Abigail Cross on January 31, 1671.

3   **about my last:** Lydia corrected herself: first writing "abaut," then "about." She referred to her last lengthy letter of January 16.

13–14   **... sent you back your letter:** Samuel sent Lydia's letter of January 16 back to her as she requested and now he desired her to return it to him for safekeeping. See Letter **22**.

21   **cōmendations:** For the first time in her letters, Lydia followed the convention of drawing a line over the first "o" to indicate the "m" should be doubled.

21–27   **the women . . . as very fooles as you doe:** Lydia referred here to the "Mistrises" or admirers of Samuel mentioned on January 16. Clearly, Samuel and Lydia had a clear commitment to each other and enjoyed joking about the various matches people were trying to put before each one of them. See Letter **22**.

28–29   **<I ┼should┼ . . . for your self I should>:** eight or nine words are crossed out; these words can be read with reasonable certainty, but it looks like Lydia changed her mind many times. The cross-outs are vigorous.

30   **leading Apes in hell:** This is a common proverb meaning "being an old maid." Samuel also used the expression in his treatise on cousin german marriages, which he must have written about this time (Tilley, M 37).

23–3

peice of news to tell you that I beleive you won't be sorry to hear, viz, that
my Cousin Ashbys troubles with her tenant ferriman are at an end. her son
Bagnall came down from london last week and partly out of love to his
mother, and partly out of self intrest; would +needs+ have diferencys
35   composed between them without a Iudg and Iury. I am very glad it is so,
for she has troubles enough besides. and has enough to doe to grapple
with the ill nature [. . .] and most unworthy caraiges of Nick: Bagnalls
freinds. but of this when I see you. I am glad there is some hopes of
Abigall; pray God restore her to her former health. youl present my duty
40   and love to all +of+ there [vertically in left margin] and asure your self I
am, My Dearest Cousin, your most afectionate and faithfull L. D.

pray Cousin present my Service and thanks to m^r Cudworth and to m^r
DuGard to. freinds here are well and salute you.

[addressed on verso:]   For Her Dearest
45   Cousin.

23–4

33   **Bagnall:** Nicholas Bagnall was Anne Ashby's son-in-law, the husband of Elizabeth Ashby.

37   **[. . .]:** There is a hole in the paper at this point, so one word can not be read.

39   **Abigall:** Lydia was certainly concerned about her friend, Abigail Cross. See Letters **19 and 21**.

42   **m^r Cudworth:** John Cudworth was a Trinity College friend and colleague of Samuel, still living in Oxford. He had received his B.A. in 1667. See Letters **29** and **30** and the Biographical Appendix.

42–43   **m^r DuGard:** Lydia is referring to her cousin, Henry Dugard. She had inquired about him a month earlier, wondering if he had left Oxford. Apparently, he had not. See Letter **21**.

24–1

[Folger X.d. 477/24]   [Worcester, mid-February, 1671]

My Dearest Cousin

I am glad my letter came so soon to your hands: for I was half afraid
cousin sam: would not have diliver'd it that night. on fryday I came I
5   thank God safe and well to Worcester, where I had bin but few <owers>
oures but in came your letter, which I read very cheerfully till I came to
+the+ bad news of Abigails death. I am very much troubl'd at it; and you
must excuse me if I say I shall now have less mind to live at Barford then
I should if she had lived. I am sure I have lost a very good freind, and if I
10   should goe thither to stay I should dearly miss her. I dont much wonder
to hear of Robin Eedses death; his countenance did not promise a long life.
but it may be he hoped to out live my Uncle. freinds at Whittford are well
and salute you. they are very hearty people; and made mighty much of
me. there is very good company, and I think I had more mirth in ten dayes
15   there, then I have had in twice ten weeks before. but I am glad I am at
home again: for I had as like be in my Chamber alone as in any company
where you are not. I had allmost forgotten a business that my Cousin
kimberly gave me an espicall charge to remember. looking among some
writeings he found severall <wh> that belong to me: some of which he
20   thinks may be of some concern<m>ment. he wish'd me to write to you
about them, and to desire you, if you think it convenient, to aquainte my
uncle. they lye very safe but perhaps my uncle may have a mind to peruse
them. I am glad my cousin is no worse but I'm afraid he is not so well as
I desire he should be, since he speaks of his health only from anothers
25   mouth. I pray God in heaven keep him well: or els Im sure I shall take but
little pleasure in my life. my Dearest Cousin

your most afectionately faithfull
LSydia DuGard.

24–2

1   **[Worcester, mid-February, 1671]:** This letter was sent to Barford early in February. It is dated by the reference to Abigail Cross's death, which occurred on 31 January 1671.

4   **cousin sam:** Samuel Kimberley was Lydia and Samuel's second cousin. Their grandmother was Elizabeth Kimberley, married to Henry DuGard. He was a student at Pembroke College during this time. See Letter **32** and Biographical Appendix.

5   **safe and well to Worcester:** Lydia had been visiting her relatives, the Kimberleys, in nearby Whitford.

7   **Abigails death:** Abigail Cross died from complications of childbirth. Lydia first mentioned that she was not well in mid December, 1670. See Letters **19, 21,** and **23.**

11   **Robin Eedses:** I have been unable to identify Robin Eedses, but he may have been related to William Eades from Warwick, who was involved in Warwick School. He was presumably about the same age as Lydia's uncle, Thomas DuGard (*VCH*, 2:310).

12   **friends at Whittford:** These friends were the William Kimberley family including William and Elizabeth Kimberley and their five children: Samuel, Jonathan, Benjamin, Hannah and Elizabeth.

17–18   **Cousin kimberly:** Most likely this was Cousin William Kimberley, who was Lydia's father's first cousin.

19   **writeings . . . me:** These were probably some of William DuGard's writings. If they included financial records, they would have been especially useful to Lydia.

20   **<m>:** This letter is crossed out with two lines, "=", and the word is continued on the next line.

23   **well:** This word can be read as "well" or "good," since one is written on the top of the other.

28   **Lydia DuGard:** The paper is torn at the bottom of the page so that this signature is partly destroyed.

24–3

[vertically in left margin] I have not seen my Master yet nor M^rs lucy. when
30 I see her she shall know how kindly you took her letter. her brother was
to blame to <tells> tell tales of her mistakes. if she had made none she
might have bin in some dainger for ought I know: for they say all true
prickers must be hanged. good Cousin desire my Cousin Ann (for I am
resolv'd I won't write till I hear from her) to send for +home+ 2 dosen of
35 yarn of mine that is at Abigails: and to be kind to my little bitch if she be
alive.

24–4

29   **Master:** Lydia's music master in Worcester was Mr. Wright, but I have been unable to locate any biographical information about him.

29   **Mʳˢ lucy:** I have not been able to identify Mrs. Lucy. Presumably, she is a friend of Lydia and Samuel living in Worcester. She may be related to the Lucys of Charlecote; certainly, Thomas DuGard knew this family. All of the women that Lydia mentions were able to write, even though apparently Mrs. Lucy's letters were not error free.

32–35   **all true prickers must be hanged:** I have not been able to find the source for this saying . Clearly, the implied meaning is that to make mistakes is only human.

25–1

[Folger X.d.477/25]   [Worcester, mid-February, 1671]

I have bin to day admireing peter young, who to morrow sets forward for
london, being to play before the king with Pool. M^r wright's afraid his
musick is not airey enough for the Court, but youngs resolv'd to doe his
5   utt-most endeavours to pleas the laydies. if I were as you I would goe up
to london and hear um: if this weather hold I beleive it would be a very
pleasant Iourny for you. my Dearest Cousin once more

                                        yours &c
                                        L. D.

10   [addressed on verso:]   For Mr Samuel DuGard
                                Fellow of Trin: Coll:
                                     these.
                          oxon

25–2

1   This is actually a postscript written along the left margin of the paper. Laetitia Yeandle, who originally catalogued all the DuGard letters for the Folger Shakespeare Library, recently reevaluated 477/24 and 477/25 and concluded that Letter **25** is a continuation of Letter **24**. She says, "The watermark, the chain lines, and three letters, including two descenders, match in the two parts of the postscript."

2   **peter young:** Peter Young is obviously a musician, but I have been unable to identify him.

3   **Pool:** Anthony Pool was an English composer (fl. c. 1670–90). His work was primarily for base viols; solos by him were mostly divisions on a ground, but included some dance movements grouped into short suites (*New Grove*, s.v. "Poole, Anthony").

3   **Mʳwright:** Lydia's music teacher.

4   **airey enough for the court:** This is a reference to the musical style then current, coming out of France. Lydia was certainly up to date in her musical taste.

5   **utt-most:** "tt" is written on top of "d."

26–1

[Folger X.d.477/26]   [Barford, late September, 1671]

My Dearest Cousin.

though I could not but expect to hear of my Cousin Harrys Death, and
hear he made so good an end, yet it aflicts me very much: and the more
5   since it so much afects you. I am heartily greiv'd to hear you say you have
lost your health. I'm afraid you have taken cold by too much siting up, and
have done your self harm as well that way as by your greife. I am glad you
are like to come home this week: my uncle was very willing to it and sent
to Pestell to take up an horse for you – but can't you make somthing a
10   longer stay then ordinary this time< . . . > sure your President and Pupils
will excuse you for once, and perhaps it may doe you good to be alitle in
the country. if you hasten away I must bear your short stay and long
absence as well as I can, but if you can contrive to give me more of your
desir'd company you will very much satisfie, My Dearest,

15   your most afectionately faithfull
                                       L.D.

all hear salute you and desire to see you. pray be carefull of your self and
be sure to put on winter cloaths when you come.

26-2

1   **[Barford, late September, 1671]:** The dating of this letter is based on Henry DuGard's death on September 27, 1671. Lydia had moved back to Barford from Worcester in the spring of 1671. See Letter **21**. No letters have been preserved between February, 1671, and this one in September, 1671. Lydia was now of age, having had her twenty-first birthday on September 30.

3   **Cousin Harrys Death:** Henry died in Oxford and was buried in St. Mary Magdalen Church, Oxford. This was the first mention of Henry's illness in Lydia's preserved letters, although obviously the death was not a surprise to her.

9   **Pestell:** William Pestell, Warwick, servant and carrier, served the DuGard household after 1671.

10   **< . . . >:** A blotch of ink cannot be read.

10   **President:** Ralph Bathurst (1620–1704) was president of Trinity College from 1664 until his death. His entire academic career was at Trinity College: scholar, B.A., 1638; M.A., fellow, 1640; ordained 1644; M.D. 1654; divine, classical scholar, philosopher. See Letters **28** and **32** and Biographical Appendix.

27–1

[Folger MS X.d.477/27]   [Barford, January 22, 1672]

Ian: 22 1672:

My Dearest Cousin.

Acording to your order I have sent you up my viol: which though I cannot
5   skillfully handle yet I can't well be with=out. and I shall miss its company
as much as some would a freinds; but it wont be long ere I shall see it
again: and its absence will make me the better husswife, and hardly the
worse Musisian. I am glad to hear you got safe to Tadmarton and <f>
oxford; and youl beleive me if I say my thoughts and best wishes atended
10   you to your Iournys end. nor have you a less share in them now then if
you were present. I need not tell you how you left me, for you know my
afection to be soe great that you may well think I was troubld more then
a a little at parting; that I miss you still; and that I pleas my self with the
thoughts of seeing you again. you seem to be much concern'd at some
15   words of mine. I'm sorry I should give you any trouble so much as in a
thought: I must confes from your great willing=ness to leave me a week
before you did, <and from> I was apt to fancy you had enough of my
company and would gladly see oxford again. but you tell me (and I may
beleive you) that you have as great a respect for me as ever: if I thought
20   you had not, and should find you were apt to slight me, <so long> since
I <le> am not concious to my self of any thing that may Iustly lessen your
esteem. it would be a real greife to me, and +I+ should count my self
strangly unhappy. but I dont in the least fear it will be so, nor that my
Cous[in] who all this while has bin so constant and afectionate will now
25   at last grow weary of and repent his love to me. though perhaps some
would doe so, and I have told you and doe realy think that in some
regards you would have bin a far happyer man had you never known me.
you wish you could live with me soe that I might not suffer inconven=
iences and hardships upon <my> +your+ account which I don't fear I shall
30   and if I had nothing to wish but Iust my own content I could live with you

102

27–2

2   **Ian: 22 1672:** Four months elapsed since the last preserved letter (**26**).

4   **viol:** Lydia sent her viol to Samuel in Oxford to be repaired. She hinted that she probably spent too much time playing her viol at the expense of daily chores.

8   **Musisian:** It looks like Lydia has written a "c" on top of the second "s" in "musisian."

8   **Tadmarton:** Samuel most likely stopped in the village of Tadmarton, Oxfordshire, to stay with the Whately family. Mary Whately, who had cared for Samuel when he was a child, had died in 1667, but Samuel still maintained his connections with the Whately family. Mary's son, Samuel Whately, was a student at Trinity College at this time. See Letter **4**.

9   **thoughts:** Underneath this word are the letters "wi."

25   **grow:** Under the "g" is a "w."

27–3

in a Cottage without the least murmure. but I shall never +be so+ great a
self loveer, or so ill natur'd to you as gredi+l+y and foolishly to desire my
own happyness without regard to yours. and if I should anyway hinder
your better fortune and preferment in the world, (as I fear I shall) I shall
35   not need to be troubl'd upon my own account, for I am not so highly
conceited of my self as <not> to think, be your fortune what it will, it will
be below me, but I shall be concern'd upon yours. and if ever you should
suffer inconveniences and hardships upon my account, (give me leave to
<you> use your own words) I should be truly miserable. so that if by
40   endeavouring <to> my content you should lose your own, I'm sure mine
would soon vanish and we should both be in a farr worse condition then
now. you say we must endure with patience, as much as to say I am, Im
patient. I dont love to be thought so, for I am not soe. and though your
absence is not pleasant to me, yet I can and doe bear it, as you doe your
45   headach, silently. will be as chearfull as I can, and if I cannot be so cheerfull as I should, you may blame me if you pleas, but I know not how to
help it. youl pardon me for loveing you so much, and not esteem me the
less because I am afectionately as well as faithfully

yours

50   L. D.

[vertically in left margin] my uncle and I have sent you all those books you
desir'd with all others things of yours that were to be sent. pray give my
respects to Mr twithy, with thanks for his kindness, which youl [. . .] in
your sermon book. pray send the coarse cloath again or els Marian will
55   grumbl

27–4

32   **gredi+l+y:** There is a "g" written under the "d."

42   **you ... patience:** Samuel had just lost the appointment at St. Nicholas in Warwick; he was getting very impatient. On 21 January 1672 he wrote to Bishop Blandford of Worcester saying he had not gotten the St. Nicholas position and would be grateful for any help he could give him in securing another (Bod., Tanner MSS XLIV, fol. 282). The position went to Samuel Jemmatt. See note 40 in the Introduction to the Letters.

45   **chearfull:** Lydia wrote "pl" and then changed her mind and wrote "chearfull."

53   **Mr twithy:** Thomas Twithy, from Worcestershire, was an Oxford friend of Samuel and the son of friends of Thomas DuGard. See the Biographical Appendix.

53   **[. . .]:** The corner of the paper is torn off at this point, so one word can not be read.

54   **sermon book:** Samuel kept a book for recording thoughts and experiences useful for writing his sermons.

54   **Marian:** Marian Hawkes was a longtime servant to the DuGard family. She was clearly friendly with Thomas Eliot, another of the DuGard servants, for they were married on 4 December 1673. The two served the family long and well. See the Biographical Appendix.

28–1

[Folger MS X.d.477/28]   [Barford, February 13, 1672]

My Dearest Cousin.

I beleive you expect some litle chideing from me, and though youl <make
it> only laugh at me and make it your sport, yet I must tell you, and you
5   can't but think, I am not very well pleas'd with you. you have told me
heretofore that while I spoke to you I did but think aloud: and I, as readily
beleiveing it, as willing to have it soe, upon that Confidence made use of
my liberty, and have ever since both spoken and writ more freely and
unconcern'dly then otherwise I would have done. I was strangly startl'd
10   at the unexpected news of the Presidents seeing one of my letters: and I
was as much asham'd to think hee <person whome I have often heard you
speak so advantageously of (as I have not more of any) for learning and
other accomplishments,> should see any thing of my scribling; as if I had
committed +some+ crime. realy my Cousin I have noe reason to take it
15   kindly from you nor can I imagein to what end you should doe it. if you
had ow'd me a spight and would <have> have studdied a way to lessen
the Presidents good opinion of me, (which posibly your too large praises
of me in your little treatise may have given way to): you could not have
pitch'd upon a more likely one, then to shew him my ill dressd thoughts
20   to you. I am sure there was nothing in +that+ paper worthy the sight of
soe Iudicious and Criticall a man <as you have told me the President is>
and if you commended it to him (and your shewing it tells me you did)
I'm afraid hee'l think your love has soe far blinded you, that it has gotten
the upper hand of your Iudgment; and he will hardly again beleive a lover
25   [. . .] praises. from those he would expect to find me inIenious as well as
loveing, and Artfull enough to express my thoughts more handsomly then
I did in that letter. The truth is <of late> I am grow'n soe well accquainted
with you, that I have us'd my self to write as familiarly and freely as I talk
and of late (though at the best my writeing is very mean) have taken soe
30   little paines with my letters, that they are unfit to be seen by any but by

106

28–2

1   This letter was written with deliberate care, revealing Lydia's self-consciousness about her writing after Samuel had shown one of her letters to the president of his college.

10   **President:** Ralph Bathurst had been President of Trinity College since 1664. Samuel knew him well and greatly respected him.

18   **treatise:** This could very well be the treatise Samuel was writing defending cousin-german marriages, which he had published in 1673 and which is included in this book.

23   **your:** Lydia started to write "youl," then wrote an "r" under the "l."

24   **lover [. . .]:** The edge of the letter is torn; some letters may be missing here.

28–3

him alone, whose love will teach him rather to excuse then laugh at, the
falls spellings, bad Inglish, im=pertinencys, and perhaps nonsence that
some of them may be fill'd with. and if the President was pleas'd not to
find fault with that letter, I may fear it was rather not to disoblidg you then
35   because he realy thought there was any thing in't (more than my love)
worthy his least approbation. now I shall write in fear, and like a stam-
merer who never fallters more then when he intends to speak best, shall
instead of writeing better, doe soe much worse that you will not think it
worth the while to take any more of my letters out of your own lodgings.
40   I am very glad you have soe worthy a freind, <as the President, I have
often heard you say how much he has oblig'd you; and before as well as
since you have bin happy in his aq accquaintance and esteem;> I have
heard you speak of him with the greatest respect, and I doubt not (for I
dare take your Iudgment in any+thing+ but your love) but he is a person
45   truely deserveing it. I reseav'd my viol safe, and return you my thanks for
it. and though it was rather my ill happ then carelessness that <In> inIur'd
it, yet Ile promise you that for the future, my care of it shall be equall to
my love to it; and then you need not doubt but it will be secure from all
harm and daingers. the weather has bin very unkind to me, in hindering
50   me from hearing the good news (I should have hoped for at the carriers
return) of your health. and the last silent week seem'd as long and tedious
as it was cold and unpleasant. but I hope this will make me amends and
will bring me a letter from my Dear Cousin then which in his absence
nothing can be more wellcome to his
55

Feb: 13   Afectionate and faithfull
1672.   LS. DuGard.

all salute you. and my Aunt thanks
you for her book.

60   [addressed on verso:]   For Mr Samuel DuGard
Fellow of Trin: Coll:
these.
oxon.

28–4

45–49 I reseav'd . . . daingers.: On 22 January 1672, Lydia had sent her viol to Samuel in Oxford to be repaired. See Letter **27**.

29–1

[Folger X.d.477/29]   [Barford, February/March, 1672?]

My Dearest. Cousin.

That my uncle seems to others soe unconcern'd in our afairs I can not
much blame him, but why he should be so shy and silent to us I know no
5   reason: since his greater freeness would be very oblidging to us and could
no way pregdudice him. in deed if I had bin a fortune, or such an one in
other respects as his son could not els where have hoped for; and he had
5 or 6 years agoe seem'd well pleas'd in our loves and incourag'd us to
continue them: – posibly I my self by this time might have though[t]
10   providenc had order'd it to his desires; and people might then have said
it <wh > was rather his design then our love +that+ brought us together.
but since my fortune is soe +mean+, and I am every way els a very ordinary person, I think no body that is well in therr witts will think he design'd it, and therefore what great policy can it be to carry it so strangly?
15   I beleive folks are so far from thinking him well pleas'd, that some will
imagin <f > (as they may from his own words) that he realy dislikes it and
could wish it otherwise. I have often thought soe my self, and it has of late
so much aflicted me that I have had much adoe to forbear speaking to him.
he was never the man that has spoke one kind word to me yet though he
20   has observ'd how deeply melancholy I have sometimes bin; and yet when
my Aunt <has-> told him I took his silence a little unkindly, and that I
beleiv'd had you made another Choice he wo+u+ld have bin better
pleas'd, he said I had no reason to think soe. and what ever is the cause,
he is very Cheerfull, and as pleasing to me within this fortnight or 3 weeks
25   as <every-> ever he was. my Aunt cannot get a sight of your last Letter to
him, but I Eyed him while he read it, and took notice he smil'd much and
seem'd very well pleas'd. my Aunt sais he speaks the worst to our faces;
that he often talks of us and of our being at Barford, but fears he shall be
streighten'd for room. if we should be here (and it will not be well in some
30   respects we should be any where els) I pray God we may pleas him; I don't

110

29–2

10–11 **People . . . together:** Lydia seemed to think that her uncle was worried that people would say he had pushed her into a relationship with his son for the sake of her inheritance. Lydia finds this very unlikely since her fortune was so "mean."

13 **I think:** This "I" is written on top of an "n."

15–16 **I beleive . . . dislikes it:** This is clearly a reference to the controversy over the marriage of first cousins and Lydia's uncle's displeasure with the marriage plans.

21 **Aunt:** Lydia had talked about her love for Samuel with her aunt, Anne DuGard, and even shared Samuel's letters with her and her cousin Anna.

28 **our being at Barford:** Lydia anticipated that she and Samuel would live in the rectory after their marriage.

29–3

love to see him frown, and I'le promise you Ile doe as little as tis posible
to deserve his displeasure. I read your last (good part on't) and 2 or 3
before it to my Aunt and Cousin, who think you have a mighty mind to be
married, of a sudden since you write so Earnestly; and that you won't
35   willingly be put of any longer then Easter. they wish it were over, but are
afraid it will not be kept so private as you would have it, and in that
regard they as well as I, think better of Iune. but you may doe as you pleas
if you stay seven years longer my Aunt sais my Uncle will not wish you
to marry, but yet will leave you to your self and not hinder you at Easter.
40   as for Ioynture, Ile leave it <who kno-> wholly to my Uncle, for I am
confident hee'l deal handsomely by me; and I beleive no body that knows
him will count me imprudent in soe doeing. you are cruelly kind in talking
of dyeing and leaveing me to another rather then bring me into troubles.
I don't love you should so much as men=tion leaveing me, and if you ever
45   should doe soe, which God in mercy forbid; what other in the world doe
you think could be so dear to me as my belov'd Cousin ? surely none; I
don't fear your bringing me into troubles, but if you should, my love to
you would make me bear them patiently. and though you had nothing
<+to cr. . . to,+> but your books, I had rather trust providence – with you,
50   and should think my self much more happy, then I should in being
match'd to an other though he could love me as much as you doe, and his
estate did deserve the greatest fortune. I don't doubt but it will be well
with us, but however things goe you shall not hear me complain, and you
shall never be made unhappy by that greatest plauge of some men; I mean
55   a disrespectfull illnaturd woman. if loveing you will render you blesst you
shall, I dare say, yield to none upon Earth. for I allways shall be as I now
am

                     your truly afectionate and faithfull
                     L.D.

60   +Mrs Millbourne+ Mrs Millbourn sends you service and many thanks for

29–4

35   **Easter:** Easter fell on April 7 in 1672.

35–37   **they . . . Iune:** This would enable Samuel to finish the term at Oxford before loosing his fellowship upon marriage. College rules specify that college dons could not be married.

36   **private:** Apparently, Samuel thought he could keep his marriage a secret and return to his Trinity fellowship until he was successful in gaining a living as vicar of a parish.

40   **Ioynture:** A jointure is a provision of land or income made in a marriage settlement for the wife should she survive her husband. As the father of Samuel, Thomas DuGard was responsible for arranging Lydia's jointure. Clearly, she trusted him to do well by her.

46   **Cousin?:** The punctuation mark (two small c's on top of one another) is not a recognizable one; maybe it is meant to be a question mark.

49   **<+to cr. . . . to,+ >:** There are several words written above the line. Only these letters can be read.

55   **woman.:** A colon was written and carefully crossed out and replaced by a period.

60   **Mrs Millbourn:** She was a neighbor and friend living in Barford. Samuel, having access to book sellers in Oxford sent books to many people in Barford.

29–5

your book. I intended to have sent Pestell for Betty to day, but she sends
me word she cannot come at present, and she shall not be here at Easter (if
you are) if I can handsom[l]y put her off for I would have no more company here then ther needs must. I have sent you up a ring that may be
65   your pattern. tis full big enough and so ~~and~~ a wedding ring should be, or
els they say ones husband won't be kind. let it have that posey you pleas
but dont let it be such a one as will make me blush to tell it, for so that you
sent would. Youl laugh at me for sending the Mothers blessing, but I could
find never another +book+ I could so well spare and I thought it would
70   serve well enough to hide my ring. I should be glad to see mr Cudworth
before Easter that I may fully know my uncles mind. <~~I hope my Uncl~~>
I hope Pestell will tell you I came saffe to lighthorn, for I am goeing thither
this morning behind him; pray will you engage him either to call there a
fryday or els to leave my letter soe that I may have it as soone as posible
75   for I shall long to hear from you. once more my Dearest Cousin"
Youre &c
LD.

29-6

61   **Pestell:** Pestell served the DuGard family as servant and carrier after 1671.

61   **Betty:** Betty Millbourn was the daughter of Mrs. Millbourn and about the same age as Lydia. See Letters **17** and **18**.

65–66   **tis . . . kind:** This bit of folklore was explained in 1697 as follows: "For if it be streighter than the finger, it will pinch and if it be wider than the finger it will fall off; but if it be fit, it neither pincheth nor slippeth; so they which are well, strive not, but they which are unlike, as wife and water." Master Henry Smith, "Preparation to Marriage" in J. C. Jeaffreson, *Brides and Bridals*, 2 vols. (London: Hurst & Blackett, 1872), 1:149. See also David Cressy, *Birth, Marriage, and Death* (Oxford: Oxford University Press, 1997), 342–47.

68   **the Mothers blessing:** Dorothy Leigh, *The Mother's Blessing* (London, 1616). By 1670 there had been fourteen editions of this very popular book written as "the godly counsaile of a Gentle-woman not long since deceased, left behind her for her children." Lydia apparently found the advice given in this book both old-fashioned and unnecessary.

70   **mr Cudworth:** John Cudworth was a friend of Samuel's from Trinity College. See Letters **23** and **31**. Lydia apparently hoped that if John Cudworth came to visit, he would be able to tell her what her uncle really thought.

72   **lighthorn:** The village of Lighthorn is approximately six miles southeast of Barford. Lydia often stayed there to care for the ailing Margaret Dodds, wife of the vicar, John Dodds, a close friend of Thomas DuGard. See Letters **18**, **30** and **31**.

30–1

[Folger MS X.d.477/30]   [Lighthorn, March 15, 1672]

March. 15 1672.

My Dearest Cousin.

Mr Dods man comming to oxon I can't but ask you how you doe and tell
5   you I am well. Mrs Dod <gives> +sends+ you her service and begs your
prayers. she is grown very weak, is still in miserable pains, and in all
probabilitys cannot continue many weeks. I know not certainly when I
shall goe home, I am loath to leave the poor woman before she has a better
nurse: and that I hope will be some time next week. I can say no more to
10   you about Easter then I have allready and I shall tire you and myself too
to write one and the same over and over. I thank you for your wine. and
Ile promise you it shall not be open'd till I see the doner; if it be not this
half year. I'de fain see you at Easter but I would not be married then. you
did not considerately make that resolution you tell me, of and soe may
15   <the be> the better be allow'd to break it. and yet I cant live contentedly
without sight of you till Iune, and therefore you had as good come at
Easter; and if you'l take me for better, for worse in my old Cloaths, and
with an empty purss you may if <th> you think well on't. this is out of
pure good nature <now> that I write to you now, for you don't deserve a
20   letter extrordinary be=cause you have put such a trick upon me to mr
wills. a tuesday morning I was thinking if my cousin An should know of
that book she would have made you beleive I had sent it to him, but I did
not imagin you would ever have let him seen it. it's no great matter, Ile
come out of your debt and serve you as good a trick one time or other. I
25   must confess this letter does not deserve an answer, but if youl <if youl>
send by this bearer, I'le write more <serious> seriously (if at all) next
week. tis late and I must not take more time for fear of disturbing Mrs Dod.
I pray God keep you in health my Dear Dearest Cousin.

your most afectionately faithfull LD.

30–2

5–7   **Mrs Dod . . . weeks.:** See Letter **29**.

10   **about Easter:** Lydia was referring to the possibility of getting married when Samuel came home at Eastertime.

20–21 **mr wills:** John Wills was a Trinity College friend of Samuel. Lydia and Samuel enjoyed playing tricks on one another. Cousin Anna was often involved as well as Samuel's college friends; however, I do not know exactly what their tricks were. See the Biographical Appendix.

30–3

30   [vertically in left margin] if you can send me any news from Mr Cuddworth next week pray doe. and whether I write or noe <dont> let me hear
from you on fryday. Service to mr wills.

[addressed on verso:]   For Mr Samuel DuGard
                          fellow of Trin: Coll:
35   These.
                oxon.

30–4

30–31 Mr Cuddworth: Lydia had hopes that John Cudworth would come to Barford to help her understand what her uncle was thinking. See Letter **29**.

31–1

[Folger MS X.d.477/31]   [Barford, March 25, 1672]

March 25 1672.

My Dearest Cousin.

You'l Easily believe me <if> since I never use to fail you, if I say I was not
willingly silent last week. I was troubld I was so far out of the Cariers call,
for I love to be talking to my Dearest freind; and as it is my great pleasure
to hear from him; so it is no little one to write to him, and think (for soe I
doe) that my letters are wellcome and are esteemd if not for their own yet
for the senders sake. I came home a wedensday; not sorry to leave lighthorn, you may well im=agin, since you know Mrs Dods distemper and
worss temper; she is likely enough to die but, if fretting, and chiding will
prolong her life she may out live me or a stronger body. my Uncle sais she
is a bad example <f> to young women. but I hope you will not find me
allterd for the worss since my being with her. her way is not so commendable or soe takeing that I should strive to be like her. and pevishness looks
so ugly in her that instead of imitating, I think I shall be the more out of
love with it as long as I live. I'm glad you have heard from Dr Waterhouse.
a while agoe we had a letter from M^r lloid the printer, who pleads poverty;
and soe Im afraid we shall not have our hunderd pound quickly. I thank
you for my Gloves. one pare I gave my Cousin Ann; who sais she will
thank you her self. I should have bin glad to have seen Mr Cudworth, but
am not sorry he comes not hither at Easter. pray will you tell me whether
youl come or noe; and if you doe, what day, whether fryday sat=erday or
not till munday. <Im afraid that your> one rubb or other still comes in the
way, and this of lisences is an unthought of one. if one cannot be had at
present without dificulty you must be content +to+ stay longer. but if M^r
Rogers can furnish you, I think my Aunt gives you good counsell. she is
as much our freind as <can> posible, and as much desires our happiness
as her prediceser would. pray Cousin have a care what you write to my
uncle. he told me you in your last writt him a displeasing passage: and

31–2

9 **wednesday:** I.e., Wednesday, March 20, 1672. Lydia had been caring for Mrs. Dodds for at least two weeks. See Letters **29** and **30**.

10–12 **Mrs Dods . . . stronger body:** Margaret Dodds died June 5, 1672. See the Biographical Appendix.

12 **life:** This word is first written "live."

16 **think:** A "k" is written on top of "g."

18 **Dr Waterhouse:** This is a most puzzling reference since the Dr. Waterhouse, named by Lydia's father in his will as her guardian, died 30 May 1670 and was buried in Greenford Church, Middlesex, on 2 June 1670. See the Biographical Appendix.

18 **Mr lloid:** Henry Lloyd was a printer for William DuGard and was still flourishing as a printer in 1675. Presumably, he acquired the printing effects at DuGard's death and owed Lydia money as a result (Plomer [1907], 119, and Plomer [1922], 191).

25 **lisences:** A marriage license, costing about 10 shillings, exempted a couple from having banns called and, if specified, allowed the marriage to be solemnized outside the couple's parish. See Introduction to the Letters, p. 15.

27 **Mr Rogers:** John Rogers was a friend of Thomas DuGard and his wife and rector of Hampton Lucy, a neighboring village; he was authorized by the Bishop of Worcester to issue marriage licenses. See the Biographical Appendix.

29 **prediceser:** The "c" is written over an "s." The reference is to Mary DuGard, Thomas's second wife, who died in 1669.

30 **writt:** "write" is changed to "writt."

31–3

gave me a fair way to talk freely to him (which I long to doe) but sombody
came in and unluckily prevented our discourse. I wish he <were-> and I
were better aquainted; and could be less strange one to another. he must
have his own humore; but let him take heed, he thinks I am of a very
35   sturdy spirit, but he is alittle misstaken, and if he should be too unkind
and harsh to me perhaps he may have more cause to repent it then hee's
a ware of. methinks you and I are prettyly concernd one for another. you
fear, you say, my happiness should be impar'd from you. and I as much
fear yours will be impar'd from mee. you need not be concern'd for me. I
40   shall be happy enough in haveing a freind whome I love as my life, and
who unfainedly loves me, more happy then any man els could make me.
but I am troubld for you, least I should make you less happy then otherwise you would have bin. and if you did not love me soe much as I beleive
you doe, I would not give you the least encourage ment to leave the Coll:
45   (and I think I never desir'd you soe to doe) till you were call'd thence by
good preferment. I wish you don't repent it, and then you need not fear
my doeing soe; for your Ioys and happinesses, troubles and discontents
will allways be as much mine as your own. my Dearest Cousin

                    your most afectionate and faithfull,
50   LSydia DuGard

I never spoke word to Marian about the business till yesterday. I don't
doubt but shee'l be close. shee's a good honest wench. and though alittle
churlish som=times; yet she loves us both. and will deserve a pare of
gloves. am glad you have undeseavd Mr Wills, and not sorry he has a little
55   laught at him self as well as he did at me.

31–4

50   **LSydia:** The intertwining of "L" and "S" is particularly pronounced in this signature.

51   **Marian:** Marian Hawkes was a servant in the DuGard household. The "business" obviously referred to Lydia and Samuel's marriage plans. See Letter **27**.

54   **gloves:** Elbow-length gloves made of leather or silk were fashionable for women during the last half of the seventeenth century. Gloves of all kinds and prices were frequently given as gifts. In the 1670s, Rev. Giles Moore of Horsted Keynes, Sussex, was often given gloves in payment for performing a wedding. The cost was as little as two shillings (*The Journal of Giles Moore*, 350–51). Samuel sent gloves to Lydia but also to other members of the family.

54   **undeseavd Mr Wills:** This is a reference to Lydia's comment about Samuel putting "such a trick upon me to mr wills." See Letter **30**.

32–1

[Folger Ms X.d.477/32]   [Barford, late April, 1672]

My Dearest freind.

I am glad you came safe and well to oxford; where if my heartiest wishes
and most Earnest prayers may prevail, you shall continue soe, till you
5   intend to bless Barford and me again with your Presence. I thank you that
you would somtimes in your Iourny send back a thought to me, +twas
fondly don+ but I beleive they did +not+ come quite home, for I hasten'd
agreat many after you, and noe doubt but yours and mine mett upon the
road. I had noe company all the afternoon but my viol and it had bin well
10   I had bin without that too, for it prov'd such as Enimie to a cut finger that
they have bin at too great a distance ever since and soe Im afraid will
continue this week yet. you tell me you hope you never shall be of less
esteem with me, because you are wholly mine, then you were before, you
need not in the least fear it, and I hope you doe not. I should be much to
15   blame, nay I should be <yo-> unworthy [of] your love should I abate any
thing of mine. and (till you give me cause, as Im confident you never will)
should deserve your slights as much as you are +now+ pleas'd to think I
doe your [...] I am, and allways +shall+ be the same, and if I doe not tell
you I love you more then ever I did, you need not take it ill since I can say
20   with the greatest truth, that I have for a long time before, lov'd you as
much as posibly I could. tis well there is no news of us at oxford. but tis all
about the country and tis to be feard some body or other will bring it to the
Coll: before you'd be willing to have it known there. you would have me
be cheerfull, and merry that I may pleas my father which I will allways
25   endavour to doe though I cross my own humore. and will be sure to look
plesantly, when my heart is either with you, or heavy at home. I pray God
keep you well and then Im sure I shall doe the better. all salute you. my
Dearest

your most afectionatly faithfull
30   LSydia DuGard

124

32–2

1   **[late April, 1672]:** This letter was written soon after Lydia and Samuel's marriage, which took place on 18 April 1672.

3   **and:** "and" is written on top of "to."

13   **you are wholly mine:** This is certainly a reference to their being married.

15   **[of]:** The paper is torn at this point.

17   **should:** Originally Lydia had written "w" and then changed it to "sh."

18   **[. . .]:** The paper is torn; one word is missing.

21   **tis well there is no news of us at oxford:** The news of the marriage had not reached Oxford yet, so Samuel still had his position at Trinity College.

24   **father:** Since she was now married, Lydia could call Thomas DuGard, "father" instead of "uncle."

32–3

[Written in the left margin.] I should be glad to hear what the President
had said to you. service to Mʳ and Mʳˢ Twithy and to Cousin kimberlys,
and pray tell Cousin Sam: I was not such a fool as to thank him for procur-
ing my ring. though I must confess it was a very freindly ofice and any
body would take it kindly. I have mended the matter much; for I don't
doubt but youl tell him what I say next time you see him. L

32–4

31   **President:** The president was Ralph Bathhurst. By now Samuel had known him for at least eight years, and they were quite friendly. See Letters **26** and **28**.

32   **Mᵣ and Mᵣˢ Twithy:** These were friends of the DuGard family from Worcestershire. They must have been in Oxford where their son, Thomas, was a student. See Letter **27**.

32   **Cousin kimberlys:** Presumably, Lydia was referring to Jonathan and Samuel Kimberley.

33   **Cousin Sam:** This was Samuel Kimberly, who must have assisted Samuel in getting Lydia's wedding ring.

33-1

[Folger Ms X.d.477/33] [Coventry, June 10, 1672]
Iune. 10 1672.

My Dearest.

Im sorry I must send you another hasty letter, but there being some
5   warrwick men in town, I would not lose my opertunity of sending by
them. I should be to blame if I should tell you I am sorry you have lost
your title of ffellow. for tis the best news I have heard agreat while since
it will not be your disadvantage: and you may well think I am more then
a little proud to think I shall see my Dearest sooner then I expected, and
10   that he comes not to give me a visit and a way again but to stay with me.
I heartily wish, +you may,+ nay I hope you will be as well pleasd in a
country life as I, and then I doubt not but we shall both think our selves
happy. I told Sam: Wattson and his wife I thought you would be here
about a fortnight hence. but how can I hope it since <that will> you told
15   me when we parted; upon the account of your pupils you could not come
till after middsummer. Sam: Watson sends you his service <to you> and
wishes me to tell you he is resolvd to keep me till you come. but unles that
can be the latter end of next week I shall be willing to see barford at the
begining of it. not that I am weary of Coventry, for they are all so exced=
20   ingly civil to me that I can't but be pleasd in being amongst um, <but yet
it will> but I can't in civility stay longer then I have business here, nor
would they at Barford be pleasd if I should doe soe. pray will you tell me
this week, if I may hope for you the next. I would fain see you here, and
soe would a great many more who have a great respect for you: and I as
25   well as otheres should like it better to have you fetch me home then to be
sent any other way. [vertically in left margin] I would have sayd agreat
deal more to you, and have put my thoughts in to better words but that I
dare not venture to take a longer time. My Dearest

your most afectionate and faithfull Wife
30   Lydia DuGard.

33–2

5	**warrick men:** This letter was sent from Coventry by post to William Pestell in Warwick and then on to Samuel.
6–7	**Lost your title of ffellow:** The news had finally reached Oxford, and Samuel had lost his position at Trinity College.
13	**Sam: Wattson and his wife:** The Wattsons were friends of Lydia and Samuel living in Coventry. I have not been able to identify them further.
17	**resolvd:** This word is written as "resold" and then corrected to "resolvd."
20	**pleasd:** The "d" is written over a "g."
20	**I can't:** A lower case "i" is replaced by an upper case "I."
20–21	**I can't . . . business here:** Lydia had now been married nearly two months. She went to Coventry to do some sort of business, which I can not identify, but she was still living with her uncle in Barford, and Samuel was still at Oxford.
22	**pleasd:** The final "d" is written over a "p."
25	**otheres:** Lydia used the common abbreviation to indicate "es."
29	**Wife:** Since Samuel was no longer a fellow, Lydia no longer had to hide the fact she was his wife.

33–3

I can give you no account of your division book, for I came a way as soon
as I had took a napp and made myself ready. Sister will have her service
to you though I have hardly some talk. pray wish Pestell to send my letter
before sunday morning. L

35   [addressed on verso]   For M[r] Samuel DuGard
                    Fellow of Trin: Coll:
                      these.
                            Car: pd
              oxon

40   leave this with William Pestell
                            at Warrwick, to be sent as above.

33–4

31   **Division book:** The most popular division book at the time was Christopher Simpson, *The Division-Violist, or An Introduction to the Playing upon a Ground divided into two parts* (London, 1665).

32   **sister:** Lydia's sister, Elizabeth , was still living in Coventry.

38   **Car: pd:** This is the only letter for which specific carriage was paid and noted. "Letters of one sheet were charged 2d., if sent to any place not exceeding eighty miles; for a letter of two sheets 4d" (Picard, *Restoration London*, 70–74).

34–1

[Folger MS X.d.477/34]

[Grafton Flyford, Worcestershire, August 11, 1698]

When there is a Division of our Goods, I doe authorize my Sis=
ter Lydia to sell 'ym

5   witness my hand
                      Tho: DuGard

Aug't 11:th 1698

34–2

2   **Grafton Flyford:** Thomas DuGard was living on lands in Worcestershire that he had inherited from his mother.

4   **Lydia:** This was Lydia Cotton, the daughter of Samuel and Lydia, born 20 August 1675.

6   **Tho: DuGard:** Thomas DuGard (born 1673) was Samuel and Lydia's first child. He married Catherine Gower in 1698. He may have died before 1705, for he was not mentioned in the will of his sister, Lydia Cotton, dated 26 February 1705.

7   This note was written after Samuel DuGard's will was proved on 29 April 1698.

35–1

[Folger MS X.d.477/35]   [February 26, 1704/5]

ffeb ye 26th 1704

If it please Allmighty God that I and my child both die I desire that
what I have to dispose of may <go> be as I shall apoint, hopeing that my
5   dear husband M^r. Cotton will not be against it. Shou'd the child live that
I am now ready to lie in of I've little that I can leave from it; shou'd it be
boy or girle I desire my dear husband to let my dear and Hon.rd Mother
M^{rs} DuGard have all my wearing Close in generall to dispose of as she
shall think fit amongst my dear sisters, I desire that my dear sister Janne
10   may have as good a share as any of them. my black cloth and anything else
that is fit for my dear and Hon.rd Mother's wear I desire she will accept of.
Shoud it be a girle that I leave behind me I desire my trunk of linin, ring's
and necklace may be kept for her but shou'd it be a boy such things will
be of little value to him, I wou'd therefore have them dispos'd of as my
15   dear and Hon.rd Mother shall think fitt; I desire my little Goddaughter
Hannah Adams may have somthing of value that was mine. Shou'd I die
and leave no child, then there is three 100 pound to be dispos'd of the one
as my dear husband shall think fit to which of his chilldren best please
him, or to be eaqaly divided betwixt them both. ten pound out of y^e
20   remaining two hundard I desire my dear husband will take to bie rings
[w]ith to give to my mother niccols, Bro an' sister Hall and to Sister Cotton
(that is with them) and to who elce he shall think fitt I desire they may be
made with my hare in. one hundard pound I desire my dear an' Hon.rd
Mother may have and dispose of it at her death as she pleases, and to my
25   two dear Brother's Samuel an' Charles each of them five pound and five
pound a peece to my fore dear Sisters, and five pounds a peece to my two
Goddaughter's Hannah Adams and Susanah Cotton. to poor M^{rs}: Key and
her children five pound; if my Aunt ffairfax be liveing I desire she may
have ten pound, if not I desire Jone our old servan+t+, may have five of it,
30   and the other five given to the poor of fforton, or as my dear mother shall

35–2

1   This will was written 26 February 1704/5 by Samuel and Lydia's daughter, Lydia, born 20 August 1675. Soon after, she gave birth to a son whom she named Dugard. Both Lydia and her son died 3 March 1705 and were buried in Holmes Chapel, Cheshire.

5   **husband:** Lydia DuGard and Daniel Cotton of Holmes Chapel, Cheshire, were married on 13 May 1704 in Tong, Shropshire. Daniel's first wife, Sarah, had died on 10 August 1701, leaving two young children for Lydia to help raise.

7   **Mother:** Elizabeth Kimberly DuGard was Samuel's second wife and the one who raised Lydia.

9   **sisters:** Lydia had four half sisters, the daughters of Samuel and Elizabeth DuGard: Elizabeth (age 26), Hannah (age 22), Phebe (age 20), and Susanna (age 16).

9   **Janne:** Janne might have been a sister of Daniel Cotton; she was not Lydia's sister by birth.

16   **Hannah Adams:** Most likely Hannah was the daughter of her sister, Elizabeth, who married John Adams of Bromsgrove in 1703.

18   **His children:** Sarah and Thomas Cotton, children of Lydia's husband by an earlier marriage.

21   **mother niccols:** This is mostly likely Alice Nichols, mother of Daniel Cotton; she died in 1715 and was buried in the Church of Holmes Chapel.

21   **Hall:** The Hall family lived in Holmes Chapel and was related to Lydia through her husband.

21   **Sister Cotton:** Sister Cotton is Lydia's sister-in-law, who must have lived with the Halls.

25   **Brothers:** Samuel DuGard (age 18) and Charles DuGard (age 13), the youngest sons of Samuel and Elizabeth DuGard. There is no mention of her two older brothers, Thomas and Richard. They may have died before this will was written.

27   **Susanna Cotton:** Susanna Cotton probably was the daughter of Daniel's brother, but I have not been able to trace down any record of her.

27   **poor M^rs: Key:** I have been unable to identify Mrs. Key.

28   **Aunt ffairfax:** Anna DuGard Fairfax, Lydia's father's sister. She was fifty-eight years old in 1704 and still living in Barford.

35–3

direct; to my Hon.rd Uncle <M> Mr Kimberley of Coventry I desire twenty
pound may be given to bie two peeces of plate which I desire may be left
to cosen Matty and dear Janne. I desire the remaining fiffteene pound may
be dispos'd <. . .> of to bie rings for my dear +Mother+, Brother's and
35   Sisters, and my good Uncles an' Aunts, I think it will be twenty shillings
rings for as many as I have named, besure let good ones go to Coventry.
I know not whether I have exprest my self so as to be understood, but my
dear husband and Hon.rd Mother will find out my meaning; I hope my
dear husband will not take it ill that I +have+ so as this dispos'd of what
40   I have, I am sure he would not did he know what obligation I lie under to
them all. I desire my dear husband will allways aprove him self a true
friend to my dear an' Hon.rd Mother and to my dear Brother's and Sister's
it is the earnest desire of your affectionate wife

45   Lydia Cotton

35–4

31   **Uncle:** Jonathan Kimberley, vicar of Holy Trinity, Coventry.

33   **Cosen Matty and dear Janne:** I have not been able to identify these two, although Janne could be Daniel's sister. See line 9 above.

34   **< . . . >:** One letter is crossed out and is indecipherable.

40   **obligation:** Since Lydia's mother died at this Lydia's birth, she was raised by her father and stepmother. Here she acknowledged that she had been treated well, perhaps not always the case with step-children.

Introduction to
The Marriages of Cousin Germans

I n 1673 there emerged from Henry Hall's press at Oxford a small book entitled *The Marriages of Cousin Germans, Vindicated from the Censures of Unlawfullnesse, and Inexpediency.* Though no author's name appears on the title-page, Anthony à Wood's reference in *Athenae Oxonienses*,[1] together with internal evidence and some surviving correspondence between Samuel DuGard and Thomas Barlow concerning its imprimatur, leave no doubt that the book was written by DuGard. At the time of publication, Samuel was twenty-nine years old and married; he had been a fellow of Trinity College, Oxford, for four years but was dismissed in June 1672 when news of his marriage reached Oxford. He had taken holy orders in 1672 and was desperately looking for a position in a parish.

References in Lydia's letters make it clear that Samuel had been working on this treatise since 1672 and that it was part of his campaign to win consent from his father, from his superiors at Oxford, and from the family's neighbors in the Warwickshire countryside to marry Lydia.[2] Samuel admitted as much when, just prior to publication, he wrote Thomas Barlow, then provost of Queen's College and vice-chancellor of Oxford, that "my affairs are in such a state that I am compelled to use this little book in the place of a shield."[3] Barlow had loaned Samuel some of his own writings on the subject and had given his imprimatur on 26 March 1673. Dedicating the book to "his much Honour'd T.D.," that is, to his father, addressed one of Samuel's problems. His anxious

---

[1] Wood, *Athenae*, 4:679.

[2] Lydia DuGard to Samuel DuGard, 13 February 1672. See Letter **28** above.

[3] Samuel DuGard to Thomas Barlow, 8 April 1673 (Oxford, Queen's College, MS 275, fol. 36). Barlow answered that to have prohibited the printing of Samuel's book would have been "discouragement to the author and a wrong to others, for it would deprive them of the benefit of a considerable truth ingeniously and rationally explained and proved. If any who have read your discourse are (by ignorance or prejudice) of the contrary opinion, and (as it seems some are) angry with you; tis their fault, not yours." Thomas Barlow to Samuel DuGard, 10 June 1673 (Oxford, Queen's College, MS 275, fol. 38).

circulation of the manuscript among his university friends, to gain their assistance and perhaps their acquiescence, addressed another. There remained the more difficult obstacle of convincing the literate laity.

That Samuel's marriage to his first cousin was *legal* was beyond doubt. Marriages within the third degree, as determined by civil law, were illegal; first cousins are related in the fourth degree.[4] Nevertheless, there is good reason to believe that seventeenth-century people had not relaxed their concern about the propriety of first cousin marriages. Sir John Bramston's contemporary response to his daughter's marriage to her first cousin may serve as an example:

> Elizabeth my youngest daughter maried first, bestowinge her selfe on Moundeford Bramston, her cousen german. This mariage troubled me extreamely, not only because I knew my brother had very manie children to provide for . . . , but in truth my concernment was cheifly the neerenes in blood, it beinge but one degree from incest (brother and sister); yet tyme, and the perswasion of freinds, prevailed with me to forgive that which was past remedie. I found too that the prohibitions of the church had varied as to the degrees, and was rather politicall, then for any prohibition in the Leviticall law.[5]

The nagging doubt remained even after her death in 1689, with Sir John's continuing hope that "God hath fully wiped it [the sin] so out that He will not lay it to their charge."[6] Similarly, Roger North abandoned any hope of marrying his cousin german, whose company he much enjoyed, because he feared breeding with so close a relation.[7]

Centuries of tradition running the other way could not be easily overcome. The tradition against first cousin marriages goes back at least as far as Saint

---

[4] By canon law reckoning, first cousins are related in the second degree, but after 1540 this system of reckoning was no longer used. Sybil Wolfram, *Laws and Outlaws: Kinship and Marriage in England*, (London and Sydney: Croom Helm, 1987), 14.

[5] Bramston, *Autobiography*, 105.

[6] Bramston, *Autobiography*, 348.

[7] *The Lives of the Right Hon. Francis Baron Guilford; The Hon. Sir Dudley North; and the Hon. and Rev. Dr. John North*, ed. Augustus Jessopp, 3 vols. (London: G. Bell and Sons, 1890), 3:28–29. Alan Macfarlane, in his study of the parish of Earls Colne over two centuries, found only two cases of first cousin marriage. *Marriage and Love in England, 1300–1840* (Oxford: Basil Blackwell, 1986), 249–50.

Augustine. In *The City of God*, Augustine maintains that even though the divine law does not prohibit marriage between first cousins, few cousins actually marry because "to have to do with a cousin did not seem very different from having to do with a sister," which was certainly against the law.[8] In 1215 the Church passed laws extending the prohibition to the fourth degree, using the canonical system of reckoning. By that standard even marriages between third cousins were illegal. Under Henry VIII in 1540, English law returned to the more narrow Levitical prohibited degrees, saying "all persons may lawfully marry except those that were prohibited by God's Law." Furthermore, "nothing shall impeach any marriage, but within the Levitical degrees."[9] It was, therefore, illegal to marry close relatives, meaning members of the nuclear family, uncles and aunts, nephews and nieces. In 1563, Archbishop Parker put forth a table showing Degrees of Prohibition to help the clergy control incestuous and unnatural contracts and marriages. This table was explicitly reaffirmed in 1603 when the Church of England established in law that "No Person shall marry within the degrees prohibited by the Laws of God and expressed in a Table set forth by authority in 1563."[10] This law used the civil law means of reckoning and made clear that first cousin marriages were not within the prohibited degrees. Thomas Fuller (1608–1661) supported first cousin marriages when he said,

> The greatest good the land got [by the 1540 statute] was a general leave to marry cousins-german, formerly prohibited by canon and hereafter permitted by common law; a door of liberty left open by God in Scripture, shut by the Pope for his private profit, opened again by the king, first for his own admittance[11] and then for the service of such subjects as would follow him upon the like occasion.[12]

---

[8] Saint Augustine, *The City of God*, trans. Philip Levine, 7 vols. (Cambridge, Mass: Harvard University Press, 1957–72), 4:507.

[9] Edmund Gibson, *Codex Juris Ecclesiastici Anglicani*, 2nd ed., 2 vols. (Oxford: Clarendon Press, 1761), 1:411–12.

[10] O. D. Watkins, *Holy Matrimony* (London: Rivington & Co., 1895), 708. Also see Cressy, *Birth, Marriage, and Death*, 311–15.

[11] King Henry VIII needed the statute to make his marriage to Catherine Howard legal in 1540, since Catherine was cousin german to Anne Boleyn, his former wife.

[12] Quoted in Jack Goody, *The Development of the Family and Marriage in Europe* (Cambridge: Cambridge University Press, 1983), 172–73.

On the other hand, Robert Burton thought that human and divine laws had conspired to avoid hereditary diseases, forbidding such marriages as were "any whit allyed and to make choice of those that are most differing in complexion from them if they love their own and respect the common good."[13] And the Roman Catholic Church reaffirmed the broader church law in the decrees of the Council of Trent: "If any say that only those degrees of consanguinity and affinity which are mentioned in Leviticus can hinder a contract of marriage, or dissolve a union already contracted, and that the church cannot dispense in some of these or lay down that a greater number shall hinder or nullify, let him be anathema."[14] The lines were clearly drawn between the Catholics and the Protestants, but the attitudes of the English people still reflected confusion.

The result was that the issue was still very much alive in the years immediately preceding Samuel's book. The Rump Parliament's Act of 1650 reflected the continual concern over adultery and incest by reaffirming the details of prohibited degrees, but it did not change them.[15] John Hales's "Concerning the Lawfulness of Marriage Betwixt First Cousins, or Cousin Germans," although written in 1630, was only published posthumously in his *Golden Remains* in 1659.[16] Similarly, the judge, Sir John Vaughan, with a special interest in legal matters touching upon prohibited degrees, took the strict but clear position that to marry within the prohibited degrees was absolutely unlawful, and it was a person's obligation to know his or her kin relationships, but that first cousin marriages were not within the prohibited degrees and therefore were legal.[17] Perhaps the clearest statement in favor of Samuel's position came from Jeremy Taylor, chaplain to Charles I, Bishop of Down and Connor (Dublin), casuistical preacher and anti-papist, who took up the cousin germans argument in *Ductor Dubitantium*, first published in 1660, with a second edition appearing in 1671, just as Samuel set to work.

Taylor's book, however, was addressed to a scholarly audience. His learned

---

[13] Robert Burton, *The Anatomie of Melancholy*, 6th ed. (Oxford, 1652; Wing B6181), 62.

[14] Watkins, *Holy Matrimony*, 705.

[15] *Acts and Ordinances of the Interregnum, 1642–1660*, ed. C. H. Firth and R. S. Rait, 3 vols. (London: Stationery Office, 1911), 2:387–89, 10 May 1650.

[16] John Hales, *Golden Remains*, "Concerning the Lawfulness of Marriages betwixt First Cousin, or Cousin-Germans, Septemb. 8. 1630" 2nd ed. (London, 1673; Wing H271), 262–72.

[17] *The Reports and Arguments of that Learned Judge Sir John Vaughan.* (London, 1677; Wing V130), 302–29.

disquisition went through the issue step by step, demonstrating that cousin german marriages were (1) not against the law of nature, (2) not prohibited by Levitical law, (3) not against Christian law, (4) not against Roman law, Greek law or Theodosian law, (5) not prohibited by canon law, (6) not against English law and, finally, (7) not against prudence and reasonableness. Taylor recognized that too many first cousin marriages would be detrimental to the well-being of society, for they would constrain widening friendships, but this did not make such marriages unlawful. In fact, he gave strong reasons for encouraging these marriages. Allowing first cousins to marry would be a remedy for natural lust, because it was natural for them to love one another, and it would bring family solidarity. Thus, he concluded,

> No person ought to be affrighted with the pretenses of any fierce and misperswaded person that the marriage of Cosen Germans is against the law of Nature. . . . The law of nature hath nothing to do in the marriage of Cosen Germans save only she hath left them to their liberty.[18]

Samuel's problem was how to convert all this to arguments his neighbors could comprehend. Here he took advantage of a university education, described by one contemporary as the art of "methodizing what others of excellent parts have invented."[19] He began by following standard conventions, setting forth his small treatise as an anonymous letter and relying heavily on biblical and classical references. While a veneer of learning was essential, there was no need or occasion for originality, a point Samuel conceded explicitly. So much of the argument came from Taylor; and, for those interested in pursuing matters further, Samuel added appropriate references to other, still more erudite works,

---

[18] Jeremy Taylor, *Ductor Dubitantium*, 2nd ed., (London, 1671; Wing T325), 229. Jeremy Taylor (1613–1667), M.A., Cambridge; Fellow, Oxford; chaplain to Charles I. He was sent to Wales by Cromwell, but returned to London in 1660 in support of Charles II. He dedicated *Ductor Dubitantium* to Charles II, who created him Bishop of Down and Conner (Dublin). (*DNB*, s.v. "Taylor, Jeremy.")

[19] Roger B. Miles, *Science, Religion, and Belief: The Clerical Virtuosi of the Royal Society of London, 1663–1687* (New York: P. Lang, 1992), 20, quoting the clerical virtuoso and member of the Royal Society, Robert Wood.

like those of Charles Butler[20] and Jacques Godefroy.[21] Overdoing the learning, however, would have been counterproductive. The audience for this small, self-contained book was the common reading public. Samuel wished to correct "the error of the multitude in the Case of Cousin German Marriages," not to tell them how much they were mistaken. His stated goal was to strengthen some, to inform others, to get still others to lay aside prejudices and correct their mistakes. "He hoped the vulgar would be willing to accept this paper, and others not unwilling to excuse it."[22]

So Samuel frames his treatise from religious and historical sources. He begins by explaining his views on why people insist on thinking cousin german marriages are wrong. The answers he gives in reply are derived from common sense. He says people copy the thoughts of their fathers and masters without thinking; people take pleasure in opposition to sound learning; and people condemn things in order to sound more zealous and holier than others. He then makes the case that each one of the nine arguments that has been made against cousin german marriages is fallacious, and he concludes with an argument for such marriages and an appeal to his father to assist him in convincing others of the correctness of his position.

So much is explicit. But the constant harping on ostensibly common fears leaves the reader wondering whether, in the end, the treatise is not intended to convince Lydia, and indeed Samuel himself, that it is all right to marry. Perhaps they saw themselves in the picture of a young couple who

> in a Blind passion rush into Matrimony, and hamper themselves in *Cords* which must not break till with the *Thread of Life*. And now when the *Hony Month* (as they say) is over, and their cloy'd love will give them leasure to think seriously, they begin to question whether they Marryed lawfully or no; They now can hearken to folks who say that First Cousins never thrive; and they are almost persuaded they have

---

[20] Charles Butler, *Syngenia, De Propinquitate Matrimonium Impediente* (Oxford, 1625; *STC* 4201). Charles Butler received his M.A. from Oxford in 1587, was a schoolmaster and then a vicar in Wotton, Hampshire. He died in 1647.

[21] Jacques Godefroy (1587–1652) was a lawyer, editor, and professor of law in Geneva. *Codex Theodosianus*, his most important work, was published posthumously in Leiden in 1665. Godefroy's contributions to the cousin german issue are limited to his analysis of the codes of Theodosius and Arcadius.

[22] See *Marriages of Cousin Germans*, below, 154.

been too rash in that which is the greatest affair of a mans life. Their Hearts which knew nothing but love before, now begin to let in remorse . . . and, gradually, they blame every ill in their lives on this one false step, and end in misery.[23]

Samuel's answer is clear. He and Lydia will not "think their Love is the cause of their afflictions."[24] Instead, "if they suffer some affliction they will endeavour to chear one another in the bearing of it, and contrive by an active industry to prevent ill thriving for the future."[25]

Samuel's book was published after he and Lydia were married. Whether it had a hand in changing Samuel's father's mind is impossible to ascertain. Thomas DuGard did not perform the marriage ceremony in his church in Barford; however, he allowed the newly married couple to live in the rectory with him, and he baptized their first child. Neither Samuel's treatise nor his (and Lydia's) experience ended the debate.[26] The controversy continued throughout the eighteenth century and beyond. Treatises in England were almost always written to support any marriages between kin not prohibited by the law as clarified in 1603, and gradually pressure has been exerted to make the prohibited degree rules even less strict, though of late the argument has been based on genetics rather than on religion or custom.[27]

---

[23] *Marriages*, below, 174–75.

[24] *Marriages*, below, 175.

[25] *Marriages*, below, 175.

[26] In 1674, Robert Dixon supported DuGard's position stating, "The Case of cosin Germans is no ways reached at as to a prohibition in the Levitical Law, because there is no degree equally near unto it that is forbidden, except of such persons as are as it were parents or in the place of parents. . . . The Christian Law or the Gospel nowhere forbids these marriages." Robert Dixon, *The Degrees of Consanguinity and Affinity* (London, 1674; Wing D1746), 7. A few years later John Turner published two treatises, which adamantly disagreed with Samuel's position. John Turner, *A Letter of Resolution to a Friend Concerning the Marriage of Cousin Germans* (London, 1682; Wing T3310), and *Two Discourses Introductory to a Disquisition Demonstrating the Unlawfulness of the Marriage of Cousin Germans From Law, Reason, Scripture, and Antiquity* (London, 1682; Wing T3319).

[27] In 1907, it became legal in England to marry a deceased wife's sister. In 2002, first cousin marriages remain legal in England. Their legality is a matter of state law in the United States; they are legal in thirty of the fifty states. See Wolfram, *Laws and Outlaws*, for a discussion of the changing response to laws of prohibited degrees in the nineteenth and twentieth centuries.

Textual Notes

It is impossible to say what the original press run was, but there are at least seventeen copies of *The Marriages of Cousin Germans* preserved in libraries in the British Isles and the United States. The book is an octavo, containing a title page, an Epistle to the Reader, and 116 numbered pages of text. I have provided signature numbers when no page numbers were given. For this edition I consulted both the British Library and the Folger Shakespeare Library copies and found them to be identical. The quality of printing, while perfectly readable, contains a number of minor printer's errors. For sake of readability I have silently emended these errors, for example, omitting spaces in such words as "a gain," "a fraid" and "a lone," adding spaces when words are run together and correcting obvious typographical errors. In dropped capitals I have capitalized only the first letter of each word. Although the printer often used italic and roman letters for emphasis, he was careless in the font used for punctuation marks. I have matched the punctuation with the text, so that if the text is in italics, the punctuation is as well. The font for the italic and roman letter S is particularly difficult to ascertain both for me and for the printer. Again, I have used the font that matches the text surrounding it. I have supplied notes in the text for the corrections called for in the Errata, which is found at the end of the book. Other than these minor changes, I have been faithful to the original text, maintaining the spelling, abbreviations, equal signs used as word dividers, the use of italics, and paragraphing.

The

MARRIAGES

OF

Cousin Germans,

Vindicated from the Cen-

sures of Unlawfullnesse,

and Inexpediency.

Being a Letter written to his much

Honour'd T.D.[1]

Nescio quomodo pleriq; Errare malunt;
Eamq; sententiam, quam adamaverunt,
pugnacissimè defendere, quam sine perti-
nacia, quid constantissimè dicatur, exqui-
rere. Cic. Acad. Quæs. lib. 2.[2]

OXFORD.

Printed by HEN: HALL[3] for

Thomas Bowman.[4]

Book-seller. 1673.

[A1v]

---

[1] These initials must stand for Samuel's father, Thomas DuGard.

[2] "But somehow or other most men prefer to go wrong, and to defend tooth and nail the system for which they have come to feel an affection, rather than to lay aside obstinacy and seek for the doctrine that is most consistent." Cicero, *Academica*, trans. H. Rackham (New York: G. P. Putnam's Sons, 1933), 476.

[3] Printer at Oxford, 1642–79(?). Elected printer of the university 21 November 1644. Plomer (1907), 88.

[4] Book-seller of Oxford, 1664–1678. Plomer (1922), 43.

Imprimatur[5]

THO. BARLOW[6]

Pro-Vice-Can: Oxon:

Mar. 26. 1673.[7]

[A2]

THE EPISTLE

TO THE

READER.

READER.

This following Letter, at the first, I assure thee, was intended only for the eye of some private persons and Friends; and in thinking [A2v] *upon the Error of the* Multitude *in the Case of* Cousin Germans Marriages, *I wish'd indeed their mistake corrected, but did not design to tell them how much they were mistaken. For I am not ignorant how little even things of greater consequence will prevail, when there are great numbers set against them; whom the Reason that cometh from one man can as little conquer, as a single man's Sword can whole thousands, engag'd by Heat and Ignorance in a wrong Cause.* [A3] *Besides, some who may be my Friends in the Case, will not perhaps be so in my handling of it, but will think me either* flat *or* triviall; *and so the Criticalnesse and curiosity of these, will hurt me no lesse then the rude prejudices of the other. But at the solicitations of some Persons, who would not wittingly desire any thing of me that might be my injury, I was at last persuaded not wholly to refuse, what I had not the Confidence so much as to think of before. And indeed when I consider* [A3v] *how much some* Cousin Germans, *whose prudent Love may have engag'd them in Marriage, have been worryed by the Censures of the* Many; *how some also to their great misery, and somtimes to almost their Ruin, have been crost by their Friends, who have either thought*

---

[5] "Let it be printed" (Latin): official license, authorizing the printing of this book.

[6] Thomas Barlow (1607–1691), Provost of Queen's College, Vice Chancellor of Oxford, later Bishop of Lincoln. See the Biographical Appendix.

[7] While this book received its imprimatur March 26, 1673, there is reference made to it in manuscript form in Lydia DuGard's letter to Samuel, dated 13 February 1672. See Letter **28** above. Based on internal evidence in Lydia's letters it is clear that she dates her year from January 1, so Samuel was certainly thinking about this book for over a year.

such Wedlock unlawfull, or else who have set themselves against it out of a Scrupulosity of their own Credit, or perhaps too great a Compliance with some men who love to be offended with many things they have [A4] nothing to do with; and lastly how others after Marriage, not being able to defend what they have done, have by the misguided zeal of some, been brought to think they have committed a great Crime, and so are made to interpret, whatever Crosse they suffer, to be a judgment upon them for their Loves; I may seem to do not an uncharitable, and ill natur'd action, *if I shall endeavour to strengthen some (who are more nearly concern'd in a good opinion of such Wedlock; and to inform others, [A4v] (who are not engaged,) that so they may not be so hasty to condemn what in it self is very lawfull, and oftentimes may be very expedient. And though I expect to be no lesse Censur'd by some, for pleading for these Marriages then if I my self were a person engaged in them,[8] yet if I can here and there prevail with a few to lay aside prejudice, and correct a mistake so generally receiv'd, I shall think it a good reward for these small Pains I have taken. But, if I may make a wish more then Ordi-* [A5] *nary for this Paper, I would Choose one place peculiarly for its good acceptance, and that upon the account of two Persons,[9] whose Credit and Interest is not less dear to me then mine own; and though their Loves are not so slight as that a Censure can shake them; nor they so ill persuaded of the lawfulnesse of such Marriage, as that they will think any affliction they may undergoe with others, or apart by themselves to be a scourge for their Wedlock as unlawfull, yet they will find the more Friends if this [A5v] Pamphlet be well accepted: for the successe of which I shall be very little solicitous, if without it They themselves will be well thought of: a thing which I can very faintly promise to them, since a Mans own Country, is for the most part the least his Friend; and, as if it had a Right so to do, will deal the most uncivilly by him. I have somtimes wondre'd how this opinion of the* unlawfulnesse of first Cousins Marriages *should be so generally received; especially since together with so many other Truths it was got* [A6] *out of the* Papists *hands, and made free by* Henry 8th, Edward 6th *and the very first Act of* Elizabeth;[10] *when before, it was a matter of* Mony, *and made unlawfull, only that by Dispensations it might increase the Popes Treasure: a thing which some, who deservedly are against the usurpations of Rome, do not think of; and if they do, I*

---

[8] By the time this treatise was published, Samuel was indeed a person engaged in a cousin-german marriage. He and Lydia were married 18 April 1672 (Wasperton Parish Register, DR208/1).

[9] These two persons were presumably his father, Thomas DuGard, and Lydia DuGard.

[10] *The Statutes of the Realm*, 32 Henry VIII c. 38, 1540; 2, 3 Edward VI c. 23, 1548; 1 Elizabeth c. 1, 1558.

know not how they will avoid their being really the Popes Friends; since there is nothing in Scripture, *the Orders of our* Church, *nor in* Reason *that does for-* [A6v] *bid it. But I will say no more since I have spoken sufficiently in the following pages; and I am afraid too largely for such a subject; unlesse it be to those who are resolv'd before hand not to Change their Opinion; and these, if they will take the pains to read, I am contented should be tir'd.*

I have been constraind to answer some Objections which an ingenious Man may think superfluous, but which I chose not to omit, lest they should be urg'd by ignorant men. As if they could not be answer'd and [A7] *so should be a means of their further Censures and uncharitablenesse. The truth of it is, very few of those who are any whit knowing, do question the Lawfulnesse of the thing; so that what I have written, is for the most part writ to the Capacity of the Common People; and if it be not such as a scholar will read, it is not such as the unlearned will not understand. And it is upon this account especially that I have avoided great numbers of Quotations; which if I had taken, as they are already used, without Con-* [A7v] *sulting the Authors themselves, perhaps I might have had as good a right to them as some others; for, as one saith true enough, they are oftentimes like Gaping, that goes from one to another, unquestion'd, and meerly out of Course. But, yet if any one would see authorityes of* Learned *men, and examples of* Cousin Germans Marriages, *he may consult* Gothofrid de nupt. Consobrin;[11] *Butlers* Syngenia,[12] *and Bishop Taylors* Duct. Dubitant.[13] *And since there are so many who are* [A8] *unknowing in this Case; and I know no Peece in English that peculiarly treats of this subject, but such as cannot be bought alone, or else such as are either too short, or not easily understood, I hope the vulgar will be willing to accept this Paper, and others not unwilling to excuse it.* [1]

Sir.[14]

I have been sometimes more than a little disturb'd at some men, whose *ignorance* hath rendered them very perverse; and could have wish'd a little more of judgement and discretion in some of those also, whose constant endeavours after knowledg, and Lives spent in *Books* and *Learning*, should one would think

---

[11] Jacques Godefroy, *Dissertatio de Nuptiis Consobrinarum* (1642) in *J. Gothofredi Opera Juridica Minora* (Leiden, 1733), 610–26.

[12] Charles Butler, *Syngenia, De Propinquitate Matrimonium Impediente* (Oxford, 1625; STC 4201).

[13] Jeremy Taylor, *Ductor Dubitantium*, 229–42.

[14] "Sir" refers to T. D. (presumably Thomas DuGard) as stated on the title page.

give them a better insight into things, then for the most part we shall find they have. [2]

The Reasons of the errors of these Latter may I think be reduced to one, or all of these Heads.

1. Their making all their *Reading* stoop to those Notions which were instill'd into them when young, by their Fathers or Masters; and the esteeming all as false, which doe differ from those principles they then suck'd in. or.

2^{d}ly. Their pleasure in opposing things received for, and which are truth, that soe they may the better be taken for men of parts and greater Learning then ordinary. or.

3^{d}ly. Their willingnesse to condemne some things as unlawfull, or, at least, uncreditable that soe they may appear [3] to be of a more rais'd *Zeal*, and greater *Sanctity* then other men.

I will content my selfe in the bare mentioning of these things, (though they might bee largely spoken to) and will onely take notice that the perversnesse of the Vulgar, proceeds from the ill example of these men I now spoke of; whether it be in an affected boasting of *Learning* or *Sanctity*, which is a great Crime; or in a misguided *Piety* which is our great unhappiness. For when they have gotten the Opinion of being Learn'd, judicious, or Zealous, whatsoever they say shall be esteem'd as Gospell; and though Reason shall be able to manifest the contrary, yet because some of them seem to act [4] by the *Spirit*, their Opinions shall be better then others Demonstrations, and the *Infallible Pope* shall be most set up in those who would be taken to be his greatest enemies.

Perchance, *Sr*, you wonder at what I drive in these words; and it may be you will think me rash in my Censures. I wish *Sr* I were, for then we should have more of candor and good nature, and lesse of *Humor* and *Prejudice* in the world then now we have. But seeing many lawfull things are cry'd down, among which none more then the *Wedlock of Cosin Germans*, (a thing which upon the account of a Friend of mine I have no reason to speak against) I thought to set [5] downe the grounds of mens mistakes in this and many other actions.

And because the Marriage of first Cosins is very innocent, and yet has so many enemies, I will in pity speake one good word for it; since from a right opinion of the thing, the lives of many would be made, not only more pleasant, but more fortunate too, and yet no injury done to any man. And surely if the lawfulnesse, and expedience of things do create them an esteem with prudent men; why, such Marriages should be so severely censur'd, I see no reason: for they are in themselves alwayes *Lawfull*, and sometimes may be *Expedient*. The proving of which shall [6] be[15] the matter of the following pages.

1. *For the lawfullnesse of them.*

Those things that are not against the *Law of Nature, the Law of God*, nor *the Law of the Land* cannot but be in themselves Lawfull; and that these Marriages are against none of these will be manifest from the answering these following *Objections* against them.

1. *Their being against Nature:*

2. *Their being forbid by Scripture.*

3dly *Their hindering of the spreading of Society, and Friendship, which is enough among Naturall Relations already.*

4. *The ill prospering of them.*

5. *Their being forbid by* Theodosius *and* Arcadius *Christian Em=* [7] *perours, with severe Punishments to Offenders in this kind.*

6. *Their not being in use with the Primative Christians.*

7. *Their being prohibited by the Apostles Canons, and the Canon Law.*

8. *It being unlawfull for Second Cousins to marry, and therefore First may not.*

9. *However, if they are not unlawfull, yet a wise man upon the account of Credit will abstain from them.*

These are the greatest arguments that I ever heard, or can think against them. And though some of them may appear plausible, yet if thoroughly search'd, will be vain enough and of no force. [8]

1. They say these Marriages are against Nature: for the Images of the Common Parents being not worn out of those who are so nearly related to them, it is a kind of incest for them to mix.

I might here have a fair Field to proceed in, and might prove the Wedlock of First Cousins not to be against Nature, from nearer conjunctions in the Earliest Generations of Man, who when all things else have had a naturall Beginning, cannot be thought to spring from an unnaturall Foundation. But I will not bring any thing here that may be thought by common Capacities to be uncouth; and since the question does not need [9] it I will go to the 2^d Objection, and shew

That these Marriages are not forbid by Scripture; where, if they were against Nature, without controversy they would be directly prohibited.

And indeed so great a Reverence have wee for that *Sacred volume*, that we

---

[15] This is the catchword on B3, inadvertently omitted from the text on B3v.

willingly acknowledge our *interest* and *affections* must vail to it; and even that of our *Love*, which can contemn Honours, quell ambition, trample upon the power of Gold, and conquer all things else in the world, shall calmly submit it self to these supreme Dictates. Nor shall we daringly, like some, inquire into Gods commands, why *He*, who is [10] all Goodnesse, should so confine men, and by his Laws make many things to become sin to them, which otherwise would not have hinder'd their well being on Earth, and would have made their Way to Heaven also more easy to be walk'd in. We acknowledge him just, in all his Actings, and will rest in his reveal'd will (though we do not understand the reason of it) as proceeding from the Highest Wisdome. Though certainly, in this thing of Restraining Marriages, we may easily discern the *Good of Society*, and the *Peace and Welfare of Families* to be happily contriv'd and commanded.

We will view a little what his will in this present Case of ours is. [11]

And surely, Sir, among those Relations who are forbid to marry, we shall not find that least mention of Cousin Germans. It is said indeed Lev. 18, *That none shall approach to any who is near of kin to him.*[16] but all those who by Blood are related, are not to be thought *near of kin*; for the Difference is very great. Only those are properly said to be near of Kin to a man, who are either his *Father*, or *Mother*, his *Brother*, or *Sister*, his *Son* or *Daughter*, or those who descend further from him, or whom he is descended from in a straight Line. And that only these are meant by near of Kin we may see from Lev. 21.1, 2, 3. *None shall be defiled for the Dead among* [12] *you, but for his Kin that is near him; for his Father and his Mother, for his Brother and Sister who is a Virgin, for his Son and Daughter; for these He may be defil'd.*[17] And if some others Levit.18, who are more remote, are forbid to marry, it is not because they are properly near of Kin, but for some other reason: for Reverence and Honour, as in the Mother in Law, and some others, or the better securing of those who are truly near, and are by no means to be touch'd. Perhaps, as there were Bounds set round the Mount; not that it was in it self unlawfull to go nearer, but if the People had been permitted that, they

---

[16] Leviticus 18:6. "None of you shall approach to any that is near of kin to him, to uncover their nakedness." DuGard quotes the King James translation of the Bible (1611) from memory; he sometimes quotes only selected parts of the verse and rearranges the words to suit his needs.

[17] Leviticus 21:1–3. "There shall none be defiled for the dead among his people: But for his kind, that is near unto him, that is, for his mother, and for his father, and for his son, and for his daughter, and for his brother, And for his sister a virgin, that is nigh unto him, which hath had no husband; for her may he be defiled."

would have been apt to profane the *Sacred Hill*. And [13] that Near of Kin is to be taken in this stricter Sense, is manifest; else how will those who are in more Remote Degrees, and yet tearm'd near of Kin, be permitted Marriage, as *Ruth* 2.20.[18] where this Phrase is attributed to Boaz[19] who was to Marry *Ruth*. and 2 *Sam* 19.42[20] where all the Men of Judah call *David* their near *Kinsman*?

And indeed had it been unlawfull for Cousin Germans to Marry, He who could not be said to forget, as Men do, who could not over look a thing which he would have observ'd by his People for ever, would have told us so in as express tearmes as he had said other things. [14]

And here we may observe that a positive Command is not necessary for the making things to be Lawfull, but the not being forbid is sufficient for that. For it is the designe of Laws to put limits and bounds to that liberty which we have by Nature, and to oblige us to the observance of some peculiar commands; and therefore Nature and Reason will tell you that where there is no particular Precept or Prohibition to bind us, we are left to our Liberty and Choice, to do, or not to do. And thus a Man may addict himselfe to Study or Learning, not that he had direct command for it (for with equall Right he might have been a Merchant, [15] or of some other Calling) but because he is not prohibited by any Law, he may follow what his own Genius and inclination lead him to. And so we may Marry a Cousin German, not because we are commanded, but because we are not forbid.

But it may be some will say that what I speak is true where there is no *Prohibition* at all; but though there be no positive nor direct one, yet if there be an indirect and Consequentiall one, it makes that action unlawfull, and such there may seem to be in our present Case. For albeit in expresse terms the Marriages of first Cousins are not prohibited, yet from some of those that are, we [16] may infer that these are no less: for where there are some who are at larger Distances remov'd whom yet we may not Marry, it may seem by no means fit that those who are nearer should be permitted. I must confess Sir, this

---

[18] Ruth 2:20. "And Naomi said unto her, The man is near of kin unto us, one of our next kinsman."

[19] Ruth 3:12–13. "And now it is true that I am thy near kinsman: howbeit there is a kinsman nearer than I . . . if he will not do the part of a kinsman to thee, then will I do the part of a kinsman to thee."

[20] 2 Samuel 19:42. "And all the men of Judah answered the men of Israel, Because the king is near of kind to us: wherefore then be ye angry for this matter? have we eaten at all of the king's cost? or hath he given us any gift?"

would be somthing if all were forbid there upon the account of Nearnesse; but there are peculiar reasons for peculiar *Persons* and *Degrees*. Thus, Sir, *my Great Aunt*, or *my sisters Neece* are as far removed from me as a *First Cousin*: and yet who grant *Cousin Germans* may Marry will deny the Lawfullnesse of the other. Nay suppose an Uncle or an Aunt to be remov'd two or three Degrees further (as we may easily suppose such a [17] thing) from the *Neece* or *Nephew*, it would be unlawfull for these to Marry, though never any denyed that *Third Cousins* might, which yet are as near as these I mention. The reason of this will be seen presently.

And surely *Fist*[21] *Cousins* are not so little away remov'd from the Common Stock, as by the most they are thought to be. They are in the fourth Degree, as the *Civil Law* do truly account;[22] for so many degrees are to be reckoned as there are persons from the common Parent, so the son is one step remov'd from the father; his son is two. This Sons Uncle is one Degree from the common Parent, his Daughter two. *So* [18] that these Degrees added together make four, whence *Cousin Germans* are four degrees distant. Nor can it in reason be thought that they are but so many Steps from one another as they are from the *Common Stock*: for to know their Relation you must run up from the Nephew to the Grandfather, and from the Grandfather down to the Neece; which is to measure four Degrees. And thus *Vlpian. in quarto gradu permittitur Conjugium extra eas personas quæ locum Parentum Liberorumque habent.*[23] Those who are in the fourth degree may marry, unlesse it be those who are in the place of Fathers and Children; as a great Uncle is to a Neece, or that Neece to her Brothers or *Si*- [19] sters Grandson. Here the more they are remov'd the lesse reason there is for their Marrying; because as a Father has a Paternall Right over ten Generations could he live to see them spring from him in a Direct Line, (his old age requiring from

---

[21] *Fist*: correct to "*First*" (Errata).

[22] In civil law, parents and children are related in the first degree, brothers and sisters in the second degree, nephews and aunts or nieces and uncles in the third degree and first cousins in the fourth degree. This method of calculating degree dates back to Roman law and differs from the method devised by canon law during the time of Pope Gregory. Wolfram, *In-Laws and Outlaws*, 14–15.

[23] "Marriage is permitted in the fourth degree between persons in the care of free parents." Ulpian further says, "formerly marriage could not be contracted between these collaterally related within the fourth degree, but now it is allowable to take a wife even of the third degree." *The Commentaries of Gaius and Rules of Ulpian*, trans. J. T. Abdy and Brian Walker (Cambridge: Cambridge University Press, 1885), 383.

the latest Grandchildren *Respect* and *Reverence* so often encreased as the name of father comes betwixt him and them) so *Uncles* and *Aunts* since they are *quasi Parentes*,[24] in the place of Fathers and Mothers, must have the greater respect by how much the more the Name of Uncle and Aunt comes betwixt them and their Nephews and Neeces, so that it would be more absurd for a Great Vncle to Marry his Neece, then [20] for an immediate uncle to Marry his.

But, Sir, could it not be prov'd by good reason (as *I* perswade my selfe it is) that Cousin Germans Marriages are not forbid by Scripture, yet the Examples of good men among the Jews, after this *Law in Leviticus* was made, are a sufficient Evidence that they are not unlawfull.[25] The Daughters of *Zelophehad, Mahlah, Tirza, Hogla,* and *Noah* were Marryed to their Fathers Brothers Sons, *Numb* 36. 11.[26] In which place God not only seems to *approve* of their Marriage, but to have *enjoyned* them to do as they did. for it is said *They did as the lord commanded Moses, and took their Fathers Bro-* [21] *thers Sons. v.* 10.[27] Where we may take notice, that this command was given to the Daughters of *Zelophehad* not as if it authorize'd them for the making of these Marriages which were before unlawfull; nor yet as if it shew'd that such wedlock was never to be made unlesse in the like Case, (for where is there the least appearance that they were before prohibited?) but what was lawfull for all before, who were no nearer of Kin, may seem to be made necessary for *Heiresses*. for you know, Sir, the cause of their Marrying thus, was that their inheritance should not passe from the *Tribe* of their Fathers; and it was thought fit it should stay in their own family too, rather then [22] goe to *Strangers*. Which thing, it is very likely, from the Jews grew a Custome amongst other Nations also. Thus Terent. in Phorm.

> *Lex est ut Orbæ, qui sunt genere proximi,*
> *Iis nubant, & illos ducere eadem Hæc Lex jubet.*[28]

---

[24] Jeremy Taylor says, "uncles and aunts are not to be married, because they are *loco parentis;* they are *quasi parentes,* images of fathers and mothers, for the reverence of which the marriage of our uncles and aunts respectively are forbidden." *Ductor,* 231.

[25] Taylor, *Ductor,* 233.

[26] Numbers 36:11. "For Mahlah, Tirzah, and Hoglah, and Milcah, and Noah, the daughters of Zelophehad, were married unto their father's brothers' sons."

[27] Numbers 36:10. "Even as the Lord commanded Moses, so did the daughters of Zelophehad."

[28] Geta says, "There's a law, that orphans are to be married to their next of kin, and the same law prescribes that the next of kin shall marry them." (Act I, lines 125–26). Terence, *Phormio,* in Terence, *Phormio, The Mother-in-Law, The Brothers,* trans. John

and for the greater credit of this Instance of *Zelophehads* Daughters, we may observe that none of the Jews afterwards, whether the *Karæi*, or the *Talmudists* (those who stuck to the words of the Law, not admitting any thing else but what could necessarily and plainly be inferred thence, or those who would have their Nicer argumentations and illations, and what is more, the Hereditary transmission of interpretations) did ever codemn [*sic*] the [23] Marriage of Cousin Germans; *Quoniam liquet ex ipsis Scripturae verbis Zelophehadi Filias nuptas esse etiam Patruorum Suorum filiis; adeoque licitum fuisse conjugium ubi quis filiam acceperit Patrui, seu consobrinam. Selden. uxor. Heb. Cap. 5. lib. 1.*[29]

But, Sir, to bring one instance or two more out of Scripture. we read 1. *Chron.* 23. *v.*21. 22.[30] That Mahli, the son of Merari a Levite, had two Sons, Eleazar and Kish. And Eleazar dyed and had no Sons but Daughters, and their Brethren the Sons of Kish took them. Persons certainly, who, since they were Levites, had reason to know the Law, and to practise it as well as any other 2.*Chron.*11.18.20.[31] Rehoboam [24] Marryed *Mahalath*, and after that *Mahachan*, who were both his Cousin Germans. A Person whom we read indeed to be a little imprudent in his refusing the old mens Councell, but who otherwise was innocent in his life. and we may say, God took an occasion from his Father Solomons sins to afflict him, rather then from his own to punish him. 1. *Kings.*11. *v.*11.12.13.[32]

Sargeaunt (Cambridge, Mass.: Harvard University Press, 1912), 16. This refers to an Attic law that required the nearest eligible male relation to marry an orphaned Athenian girl.

[29] "According to scripture, the daughters of Zelophehad were permitted to marry the sons of their paternal uncles. Thus a marriage was permitted in which one could take the daughter of a paternal uncle, that is a cousin." *John Selden on Jewish Marriage Law: The Uxor Hebraica*, trans. Jonathan R. Ziskind (New York: E. J. Brill, 1991), 54.

[30] 1 Chronicles 23: 21–22. "The sons of Merari; Mahli, and Mushi. The sons of Mahli; Eleazar and Kish. And Eleazar died, and had no sons, but daughters: and their brethren the sons of Kish took them."

[31] 2 Chronicles 11:18–20. "And Rehoboam took him Mahalath the daughter of Jerimoth the son of David to wife, and Abihail the daughter of Eliab the son of Jesse: which bare him children, Jeush, and Shamariah, and Zaham. And after her he took Maachah the daughter of Absalom; which bare him Abijah, and Attai, and Ziza, and Shelomith."

[32] 1 Kings 11:11–13. "Wherefore the Lord said unto Solomon, For as much as this is done of thee, and thou hast not kept my covenant and my statutes, which I have commanded thee, I will surely rend the kingdom from thee, and will give it to thy servant. Notwithstanding in thy days I will not do it for David thy father's sake: but I

But lastly it is not improbable that *Joseph*, and *Mary*, the Mother of our Saviour, were Cousin Germans:[33] for otherwise it cannot so well be made out how Jesus was of the Tribe of Judah, and the family of *David*, as was prophesied of him. For hee could by no means be said [25] to be the true and Genuine Son of *Joseph*, but only of his Mother. Now only *Joseph's* Genealogy is described by both the Evangelists. *Matthew* bringing it from Solomon the Son of David by Bathsheba; *Luke* from Nathan Davids Son by the same Bathsheba. (Where by the by, we may take Notice, that the Tracer of the Genealogies at the Beginning of some of our English Bibles, is much out. For that by Luke is not *Maryes*, as it is there made to be, but *Josephs*, *Heli* being his Father by *Law*, *Joseph*[34] and *Jacob* by *Nature. vid. Euseb. Ecclesiast. Hist: cap. 7. lib.*1.)[35] Some of old (since *Mary* was reckon'd to be of the tribe of Levi as being Kin to Elizabeth who was of the [26] Daughters of Aron *Luke.* 1.5.)[36] Thought this knot could not be untyed, unless they should assent[37] that *Jesus* was sprung no less of *Ioseph* then of *Mary*, and this Sect Antiquity call'd *Iosephites*. But this is directly contrary to Scripture, which sai's, [*sic*] that *Iesus* was borne of a pure *Virgin*. But if we say that *Mary* was Cousin German to *Ioseph*, the thing is solv'd beyond all exceptions; for then Josephs Genealogy, to his Grandfather, *Matthan*, will be Maries too; and so *Mary* will not only be of the *Tribe* of *Juda*, but of the *family of David* also. I must confesse *Mary* may be of the House of David, and yet not so nearly related to *Ioseph*; but then we shall take away the mutuall share [27] which they Both have (perhaps by a speciall design of the Holy Ghost) as far as lawfully they could, in the Genealogy; and we might say, that *Matthew* and *Luke* direct us indeed to *David*, from whom our Saviour sprung, but yet send us thither the wrong way.

---

will rend it out of the hand of thy son. Howbeit I will not rend away all the kingdom: but will give one tribe to thy son for David my servant's sake, and for Jerusalem's sake which I have chosen."

[33] Taylor, *Ductor*, 234.

[34] *Joseph*: blot out (Errata).

[35] This argument hinges on tracing Joseph's genealogy by nature and by law and thereby making Mary and Joseph cousins german, since Eli and Jacob were half brothers to Joseph, the former by law and the latter by nature. Eusebius, *The Ecclesiastical History*, trans. Kirsopp Lake, 2 vols. (London: William Heinemann, 1926–32), 1:55–65.

[36] Luke 1:5. "There was in the days of Herod, the king of Judaea, a certain priest name Zacharias, of the course of Abia: and his wife was of the daughters of Aaron, and her name was Elisabeth."

[37] assent: correct to "assert" (Errata).

And though indeed *Joseph*, the first step backwards in the Genealogy, in respect of Blood, has no share in our Saviour, yet so little in the whole may be allow'd upon the account of the usuall Reckoning of Generations among the Jews, who never went by the *Mother*: especially since Hee who after *Espousalls*,[38] (as our Saviour *Luke* 1.2, 7.)[39] is not unlawfully begotten, may justly be said to be the Son [28] of the Man, as he is of the Woman; and God may give Children what way he pleases. But though this be sufficient to make *Joseph* the first step of the Genealogy, yet it by no means is sufficient to make our *Saviour*, only by *Joseph*, to descend from *David* according to the *Flesh*. For the making our *Saviors* Genealogy out, it will be most convenient (might almost say necessary) to think *Joseph* and *Mary* to be *Cousin Germans*; otherwise if you make *Mary* to be of the *House of David*, and yet not nearly related to *Joseph*, our Saviors Line will be right in the End, but not direct in the Way. If you shall make her to be of another *Tribe*, (as some have thought) though *I* [29] cannot but grant that when two persons of different Tribes did Marry, the Children were reckoned of that Tribe which the Father was of, yet were there nothing but *Joseph* the imputed Father to entitle the *Tribe of Juda*, and the *Family of David* in the Messias, for ought I see, *Levi* would have more reason to boast of our Saviour then *Judah*; and some other Family might claim the Honour of his Birth, rather then Davids; which would be no mean argument in a Jewes mouth for his Obstinate Denying of Christ.

If it shall be ask'd, how then, since *Mary* is made to be of the *Tribe of Juda*, *Elizabeth* could be her Cousin, who was of the Daughters of Aaron, *Luke*. 1.[40] It [30] may be said, that *Elizabeth* also was of the *Tribe of Judah*; neither did that Law[41] which forbad *Virgins* Marrying into other Tribes, hinder that they might

---

[38] Samuel's point here hinges on the legality of a marriage contract made by a simple pledge, called "spousals." This pledge of union, though not common, was officially recognized even in the seventeenth century. Martin Ingram, "Sex and Marriage in Early Modern England" in *Popular Culture in Seventeenth-Century England*, ed. Barry Reay (London: Croom Helm, 1985), 140–41.

[39] Luke 1:27. "To a virgin espoused to a man whose name was Joseph, of the house of David; and the virgin's name was Mary."

[40] Luke 1. See note 42 below.

[41] Numbers 36:8–9. "And every daughter, that possesseth an inheritance in any tribe of the children of Israel, shall be wife unto one of the family of the tribe of her father, that the children of Israel may enjoy every man the inheritance of his fathers. Neither shall the inheritance remove from one tribe to another tribe: but every one of the tribes of the children of Israel shall keep himself to his own inheritance."

not be Marryed to *Levites*, although they were Heiresses; because the *Levites* had no Portion of their own, and so might make themselves fortunes out of any Tribe. Besides, those Virgins that had no lands might Marry where they pleas'd; so that Elizabeth was reckoned of the Daughters of Aaron, only because she was the Wife of *Zacharias. see Beza's annot: on Luke 1.5.*[42]

And thus Sir we see *C. Germans* Marriages are not such desperate things, as some folks make them to be. If they were, they would [31] not have been commanded in Zelophehads Daughters, nor have been so calmly pass'd over in Meraries offspring,[43] Rehoboam,[44] nor lastly have been contracted in that *blest Pair*, whence the greatest *Purity* and *Holiness* our *Saviour* himselfe sprung: nor do we see the least shew of a Prohibition in the Gospell, so that they must be strangely præjudiced, who will so severely condemn what is by no means forbid in the *New* Testament, and so well approv'd of in the *Old.*

But, Sir, there is another objection urg'd against these Marriages and that is. 3dly *Their hindring of the spreading of society and Friendship, which is enough among naturall Relations* [32] *already and so, by Marriages further from home, should be rais'd up and nourish'd in others.*

I am so great an Esteemer of Friendship that I wish not only that it reach'd wider then it doth, but that it were more intense and firm in those narrow bounds it has; nay even in many persons too, whom the closest Bands of nature, and those more close ones of Choice and Marriage should, one would think, teach the highest affection. And you may beleive me, *Sir*, if by so doing I could reconcile the Hatreds and Animosityes that so much rage in the world, I would give up not only my *argument*, but my *Life* too. But, Sir, let it be granted that it is better generally for o- [33] thers to Marry, then *Cousin Germans*, upon the account of scattering Friendships, yet I hope here and there one *Cousin German* may marry another, and yet no great harm be done to the common *Society* of

---

[42] "Though Elizabeth were of the tribe of Levi, yet she might bee Maries cousin: for whereas it was forbidden by the Law for maidens to be married to men of other tribes, this could not let it, but that the Levites might take them wives out of any tribe: for the Levits had no portion allowed them, when the land was divided among the people." *The New Testament of Our Lord Jesus Christ translated out of the Greeke, by Theod. de Beza with briefe summaries and expositions upon the hard places by the said auctor,* trans. L. Tomson (London, 1616; *STC* 2915), 51v.

[43] See note 30 above.

[44] Rehoboam: correct to "and in Rehobeam" (Errata).

Men. *St. Paul saies, it is better to continue single then to Marry,*[45] but he did not intend that his advice should, nor think that it would have a Generall effect: and, if all should have took his Counsel, the world must have had an end in that Generation, or else God must have continued it by a Miracle. It is better to marry others then *Cousin Germans*, as it is better not at all to marry, then to marry; but if it were so strictly observ'd; as to be thought a sin to be now and [34] then otherwise, I believe and dare affirm it would be a greater Disadvantage and injury to some single Persons, then it would be an advantage to the *Community*. That man is very unwise who would be at great Damages, and would undergoe the hazzard of losing the pleasures of his life, and, it may be, Life too (for the effects of a Frustrated Love are sometimes dismall) out of a principle of scattering Friendships abroad, which would not the thousandth part help the Kingdomes peace so much as destroy his own Happinesse. Charity and Friendship do well abroad, I confesse, but they must begin at Home; and, however some may think, I am sure those men can little look after o- [35] thers welfare as they ought, who will be slack and carelesse of their own. If Men were so much addicted to the marrying of First Cousins, as to neglect matching with others, it would be well some Law should be made by the Civill Magistrate for the prohibiting a Custome so destructive to *Society*; but so long as there is so good store of *Persons* and *Faces,* and more wealth too (that great Motive of Love and Matrimony) abroad, then there is, for the most part, at home, we need not fear the Love to our Kindred will justle out our interest elsewhere; and for one match between *Cousin Germans*, I dare be bold to say there will be thousand of another Stamp. [36]

But, for the strengthening of this and other arguments, they bring this terrible Observation, which is a

4th Reason, viz. *that Cousin Germans do not thrive, and that God shews by the ill prospering of them that such Marriages are unlawfull, and by no means approv'd of by him.* Which I will speak somthing largely to, not that the Objection needs it, but that the censorious nature of People, almost every where, may seem to require it.

I will not, Sir, wish they may want good successe, who judge of the goodnesse or illnesse of an action from the event of it; though, really, I think none

---

[45] 1 Corinthians 7:1–2. "It is good for a man not to touch a woman. Nevertheless, to avoid fornication, let every man have his own wife, and let every woman have her own husband."

deserve such a wish more then these. [37] And I would with all my heart this strange uncharitableness did not find a lodging in their Breasts who would be taken for the best Christians; I say, I wish it be not found as much, if not more, in them then in any others; as if they could not be *pious* unlesse they must pretend to be acquainted with the *Methods of Providence*; and think that God will do nothing, but what he will tell the reason of to them. And thus their vain imaginations shall be look'd upon as the *Suggestions of the Spirit*; their *Daring* and *Presumption* esteem'd as *Sanctity* and a *Closenesse with God*; and what they will interpret to be *judgements*, (and all shall be so which those suffer whose opinions [38] and actions are not just as they would have them,) shall be judgments in spite of *Charity* which they should have as *Christians*, or *Reason* which they should have as *Men*. But we will examine.

1. *Whether this be true or no, that Cousin Germans marriages thrive not.*

2. *Whether those, are alwayes Judgments which are thought to be so.*

3. *What may be the reason of those Cousin Germans improsperity, who really are unprosperous.*

1. *Sir, I can testify, it is not alwaies true that First Cousins thrive not.* For I know some who have adorn'd their Marriage by their Love, and who have had their Love adorn'd too, [39] with the blessings of the Earth, increase of wealth and Children to possesse it. And why may not I make an argument for the Lawfulnesse of these Marriages, and their being approv'd of by God, from the prosperity of some, as well as they for the unlawfulnesse of them, and their being displeasing to God, from the ill thriving of others? If we will search Scripture we shall find that those Familyes which God had a peculiar intent to blesse, were to arise from the Wedlock of first Cousins, Thus the *Daughters of Heth* were not fit Matches for *Jacob; and Rebecca's Life* would do her no good if her son should take him a wife of the Daughters of the Land.[46] [40] To Padanaram therefore he must go, and after the Tediousness of *Travell*, (which alone might seem to have deserv'd a wife) serv's seven years for his Cousin *Rachell*; and after a frustration seven yeares more; too hard a task for a thing unlawfull, for a thing that should

---

[46] Genesis 27:46. "And Rebekah said to Isaac, I am weary of my life because of the daughters of Heth: if Jacob take a wife of the daughters of Heth, such as these which are of the daughters of the land, what good shall my life do me?" Genesis 28:1–2. "And Isaac called Jacob and blessed him, and charged him, and said unto him, Thou shalt not take a wife of the daughters of Canaan. Arise, go to Padanaram, to the house of Bethuel thy mother's father; and take thee a wife from thence of the daughters of Laban they mother's brother."

carry ill *Luck* along with it. But in what was *Jacob* unblest? In nothing surely unless in this, that his Father *Laban* envyed him as being too much blest. The Flocks seem'd willing to change their Master, and would bring forth Ringstraked, Speckled, and Spotted, that *Jacobs* Blessings and wages might be greater. Thus the man increased exceedingly, had much Cattle, Men-servants and [41] Maid-servants, and promise[47] that in his seed all the Generations of the Earth should be blessed. I need not stay longer upon this, but will take notice of this one thing, viz, that never any Marriage could boast of such a Numerous progeny, and such a blest People as that Race was which sprung from the Wedlock of *First Cousins.*

But perhaps, Sir, some will say that this is an extraordinary instance; and so is unfit to be brought as an example in this our Case; for, 1. *it was before the Law was given, and so this Marriage was rather wink'd at then approv'd of. And* 2[d]*ly it was enjoynd Iacob, because none else were fit to be his wives.* [42]

To the first, viz, *that this Marriage was before the Law was given, and so was rather wink'd at then approv'd;* we may truly say, that what was not forbid when the Law was given, was not wink'd at but approv'd of before. And so *Jacobs* Marriage with his *Cousin German* is quite of another Nature from his M[a]rrying two Wives, and them Sisters. for the Marrying two Sisters afterwards[48] prohibited *Levit.* 18.18.[49] *and Bigamy,* though permitted unto them under the Law, was yet forbid them by our Savior under the Gospel, *Mat.*19.9.[50] where it is said, *whosoever puts away his wife and Marryes another commits adultery;* and why he should be forbid after a [43] Divorce to marry again, if he might Marry two or more wives before, I can't yet conceive. but *Cousin Germans* Marriages were never yet forbidden under the *Law* or *Gospell,*[51] but were once peculiarly commanded, and often had good commendations from creditable exemples, as I have before mention'd.

But here we may take notice that though *Jacob* liv'd before the writing of the Law, and upon that account was excusable in some actions, which were

---

[47] and promise: correct to "and a promise" (Errata).

[48] afterwards: correct to "was afterwards" (Errata).

[49] Leviticus 18:18. "Neither shalt thou take a wife to her sister, to vex her, to uncover her nakedness, beside the other in her life time."

[50] Matthew 19:9. "And I say unto you, Whosoever shall put away his wife, except it be for fornication, and shall marry another, committeth adultery: and whoso marrieth her which is put away doth committ adultery."

[51] Old Testament law or New Testament gospels.

afterwards made unlawfull, yet it is very probable, that there were many precepts, concerning severall things, given by God, even then; whether to *Adam* or *Noah* or to more, I [44] am not solicitous. And this is manifest in *Tamar*, whom *Gen.* 38.[52] *Onan* was to Marry, that he might *raise up seed to his Brother.* which are the words of Moses's Law afterwards. And when *Tamar* after *Onans* death was found with Child, and so was to be burnt. (which punishment denotes another Law, and would have been too severe for the fault though a great one, if she had not by right and Law been shela's) Juda understanding at last the whole business, said, that she was more righteous then himself, because he had not given her to *Shela* his other Son.[53] And thus *Grotius de jur. Pac. & Belli. Has Leges olim datas esse censent Hebræi, neque id* [45] *referre putant quod illud á Mose suo loco narratum non sit, quia salis*[54] *habuit hoc in lege ipsâ tacite indicasse, cùm Gentes extraneas eo nomine damnet.*[55] The Jews beleeved that the Cheif of these Lawes were given of old by God himself before they were written by Moses; nor does it weaken their assertion to say, that *Moses* does not openly declare so, for it is sufficient that he tacitly hints it, when he condemns upon this account the nations of the Heathens *Levit.* 18.24.[56] which he could not have done had they not acted against their knowledge and this knowledge, only *Nature*, without some *Positive Law* from God, could not in many things have [46] acquainted them with. And when it is said just after the Catalogue of Marriages *Levit.* 18. *that in All these things the Nations are defil'd, which I cast out before you,* that universall speech may be reduced to the Chief Heads of the Chapter; as the not Lying with Mankind as with Womankind; the not Lying with Beasts, nor with Parents, nor with Sisters, nor others wives; for the preserving of which the more safe, the other lawes were added as a προφυλακή or *Fence.* These greater Lawes

---

[52] Genesis 38:8. "And Judah said unto Onan, Go in unto thy brother's wife, and marry her, and raise up seed to thy brother."

[53] Taylor, *Ductor*, 230.

[54] *salis*: correct to "satis" (Errata).

[55] "And the Jews do not think that the fact that this provision was not mentioned by Moses in the proper place makes any difference. Moses considered it sufficient to have tacitly indicated it in the law itself, when he condemns foreign nations on that account." Hugo Grotius, *De Jure Belli Ac Pacis* (1646), trans. Francis W. Kelsey, 4 vols. (Oxford: Clarendon Press, 1913–27), 3:244.

[56] Leviticus. 18:24. "Defile not ye yourselves in any of these things: for in all these the nations are defiled which I cast out before you."

Jacob and the other Patriarcks observ'd fully; which thing the Patriarcks[57] did not do. Nor can we think the marrying two Sisters then, as I*acob* did; nor yet marrying an Aunt, [47] as *Amram* the Father of *Moses* did, *Exod.*6.20.[58] were the things which the Heathen were condemn'd for. For the Piety of these men would not have permitted them to have done such things which they had known to be Crimes, and to be avoided. Nor can we suppose that God would have united his People in Wedlock that was illegitimate; for this in *Iacob* and *Rachel*, would have been to make *Profanesse* administer to *Religion*, and to seperate his Chosen ones from the Heathen, by one of the *Vices* of the Heathen. But

2dly, What if I should say that *Jacobs* Marriage with *Rachel*, was upon the account of *Kindred* and not of *Religion? Esau* I [48] am sure thought so when he in hopes, to pleas his Father, took to Wife *Mahalath* the Daughter of *Ishmael Abrahams* Son, immediately after *Jacob* went to *Padanaram* to please his Mother *Gen.* 28.9.[59] and *Laban* thinks it is better to give his Daughter to his *Kinsman*, then to another, who is a *Stranger Gen.*29.19.[60] and surely had *Rachel* been a true Worshipper of the God of *Abraham* she would not so Zealously have stol'n her Father Labans Gods from him; nor have thought it worth while to lye for them too, that they might not be found out nor carryed back. Nor yet would *Laban*, if he had been well acquainted with the *Fear of Isaac*, have polluted his House with [49] such stupid Deityes, have been more solicitous for their being taken from him, then for his Daughter and Grand Childrens leaving him after so abrupt a manner, He indeed, from *Jacobs* long converse with him, if from nothing else might have learnt that *Abrahams* God was a great God, and fit to be sworn by,

---

[57] Patriarcks: correct to "Nations" (Errata).

[58] Exodus 6:20. "And Amram took him Jochebed his father's sister to wife; and she bare him Aaron and Moses: and the years of the life of Amram were an hundred and thirty and seven years."

[59] Genesis 28:9. "Then went Esau unto Ishmael, and took unto the wives which he had Mahalath, the daughter of Ishmael, Abraham's son, the sister of Nebajoth, to be his wife."

[60] Genesis 29:19. "And Laban said, It is better that I give her to thee, then that I should give her to another man: abide with me."

Gen. 31.52;[61] but from his joyning *Nachors God*[62] (which Commentators make to be the Sun) with *Abrahams,* whether he was so much to be distinguish'd from Idolaters, as I will not stiffly deny, so I cannot confidenly affirm.

But, Sr, I must confesse that these men, who so much urge ill thriving against *Cousin Germans* [50] Marriages, are in the right; and they too much make their assertions good, by being themselves, and rend'ring others such busy Censurers. For, Sir, it is one part of a Miserable condition to be thought miserable, and to have all the affairs of a mans life scann'd for the finding out ill accidents to discourse of; and Dispensations to comment upon. Thus Sir, if some ordinary neighbour had some Crosse fall'n upon him, men perhaps will not take notice of him, or else will pitty him, and think it no more then what happens to other Men; but if *Cousin Germans* have any misfortune; if an *Horse* dye or the *Orchard* does not hit,[63] you presently know whats the cause of it. If the *Flock of* [51] *sheep* be less'ned by the *Rot,*[64] the negligence or unskilfulness of the *Shephard,* or the ill temper of the *Pasture* shall not be thought of, but it is an apparent Judgment upon the Marriage. The Children are weak, it may be; grow crooked, or, what is worse, do not prove well; presently, *Sir,* it shall be said what better could be expected? an unlawfull Wedlock must have an unprosperous successe. Whilst, in the mean time, if they truly love one another, rejoyce in the joyes of each other, grieve in the greifs; if they are so intirely affectionate as to further their mutuall content by a mutuall sweetnesse of nature, and God, it may be, sends many blessings upon them as a re- [52] ward of this peacefull behavior, and virtuous converse, all this shall not be taken notice of; nothing but adverse affairs shall be Eyed and observed, and be, perhaps too, made greater by ill interpretations then really they are.

---

[61] Genesis 31:52. "This heap be witness, and this pillar be witness, that I will not pass over this heap to thee, and that thou shalt not pass over this heap and this pillar unto me, for harm."

[62] Genesis 31:53. "The God of Abraham, and the God of Nahor, the God of their father, judge betwixt us. And Jacob sware by the fear of his father Isaac." Nahor's God was worshipped by the family of Terah, Laban and Abraham's ancestors, and was a patriarchal patron deity. Laban swore by Nahor's God. See Roland deVaux, *The Early History of Israel,* trans. David Smith (London: Darton, Longman and Todd, 1978), 272.

[63] A hit is an abundant crop of fruit; i. e., one that turns out a success. *OED,* s.v. "hit," n.6.

[64] Rot refers to a virulent disease affecting the liver of sheep. *OED,* s. v. "rot," n¹. 2a.

But 2dly, Sir, it will not be from the purpose if we shall examine *whether those are to be esteemed really Judgments which are commonly thought so.*

Suppose *Cousin Germans* to have greater shares of afflictions then others, yet it will be very bold to affirm that God is displeas'd with them, and is their Enemy. We see Prosperity is not alwayes an attendant on vertue, and an uninterrupted course of [53] Delights here is not an unerring argument of the Persons goodnesse.

But, Sir, there is a *judgment* which is said often to accompany these Marriages, and that is a *Want of Children* and a *Barrennesse*. And I have taken notice of it not only from the Mouthes of some, but have seen it in print too, and that from no less a Man then the *Pope. Quædam lex Romana permittit ut sive fratris & sororis, sive duorum fratrum Germanorum, sive duarum sororum filius & filia misceantur; sed experimento didicimus ex tali conjugio sobolem non posse succrescere. Respons. Gregorij ad 6. interrog. Augustini Angl. Episcopi.*[65] We have (saies he) found by experience [54] that from such Wedlock there can be no ofspring.

I know not what power his Holyness's will, has over such Marriages in *Italy* to hinder much their Fruitfulnesse; but in England *I* am sure there is no such matter. And you and *I*, Sir, know some who may Count Children with the most of their Neighbours, and who, if that *Roman Law*[66] were in force here, which allowed Mony to the *Father of three Children*, might upon the account of their Ofspring carry away no small reward.

Somtimes we see those, who are no Kin, to be Childlesse; and I remember one Couple of *Cousin Germans* with whom it was so; and another who expected

---

[65] Pope Gregory was responding to St. Augustine's question: "As far as what generation believers ought to be joined in marriage with their kin, and whether it is lawful to be joined in marriage with stepmothers and brother's wives?" Pope Gregory's answer: "A certain earthly law in the Roman republic allows the son and daughter, whether of a brother or a sister, or of two brothers, or of two sisters, to marry together. But we have learnt by experience that progeny cannot ensue from such marriages." What follows is not quoted by DuGard. "And the sacred law forbids to uncover the nakedness of kindred. Whence it follows that only the third or fourth generations of believers may be lawfully joined together." *A Select Library of Nicene and post-Nicene Fathers of the Christian Church*, ed. H. Wace, new series, 14 vols. (Oxford: Parker & Co., 1890–1900), 13: 320.

[66] This was the Augustan law titled *Ius trium liberorum* (the right of three children), which gave benefits to men and women for having three children. See Antti Arjava, *Women and Law in Late Antiquity* (Oxford: Clarendon Press, 1996), 77–80.

167

a [55] great while ere they had a Child; but at last a Son came, and stopped the Mouthes of some observers, who had gravely pronounc'd *Barrenness* a punishment of the profane Match.

And realy, Sir, (If you'l allow me to trifle) I see no reason why they should not have offsprings numerous, as their neighbours. They may be as Strong, and of as healthfull Bodyes as other folk; nor do I see how a *Likeness of Temper and Constitution*, (according to the large talk of some)[67] should hinder Procreation; nor yet why they should be said to be of so like a *Constitution*. I have known even Brothers as Different in their *Tempers* and *Genius's* as they have been in their [56] *Faces*. And sometimes a Child may so much follow the constitution, and shape of the *Father*, that he may seem to have very little or none at all of the *Mother* in him, though she bore him. Sometimes the Mother so much prevails in his person and Temper, that it is only from the Honesty of the woman, we know who is the *Father*: and sometimes he may be so unlike Both, as if the *Father* had not begot him, nor the *Mother* brought him forth.

Now Sir, suppose two Brothers Marry two women of different Familyes, and unlike constitutions, and the Son of one, and the Daughter of the other take both after the Mother, shall [57] these be denyed Children upon the account of nearness of Tempers, which I dare say are as far distant as any others? That I may not mention how we Change our Bodyes every seventh year, and so cannot expect to be of the same constitution exactly.

But Sir, (*If I may digress a little*) what if *Cousin Germans* have not so often Children as others? what will their Censures inferre? Truly *I* have been sometimes apt to think that the want of an ofspring has not been so great an unhappinesse to some men, as commonly it is imagin'd to be. For what Father almost is there, who has not a greater vexation in his Children, then he would [58] have had in Childless condition?[68] Indeed the thoughts of gathering and laying up for a Stranger, and the apprehension of having none to continue their Names when

---

[67] Robert Burton says, because inherited diseases and conditions are so powerful, "the church and common-wealth, humane and divine laws, have conspired to avoid hereditary diseases, forbidding such marriages as are any whit allyed and as Mercatus adviseth all families to take such, *si fiere possit quæ maximè distant natura*, and to make choice of those that are most differing in complexion from them, if they love their own, and respect the common good." Robert Burton, *Anatomie of Melancholy*, 62.

[68] Ironically, in 1695 Samuel wrote a treatise growing directly out of his own situation called *Polupaidia, or A Discourse concerning the having many children* (London, 1695).

they are gone, does oftentimes damp mens Mirth, and make them Melancholy, it being Esteem'd a more then ordinary Death, to have a Name Buryed too, or else to live no where but on a *Tombstone,* or in the *Church Book;* but yet, *Sir,* I know some who would have been glad it had been so with them. Sometimes a fair Progeny surrounds the Father, and in the midst of such attendants he may think himself more happy then a King encompass'd with his Peers; but if one of them after [59] the cost, care, and pains of Education shall Chance to dye, when grown up to fulfill those hopes so long conceiv'd for him (as very often it falls out) the greife at the *Death* of that one, is greater then the pleasure in the *Lives* of all the rest. I could tell you of more then one with whom it is so at the present; who, though it be only the *Disposalls of Providence,* and not their fault in the least, are almost drown'd in their own *Tears.* But if so much sorrow follows the Death of a Son, whose innocence and Laudable behaviour may have render'd him as fit to dye as to live; the greif must needes be greater, when the hopes of a Son, towardly and ingenious whilst a Boy, shall end in an in- [60] corrigible *Loosnesse* when grow[69] a man: by which he shall be unfit for private affaires or publick imployments. This surely is more torturing then if he had dyed in a Blooming age, adorn'd with accomplishments & vertue.[70]

I might, *Sir,* Mention the great affliction that some men have from their Children when their Number increases, and they have not withall to breed them up answerable to the Love they have for them, or that condition they themselves have alwaies liv'd in; a thing, which, *I* question not, had made some persons reflect upon their once joyfull wedding day with Care and sorrow; and wish they had either never known Marriage, or [61] had been blest in a *Barren Womb.* Good Families there have been who have fallen into the pitty of some; and the contempt of others, by reason of the great number of younger Brothers, who have been constrain'd to take up with mean Courses of life; and, if compar'd with the grandure of their *Ancestors,* miserable ones: whilst some disdaining such a low condition, as unworthy their *Name* and *Descent,* have grown desper- ate, and would be any thing, rather then poor men, though at the same time they might be *Honest* and *Vertuous.* But though the Father be not overburden'd with Children, and has but what he would wish for the continuing of his Name and [62] possessing his wealth, yet if he Chance to live to a good age, it may be,

---

[69] grow: correct to "grown" (Errata).

[70] Samuel may be thinking of his own brother, Henry, who died in Oxford in September, 1671, after living what seems to have been a rather "loose" life.

his youngster may think he takes up too much room in the world, and, though he owes his life, and Education to him, will take it unkindly that he lives so long, it is well if he does not endeavour to dispatch him hence by slights and disrespect, which are more cruell then the slashings of a *Sword* and the Wounds of an *Enemy*.

But *I* forget how *I* have run from the purpose and how little I have oblig'd those who are to be Born, as well as those who are: but they look like melancholy thoughts, and not like spleen and ill nature; and from them we may somthing discern, what we were [63] to enquire after, viz.

That they may not be allwayes judgments and Displeasures of God, which are reckoned so by the most. And so they go upon very ill grounds who censure *Cousin Germans* upon that account.

3dly, *I will shew what may be the reasons of those First Cousins not thriving, who are really unprosperous;* for I should be very unwise if I should think all live happy.

There are many things in the world, Sir, that may render men unblest. *Injustice* and *Oppression* may canker[71] an Estate, and it may, by a secret hand of *Providence*, be diminish'd amidst those arts that seem to increase it. The Falling of a mans fortune is a very intelli- [64] gible consequence to *Sloth* and *negligence*, and a just punishment too. Diseases may be the effects of *Riots* and *Intemperance*, and the sickly constitution of Children also, and their immature Deaths be caused by the guilty *Delicacy* and *Luxury* of their Fathers; and so severall sins shall have their severall punishments awaiting them.

Now, Sir, if *Cousin Germans* could not be staind, with such Crimes, as well as any others, we might with more probability lay all the fault upon their Marriages. But *I* will not say but that may be as Wicked as their neighbours, and I doubt not but they have been. And so they shall have ill thriving without doores for [65] such Crimes; and if within Doores the *Curtains* shall have more *Lectures* then the Bed has Love, and quarrels and jarrs shall take place where meek and quiet affection should dwell, why may not the ill nature of the Wife, or the Cross-graindnesse of the Husband be the Cause; when, 'tis very likely, had the *Scold*[72] been Marryed to any other, the Case had been the same; or had

---

[71] To canker means "to infect, corrupt, to consume slowly and secretly like a cancer." *OED*, s.v. "canker," v. 2.

[72] A scold is "A woman of ribald speech, addicted to abusive language; a woman who disturbs the peace by her constant scolding." *OED*, s.v. "scold," n. 1.

the *Churle*[73] lighted on another Wife, her life would not have been lesse miserable then her's he now has?

But, Sir, I will not deny but *Cousin Germans* may have, and have had unhappiness from their Marriages; which they would not have had if their Choice had been made elswhere; but that these [66] have been judgments upon their Wedlock, as unlawfull, or unchristian, I will not, dare not grant; but will manifest whence these Mischiefs may take their *Rise.*

And 1. you will easily grant me that *Love* is greater somtimes then *Reason,* and renders the persons that are in Love blin'd to all things but the Faces they look upon, and it may be Cheats their sight theretoo.

2dly You will grant me that a thing though lawfull, if it be not thought lawfull, and be done either through rashnesse or willfulnesse, will afterwards not only be imputed to the Agent as a Crime, but will carry that *Remorse* along with it, and cause [67] those dire consequences, which attend and follow that which in itself is really guilt and wickednesse.

Now, Sir, I question not but somtimes the Love, which ignorant C. *Germans* have, may stifle all the thoughts of either the unlawfulness, or discredit of their Marriage. They cannot awhile to think so unpleasantly; they are willing it should be lawfull, and that is argument enough at present that it is so. A smile from a Mistresse shall conquer an ill look'd suggestion, or the unwelcome caution that a Friend gives. They are over head and Ears in Love,[74] and it shall not be said they were frighted or threatned from a long'd for Wedding Day, or, it [68] may be, an Estate which could not have been so well obtain'd elswhere. Thus they in a Blind passion rush into Matrimony, and hamper themselves in *Cords* which must not break till with the *Thread of Life.*[75] And now when the *Hony Month*[76] (as they say) is over, and their cloy'd love will give them leasure to think seriously, they begin to question whether they Marryed lawfully or no;

---

[73] A churle refers to a "male, base fellow, rude; used as a term of disparagement or contempt." *OED,* s.v. "churl," n. 5.

[74] To be over head and ears in a thing. Tilley, H268.

[75] This refers to the course of life represented in classical mythology as a thread that is spun and cut off by the Fates.

[76] "Hony Month" was used in the seventeenth century to refer to the first month after marriage. *OED,* s.v. "honey-month." As early as 1546, it was also called a "honey moon." This referred "not to the month, but comparing the mutual affection of newly-married persons to the changing moon which is no sooner full than it begins to wane." *OED,* s.v. "honeymoon" n. 1.a. See Lawrence Stone, *Family, Sex, and Marriage,* 223.

They now can hearken to folks who say that First Cousins never thrive; and they are almost persuaded they have been too rash in that which is the greatest affair of a mans life. Their Hearts which knew nothing but love before, now begin to let in remorse; and that Face, which [69] erstwhile so much pleased, now only minds them of their inconsideratenesse and guilt. And thus the next Crosse they suffer shall be look'd upon as a just judgment upon them, and a cruell earnest of more that will follow. And how shall they comfort one another in their afflictions by their Love, when they think their Love is the cause of their afflictions? And so their ignorance makes them despond, and renders them unfit for the preventing of future evils. For they think it to very little purpose to strive against those Punishments which heaven has design'd for them. And so by a sullennesse and stupidity they neglect the affairs of the world, and make themselves mi- [70] serable, when, it may be, Heaven never intended they should be so.

But these evils, Sir, are prevented when *Cousin Germans* are persuaded of the Lawfulnesse of the great affairs they undertake and go upon *sure* grounds. When they begin their Love in innocence and continue it in vertue. When if they suffer some affliction they will endeavour to chear one another in the bearing of it, and contrive by an active industry to prevent ill thriving for the future. If more crosses fall upon them, they will think it is better with them however then with many others. They will call in their Piety, as well as Love, to aid in the undergoing them, and will [71] endeavour by an innocent and vertuous convers to deserve them as little as may be.

And thus, Sir, I have at large examined that Objection against *Cousin Germans* Marriages, viz. *The ill Thriving of them.*

A 5ᵗ argument against these Marriages is a Law made against them by Theodosius and Arcadius Christian Emperours.[77] *And the great Punishments they inflicted upon offenders in this kind, which would not have been done if such Wedlock had not carryed a great deal of guilt along with it.*

It is true that there was such a Law made;[78] but the cruelty of it may be tax'd more then the justice of it commended. But yet St. *Am-* [72] *brose*, who was the

---

[77]Theodosius I was emperor from 379–395; his sons, Arcadius and Honorius, became the founders of the sub-empires in the east and west respectively.

[78] This law was made in A.D. 385. See Jack Goody, *The Development of the Family and Marriage*, 55–56; Judith Evans Grubbs, *Law and Family in Late Antiquity* (Oxford: Clarendon Press, 1995), 154.

Cause of this Law, and who ruled the Emperour, testifyes in his 66 *Epistle*,[79] that it was somtimes dispens'd with by *Theodosius*: which it is probable it would not have been, if St. *Ambrose* had thought it in all cases unlawfull. But while the St said it was prohibited, I know no reason why we may not say he was mistaken; and thus *Martyr. Class. 2. cap. 10. sect. 47. quòd verò Ambrosius affirmat Consobrinorum conjugium lege divina esse prohibitum, nullis qui verba legis Dei, & facta Patrum attentiùs considerant probari poterit.*[80] *Arcadius* also by the example of the Emperour his Father forbid these Marriages *anno* 396, yet so as that he Mitigated the pu- [73] nishment his Father appointed to delinquents in this Case, but afterwards anno 405 he repeald his own, and Fathers statutes against them, and made them as Lawfull as any others. *Instit. lib.*[1] *Tit:* 10. *Impp. Acad. & Hon. A. A. Entychiano P. P. Celebrandis inter Consobrinos Matrimoniis licentia legis hujus salubritate indulta est; ut revocata prisci juris anthoritate, restinctisq; Calumniarum fomentis, Matrimonium inter Consobrinos habeatur legitimum;*[81] *sive ex duobus fratribus, sive ex duabus sororibus, sive ex fratre & sorore nati sunt: & ex eo Matrimonio editi, Legitimi & suis Patribus successores habeantur.*[82] *We grant a Liberty for the making Marriages between* Cousin Ger- [74] mans, *by reason of the wholsomness of such a Law. That the authority of Ancient Statutes being reestablished, and all*

---

[79] *The Letters of S. Ambrose, Bishop of Milan*, ed. H. Walford in *Library of the Fathers of the Catholic Church*, ed. E. B. Pusey, 51 vols. (Oxford: James Parker & Co., 1838–85), 31:351–54. Walford has renumbered Ambrose's letters, so that Epistle 66 becomes Epistle 60 in his collection.

[80] "And in that Ambrose affirmeth there, that such kind of marriage (cousin german) was forbidden by the law of God; it cannot be proved unto anie which throughlie consider the words of the lawe and the acts of the fathers." *The Common Places of the Most Famous and Divine Doctor Peter Martyr.* trans. Anthonie Marten (London, 1583; *STC* 24669), 451–52.

[81] ". . . the law that forbad them was occasioned and fomented by calumnies; which being dispersed, the authority of the ancient law was recalled." quoted from Taylor, *Ductor*, 236. Arcadius legalized cousin marriages for the Eastern empire in A.D. 405; Honorius permitted such marriages only with imperial dispensation. Goody, *The Development of the Family and Marriage*, 55.

[82] "The children of two brothers or sisters, or of a brother and sister, may lawfully marry." *Imperatoris Justiniani Institutionum*, ed. J. B. Moyle, 2 vols. (Oxford, Clarenden Press, 1883), 2:14; see also 1:125, n. 4: "Marriage between first cousins, which originally was unknown, gradually came to be permitted, Livy 42.34, Tac. Ann. 12.6, and after being prohibited by Theodosius I, was again made lawful by Arcadius and Honorius, Cod. 5.4.19."

grounds of Murmuring and Calumny taken away, the Wedlock of First Cousins may be esteem'd lawfull. Whether they are two Brothers Children, or two Sisters, or else one the Brothers the other the Sisters; and those that are born in such Marriage shall be accounted Legitimate, and the true Heirs of their Fathers Estate. This Law is vindicated by *Gothofrid* in his notes upon the 3. *Code of Theodos. Tit.* 12.[83] Where many more things to this purpose. Before Theodosius his time they were not forbid, as that Clause in the statute (viz. *Revocata prisci juris authoritate*) shews. and St. [75] *August. de Civitate Dei lib.* 15. cap: 16. has it thus, *nec divina Lex has nuptias (consobrinorum scilicet) prohibuit, & nondum prohibuerat Humana.* But that we may be just, and not usurp a part only of what he saies, we will take in what he further adds, which is, *Raroper mores fiebat quod per leges licebat, & factum licitum horrebatur propter vicinitatem illiciti.*[84] The *First Christians* very seldom made these Marriages, though they might have done it lawfully. And they shunned this lawfull thing because it was so near to what was unlawfull; which is the.

6th Objection; viz: *Cousin Germans Marriages are to be avoided, because they are soe near to* [76] *what is forbid; and he that will go to the outmost step of a lawfull thing seldome stayes there, but falls into guilt.*

That I may the better answer this, I will first consider the *Primitive Christians* example mention'd by *Saint August.* The great Zeale they shew'd not only in this but many other things, and their confining themselves in narrower Bounds then God had done, I will say was commendable then, when they had many malicious observers, and when their more then Ordinary strictness was to commend their Profession, which had it's Birth but newly before: but I cannot say we are in every thing to imitate them now; for neither are we [77] bound to make

---

[83] Jacques Godefroy, "De Incestus Nuptiis," *Codex Theodosianus*, 6 vols. (Leipzig, 1736–45), 1:294–300.

[84] "For cousin-germans to marry was neither prohibited by the laws of God or man; and so we have a testimony beyond exception concerning the civil law, and the law of God, and the law of the church till his time." Taylor, *Ductor*, 236. DuGard's Latin version is a slight variation on the Loeb edition which states more fully, "Experti autem sumus in conubiis consobrinarum etiam nostris temporibus propter gradum propinquitatis fraterno gradui proximum quam raro per mores fiebat quod fieri per leges licebat quia id nec divina prohibuit et nondum prohibuerat lex humana. Verum tamen factum etiam licitum propter vicinitatem horrebatur inliciti." That is, "For such marriages were not forbidden by divine law and had not yet been forbidden by human law," followed by "Nevertheless, there was a revulsion from doing something which, lawful though it was, bordered close on something unlawful." Saint Augustine, *The City of God*, 4:506–7.

distribution of our Estates, nor to receive the Communion every day, nor, if Persecution should come, anxiously to seek after Martyrdom; things which They did as will be seen by any who look into the first ages of the Church. And why may we not, if God has indulg'd us a liberty, make use of it with Cheerfulness when there is an occasion, as well as avoid with detestation what he has prohibited us? upon the account of unlawfull things to abstain from things that are lawfull and sometimes expedient, shewes many times a greater *Fear of God* for his punishments, then it does a *Love* to him For his Mercyes; which is a temper that God is not[85] [78] so well pleas'd with. If we keep our selves unpolluted with those things which are forbidden, we shall not be blamed for now, and then making use of those things which are indulg'd us. And if we shall, out of an affected preciseness or prejudice, avoid at all times the doing them, and censure others that shall do them, we shall have only this as a reward, viz, *Who has required these things at your hands?*[86] and it is well if our Censuring and condemning others (although it may seem to be an *Effect of Piety*) be not more punish'd then some things that are agreed upon by all to be sins.

But yet I don't see any strength this argument has, viz. that *Cousin* [79] *Germans Marriages are to be avoided because they come so near to the Prohibition.*

There are many things that are but one remove from the unlawfullness, which yet are very usually done without offense; and, I may say, should this argument hold, even Justice, in its proper sense, must never be exercised. To give a man but just his *Due* is the next door to injuring him, and rendering him lesse then his *Right*; but there is none but will grant that I am not bound at all times to be Liberall, which is to be more then just. And though in Punishing, the Jews gave but fourty strips save one, which was one lesse then they might lawfully have done *Deut.*25.3.[87] [80] yet it is probable, that it was not that they might not goe at any time to the extremity of the Law, but that they might not exceed. For they usually beat offenders with a *Whip* which had three lashes; so that every stroke stood for three, and, if they had given one more, would not have been fourty, but fourty two. Though, if they did abstain from the exact Number of Stripes out of design, it was but a prudent prevention of their anger

---

[85] This is the catchword on F7v, inadvertently omitted from the text on F8.

[86] Isaiah 1:12.

[87] Deuteronomy 25:3. "Forty stripes he may give him, and not exceed: lest if he should exceed, and beat him above these with many stripes, then thy brother should seem vile unto thee."

which sometimes might have made them forget, and so might have urg'd them to excess: and it is probable that that *Passion* which might have carryed them on beyond forty, might have made them forget the just thirty nine, and sometimes [81] give no more;[88] which yet they were not guilty of, if, the scourge being Single, they lay'd on no more. And indeed, if we consider how many Marriages there are made which are at the greatest Distance from those Degrees forbid; and how few there are, and are like to be (though we should generally have a better opinion of them) that will reach to the very outside of our liberty, we may not I think fear our entrenching upon Gods Lawes in this Case more then in others: especially, since in this matter, there is an *Aversion*, which by early instillings, and a deep rooted consent of all, grows up together with us, and will not quickly leave us. [82]

But those that affirm *Cousin Germans* Marriages to be the very next to those which are forbid, are not so unquestionable in their assertion, as the most imagin, and though I may let them alone, whilst they think such Wedlock but one remove from unlawfull, (for they do not injure our Case in the least as *I* but now shew'd) yet not a few of the Hebrews, and some Learned men since, have been of *Opinion*, that *Unkles* and *Neeces*, who are one degree nearer then *Cousin Germans*, are not forbid *Levit.* 18. Nor does it follow by an undoubted consequence that, because *Aunts and Nephews* are forbid, therefore *Uncles and Neeces* are. For the Case is Different. If the *Nephew* [83] should Marry the *Aunt*, then she who is by nature his *superior*, is made as she is his wife, his *Inferior*; but the Neece is alwayes below the Uncle, and so the order of nature inverted.[89] *Menoch. Corn. à Lapide. Episcop. in* 1. *Cap. Mat.*[90] And though indeed the Reason mention'd *Levit.* 18. Why *Aunts* and *Nephews* should not Marry, may seem to be *Nearness of Kin*, and so may reach the *Vncle* and *Neece*, and make their Marriage as unlawfull, as the other, yet their is a Difference. The *Nephew* must not Marry the *Aunt* because, (*Verse.* 12.)[91] *she is his Fathers near Kinswoman.* It is not said *His*, but *his Fathers*; Him, whom in Her He should honour; but whom [84] he[92] could not, in making her subject to him, as a Wife ought to be. But it is other wise with

---

[88] no more: correct to "one more" (Errata).

[89] inverted: correct to "is not inverted" (Errata).

[90] Cornelius van den Steen, *The Great Commentary of Cornelius à Lapide,* trans. Thomas W. Mossman, 8 vols. (London: John Hodges, 1876–97), 1:1–41 (St. Matthew's Gospel).

[91] Leviticus 18:12. "Thou shalt not uncover the nakedness of thy father's sister: she is thy father's near kinswoman."

[92] he: blot out (Errata).

the Neece; and though indeed her Uncle is her Fathers near Kinswoman,[93] yet the Honour she should shew to him as such, will no[t] be overthrown by his becoming her Husband, since as he is her H*ead* he is to be Reverenc'd by her. Nachor he Marryed Milcah who was his Brother Harans Daughter, and so his Neece. and *Abraham* Marryed *Harans* other Daughter, who was his Neece also. *Gen*. 11.29[94] for *Iscah* there mention'd is *Sarai* as *Josephus* and the best *Commentators* understand it, and as it will appear to any one, who rightly considers the place. *Sarai* indeed is said to be Sister to *Abra-* [85] *ham*, but as Lot was his *Brother* when he was his *Brothers Son. Gen*. 12.5.[95] *Othniel* the son of *Kenaz Calebs* Brother took to wife *Achsa* the Daughter of *Caleb; Jos*.15.17.[96] Where if *Othniel* was *Calebs* Brother (as some think he was) he Marryed his *Neece. Herod* the Great Marryed his *Brothers* Daughter, and gave his own Daughter to his Brother *Pheroras. Joseph. Antiq. Lib*. 12. 16.[97] Which yet *I* bring, not as carrying any authority as being the Action of *Herod*, who was as little *a good man* as he was a *Jew*, but because Josephus does not in the least seem to condemn it, as a thing unlawfull or unusuall. We may think there were many such Marriages among the [86] *Jews* though we read not of more; the Genealogyes in Scripture being nothing in respect of those vast numbers among the Hebrews, the *Tables of whose Descents, Herod* destroy'd, that Himself might the better appear to be of the *Race* of the *Jewes*. Hence may be that of *Tacitus, nova nobis in Fratrum filias conjugia, at aliis gentibus solennia, nec lege ulla prohibita*.[98] *The Marryage of Vncles and Neeces with us is a new thing, but among other Nations it is usuall and forbid by no Law.*

---

[93] DuGard has written "kinswoman," although clearly he means "kinsman."

[94] Genesis 11:29. "And Abram and Nahor took them wives: the name of Abram's wife was Sarai; and the name of Nahor's wife, Milcah, the daughter of Haran and the father of Milcah, and the father of Iscah."

[95] Genesis 12:5. "And Abram took Sarai his wife, and Lot his brother's son, and all their substance that they had gathered, and the souls that they had gotten in Haran; and they went forth to go into the land of Canaan; and into the land of Canaan they came."

[96] Joshua 15:17. "And Othniel the son of Kenaz, the brother of Caleb, took it; and he gave him Achsah his daughter to wife."

[97] This story is told in Josephus, *Jewish Antiquities*, but in Book XVII, Sections 12–22. Flavius Josephus, *Jewish Antiquities*, trans. Ralph Marcus, 8 vols. (Cambridge, Mass.: Harvard University Press, 1926–1963), 8:379–81.

[98] "Marriage with a brother's daughter is something new with us, but it is common among other peoples and it is not prohibited by law." *The Annals of Tacitus*, ed. George Holbrooke (London: Macmillan & Co., 1882), 276.

I have mention'd these things, not that I will make any use of them for the proving the Marriage of *Cousin Germans*; nor that *I* am myself sway'd by them to an assent, (for such Mixtures are thought [87] prohibited by *Arch Bishop Parkers tables*,[99] which I by noe means question) but that They, who are so much against First Cousins Wedlock, upon the account that it is but one Step remov'd from that which is unlawfull, may see that their Reason has been question'd for the *Truth*, as well as it justly may for the *weakness* of it. *Athanasius in Synopsi scripturæ ad calcem Numeror*: very respectfully speaks of *Cousin Germans* Marriages, Πρόσταγμα Κυρίου καὶ νόμος, νόμιμον ἔιναι γάμον τὴν πρὸς ἀνεψιοὺς ουζυγίαν.[100] *It is a Law and ordinance of God that the Wedlock of First Cousins should be esteem'd Legitimate.* From which Place, and from that of *St August.* which *I* mention'd but now *(viz. Nupti-* [88] *as has nec Divinam Legem & nondum Human-am Prohibuisse)*[101] we May find an answer to the.

7th Argument; namely, *that the Apostles Canons forbid these Marriages.* For *if that Canon, at least which* prohibits the Wedlock of *Cousin Germans*, had either then had a being, or not been Spurious, Athanasius or Saint August. Would, in all probibility, have taken notice of it.

For the other part of the Objection, *viz, that the Canon law (good part of which is observ'd by our Church) is against these marriages*, we cannot but grant; but if this Law should generally prevail with us, Spirituall Kindred also, as Godfathers and Godmothers, and their Children too must [89] not Marry. But that the Pope, who for *Holinesse* sake will prohibit Marriage to such Spirituall Relations, will for *Lucre* sake dispense with it, not only to them, but to those also, who are more nearly allyed in Blood, may be seen from the *House of Austria*, and the *Kings of*

---

[99] "The Anglican table represents the authoritative mind of the English Church. First put forth by Archbishop Parker in 1563, soon after Elizabeth's accession, it was adopted by the 99th Canon of 1603. 'No person shall marry within the degrees prohibited by the Laws of God and expressed in a table set forth by authority in the year of our Lord 1563.' The table is simply the system exhaustively stated. Outside the limits of the table there are no prohibitions and there is accordingly no need of dispensation." Watkins, *Holy Matrimony*, 708.

[100] "With regard to the union of first cousins it is the ordinance and the law of God that the marriage be considered lawful." Athanasius made this commentary on Numbers 36:11, which describes Zelophehad's daughters marrying their uncles' sons. Athanasius, "Synopsis Scripturae Sacrae," 282–436 in J. P. Migne, *Patrologiæ Cursus Completus*, Series Graeca, 161 vols. (Paris, 1857–1866), 28:309.

[101] "Marriage is not prohibited by divine or human law." See note 84 above.

Spain, in a more then Ordinary Manner. For *King Philip the* 2^d might have called *Albert Arch Duke of Austria, Brother, Cousin, Nephew* and *Son; being Uncle* to *Albert* himself, and *Cousin German* to his Father, Husband to his Sister, and Father to his Wife: for he Marryed *Alberts* Sister, and then *Albert* Marryed his Daughter:[102] how many dispensations must his Holinesse grant here, and where is the poor [90] *Canon* Law when large summs appear?

But for a whole answer to what ever from that Law can be brought against *Cousin Germans* Marriages, I will cite one clause of an *Act of Parliament Anno. 32. Hen.8. cap.38.*[103]

Since by reason of other prohibitions then Gods Law admitteth, which were invented by the Court of Rome (the Dispensation whereof they alwayes reserv'd for themselves, as in Kindred or Affinity between Cousin Germans, which yet were Lawfull, and not prohibited by Gods Law, and all because they would get mony by it) many Sutes of Law with wrongfull vexations, and great Damage of the innocent Partyes have been procur'd, and many just Marriages [91] *brought into doubt and danger of undoing &c. Bee it therefore Enacted by the King, Lords Spirituall and Temporall, that such Marriages shall be taken and judg'd to be Lawfull, Just, Good, and Indissoluble.* (which Clause of the Act though the Rest of it was repeal'd was signally established anno 1° Elizabethæ. *cap.* 1.[104]

8Iy. An usuall Objection it is, and almost in every Bodyes Mouth, *That second Cousins may not Marry, and consequently that First may not.*

I would fain know where this prohibition is, for I must confess, I never yet understood whence this *Saying* should take its rise. I have heard of it often spoken, but when I have ask'd up- [92] on what grounds they have said soe, they have referr'd me to the *Bible*, and the *Table hung up in Churches.*[105] Thus ignorance and Mistakes sometimes will have Divine authority to uphold them. indeed a Readiness to beleeve, what the *Scripture* and *Church* do say, does deserve a good commendation; but it is a Sign of a great weakness, or negligence, to be over hasty of Beleef, before we are sure the *Bible* and the *Church* do say so, Though surely, as to the *Church*, there are few who erre this way; for now a dayes, That is as much slighted by a great many, (the more is our Sorrow) as the Scriptures are little understood, as they should be. And I may truely [93]

---

[102] A family tree delineating all these relationships can be found in A. H. Huth, *The Marriage of Near Kin* (London: J. & A. Churchill, 1875), 80.

[103] 32 Henry VIII. c. 38, 1540. See note 10.

[104] 1 Elizabeth c. I, 1558.

[105] Archbishop Parker's Tables.

affirm,[106] that the taking things for granted from the assertions of some men, (whose *Zeale* (that *I* may not give it a worse word) is greater then their *Knowledge* or *Reason*) and not rightly consulting the Scripture, and meekly submitting to the Judgment of the Church, has been the occasion of more mischeif, then by a great deal of piety can be took away. I need not tell you Sir, there is no such thing in the *Bible* as a Prohibition of second Cousins Marriages; and I am sure in *Arch Bishop Parkers Tables* we may find all Marriages forbid as soon as These. But since I have prov'd by reason and example, that the wedlock of first Cousins is lawfull, and have, or at least [94] shall answer the Objections brought against them, there is none sure who will read this Paper, that will question the Marriage of Second Cousins. A thing indeed which since it is an error of the *Multitude*, and had no ground at all, deserv'd to be laugh'd at, rather then spoken to. But.

The 9th, and, which is the most materiall argument, is this.

Supposing the Marriages of Cousin Germans to be lawfull, yet a wise man upon the account of Credit will abstain from them.

A good report indeed is better then great Riches; and he is very unwise who will lose it when with H*onesty* he may keep it. [95] But yet Sir to be foolishly scrupulous in some actions that are not unlawfull, upon the score of an empty praise, and to shun a considerable advantage for fear of a Censure from the giddy vulgar, is the way to lose credit with wise men, whilest we strive to preserve it. It is a sign of a very weak Soul to be over much concern'd at the Praises or Dispraises of the *Many*, when we our selves are sure our actions are in themselves just and commendable. And though, Sir, I would be loth to be spoke, or thought ill of, even by the meanest, yet I would not purchase the good opinion of the Best, with the losse of the least vertue, or what is next precious to ver- [96] tue, the greatest comfort of my Life.

I think Sir, I shall not injure their argument, if I shall consider Credit.

1. *As it has Relation to the opinions of some Learned and good men, who have been, and some who now live, that are against the Marriage of Cousin Germans.*

2dly *As it has Relation to some Weak Christians who will be offended, and Scandaliz'd in such an action.*

To the 1. Sir, *namely the Opinions of Learned and good men I can say this;* That though I reverence Piety and esteem Learning, yet,[107] in matters of Faith and

---

[106] This is the catchword on G6ᵛ, inadvertantly omitted from the text on G7.

[107] yet: correct to "yet as in" (Errata).

Religion, I must not bee led by any man against a well ground- [97] ed persuasion, so in the greatest concerns of Life (as a *Wife*[108] should bee) it would be a manifest *Folly* to be over awe'd by a grave *Look* and a *Stately saying*, when it carries only the authority of the Person, and shews me no reason for it. And I dare say for my Friend that if any man can shew him better reason against it, then he can for it, he will in point of Conscience forgoe his *Love*, which I think is not of less length then his *Life*.

Nay some there are who say that these Marriages in some cases are very expedient; and those who do dislike them, do it, for the most part, upon this account, that they are not well relish'd by the Common people. Now [98] since the *Vulgar* so much esteem these Good men they talk of, and are so stiff in urging their Authority, methinks they should conform to their more Clear judgments; and not by a Folly, and ill nature, persist to strengthen those arguments which were drawn only from the perversness, and ignoranee of the *multitude*. A frowardnesse of Humor which these good Men do, or should like a great deal worse then the common people do these marriages.

Somtimes I have thought how strangely we have lost our Liberty in a too much yeilding to the ignorance and Humors of the Vulgar. So that at first what was only our *modesty* and *kindnesse* to [99] them, is reckon'd now their *Due*; and not to obey their censures is look'd upon as our *immorality*, and *crime*. I know not whether in so doing we have injur'd our selves or Them the more. Our selves in bringing our Reputation into such narrow, and dangerous Limits, Them, in permitting them to have such erroneous, and false conceptions of things, which not only is the occasion of, but many times is sin to them. I will not undertake to prescribe a way how these things shall be remedyed, (for I am sufficiently conscious of mine own meanness, and so am fitter to be instructed my selfe then in such important dictates to teach others,) but really I know no better method [100] then that some men, who are noted for men of Piety and Learning, should act now and then some of those Lawfull things, though they are unusuall, and esteem'd by some unlawfull, that so, by their example, the common people may be undeceiv'd; and our Credit, in a thousand affaires, forced[109] from that ticklish estate it is now in. And by this means we may lay a

---

[108] *Wife*: Even though the text doesn't change, the errata says to correct to *"Wife"* (Errata).

[109] forced: correct to "Freed" (Errata).

good foundation for the strengthning of *Weaker Brethren*, which was the second thing to be consider'd.

Cousin Germans Marriages, though in themselves not unlawfull, are yet to be abstain'd from as uncreditable and inexpedient upon the [101] *score of scandalizing Weaker Brethren.*

In the considering of this we will see who are meant by *Weak Brethren*, and how these are to be dealt with, the through stating of which, would take up a great Deal more time then *I* am willing to bestow upon it at present. *I* will therefore dispatch in as few words as *I* can: for *I* fear, Sir, *I* have tir'd you no less then my self.

First Then; Those who will be offended at everything out of a Cross-graind Humour, who will make *Piety a Cloke of Maliciousnesse*, and will put on the *Face of a Saint* that they may the more securely disturb our Christian Liberty, and render others disaffe- [102] cted to us; who will willingly distort our Lawfull actions into ill Precedents for their own wicked Deeds; these *I* say are rather to be scourged then yeelded to, and are to be accounted the *Strength of the Divell*, rather then the *Weakness of Christianity.*

Those only are to be esteem'd *Weak Brethren*, who out of sincerity of Heart are Scrupulous of many things which yet are Lawfull; or who will be apt to make an ill use of our *Liberty*, and take incouragement thereby to sin.

2dly. These we must have a tender respect for, and be very carefull how we put a stumbling Block in their way.

What this carriage of ours should be towards them, I will [103] lay downe in these two positions.

First. When we see our Brother will be offended at our action, and be put in a fair way through our liberty to commit sin, although our action in it selfe be very Lawfull, yet if we can wave it without any great damage or disadvantage to our selves or others, who are related to us, we ought in Charity to do so: and this will appear from *Romans*.14.21.[110] *Rom.* 15.1,2,3.[111] 1.*Cor.* 8.13.[112] But.

---

[110] Romans 14:21. "It is good neither to eat flesh, not to drink wine, nor any thing whereby thy brother stumbleth, or is offended or is made weak."

[111] Romans 15:1–3. "We then that are strong ought to bear the infirmities of the weak, and not to please ourselves. Let every one of us please his neighbour for his good to edification. For even Christ pleased not himself; but, as it is written, The reproaches of them that reproached thee fell on me."

[112] 1 Corinthians 8:13. "Wherefore, if meat make my brother to offend, I will eat no flesh while the world standeth, lest I make my brother to offend."

2dly. If the action be of very great concernment, and such as will influence on Life and the well being of it, although our Weak Brother will be offended at it, we are not bound to forego [104] it. For this would be to give the upper hand in the world to Ignorance and unsettled Judgements: to make Weaknesse the controler of the important affaires of society, and to permit Fools to sway the Scepter over the wise and Prudent. should this be permitted, for ought I see in our present Case, the Mistress's Grant, and the Parents consent would be very small and inconsiderable things; since every Weak Brother might contradict them, and every Melancholy man in the Parish forbid the Banes.[113] Such as these must be instructed; and if they are Christians, as well as Weak, they will be willing to be taught; if they are stiffe in their Opinions, and will not yield to a good [105] natur'd admonition they are worthy of *Pity*; but a *Pity* that must be shew'd in an angry look, and cloath'd with a Chiding and a sharp Reproofe. It will be well indeed if the prosperitie of our Brothers Soul and Body shall attend our florishing Condition; but if his negligence and stubbornnesse will not permit it to be so, there is a *Scandal taken* indeed; but none *given*. He will be unhappy, but we shall not be guilty, he is to be pityed, but we not to be blamed. Thus, Sir, I have consider'd this last argument, though in short, yet in its greatest strength: and have also shewn that these marriages are confirm'd by the Lawes of the Land (made [106] by the most Reverend of the *Clergy*, and the most prudent of the *Laity*) as well as approv'd of by the Laws of God: so that the man must be strangely Obstinate or stupid, who will not yield to the Lawfullness of them.

For a Close of all, I will in a word or two shew (what at the first I propos'd) the Expedience of *Cousin Germans* Marriages, and the Conveniences of them, somtimes beyond those of others. And indeed they are very considerable.

First. *Cousin Germans have more reason to know one anothers Tempers and Humors from their dayly converse, and Education oftentimes together.* And so being throughly acquainted, their [107] Marriages are not so much Lotteryes as others are. And surely, if we should (as the proverb saies) *Eat a Peck of Salt with a Man before we Make him our Friend,*[114] it would not be amisse if we should eat two with a *Woman*, before we make her, the most important of all *Friends*, a *Wife*. I question not but the short acquaintance of so many in the world, before they

---

[113] Samuel DuGard himself must have feared that banns might be forbidden for he applied for a special license from the bishop in order to avoid the calling of banns for his own marriage. See Letter **31** above.

[114] "Before you make a friend eat a bushel of salt with him." Tilley, F685.

Marry, is the cause of so much unhappiness in *Wedlock*, before that of a *Single Life*. and *I* dare be bold to say, that the most do not *Marry* the Person they think they *joyn Hands* with. For, Sir, Men and Women are not to be esteem'd by their Faces, nor by their words; *It* is not the Fairest *Body* [108] that alwayes carryes the best *Soul*; and sometimes *I* have thought that whilst Providence has so commended some deform'd Persons by a quick and brave mind, it has set off some meaner Souls by a specious outside, and handsome Stature; that in all there might be somthing worthy of praise. And then, Sir, it is the fault of young Persons (and more then them too) to be too much taken with good words, and to esteem Persons, and things rather by their hopes (which are for the most part too high and extravagant,) then by their Knowledg, (which is too seldome sure and well grounded) which unhappinesse women are in an especiall manner inci- [109] dent to, as from some other accounts, so from their power of Choosing them Husbands only out of those who come *Suitors* to them; it being reckoned a piece of immodesty in them to look abroad, and be their own Carvers,[115] a priviledge, which men have before them. Besides, Sir, it being counted a Discredit, and a Contemptible thing to be a *Stale Maid*,[116] and some thinking the *Leading Apes in Hell*[117] to be the greatest Punishment there; Fearing also, that when such or such an admirer is cashierd they shall never have another, or, at least, not a great while, that pleases them so well, (afflictions too great to be born in this world) their Love Passi- [110] on is quickly kindled, and when it is kindled Flames vehemently; Thus having Love sworn to them in Passionate expressions, and being made acquainted that they are *Nymphs*, and *Goddesses*; and are made up of *Diamonds Rubyes, Fair Roses, Warm Snow*, and the like, (things which they never knew before, and now begin almost in Earnest to beleeve) they give away themselves the sooner, for being made so precious, and raised to so high a value, whilst on both sides the Partyes are miserably Cheat-

---

[115] To be a carver is "to take or choose for oneself at one's own discretion." *OED*, s.v. "carver," 4. fig.

[116] A stale maid is "a woman past the fitting season for marriage." *OED*, s.v. "stale," a.4.a.

[117] The proverbial fate of an old maid. Tilley M 37. Lydia also refers to "Leading Apes in Hell" in Letter **23** above.

ed, and a Cloud is embraced instead of *Juno:*[118] a Cloud that is big with Tears, and weighty with Sorrows.

2dly another convenience of [111] *Cousin Germans* Marriages is that which is urg'd by many as a great Objection against them, viz, *Their having the same Kindred, and their Equally sharing in the praises and dispraises of the Common Stock*: so that they are free, for the most part, from those jarrs that arise from the reflexions on the Meanness and Greatnesse of Parentage. There is nothing swells persons more then the thoughts of an *High Birth*, And nothing commonly shall sit more uneasy upon one unequally yok'd then the Name of Family and Relations. Which thing unlesse there be Prudence on both hands to correct it (as it canont [sic] be often expected, since there are more *Fools* [112] *then wise*) will breed Feuds and quarrels, and make Wedlock very unpleasant. But where there are Equall Descents (as in First Cousins usually there are) upbraidings are taken away. If their Births are Creditable, their Gloryings meet, and joyn in Consent. if they are low and mean, their mouths are stop'd; since they cannot lash the other, but they must wound themselves.

These two conveniencyes, Sir, are something, but when they are joynd with a *Cousin German* who is an Heiress of an Estate which hath belong'd to the Name and Family, it may be, for some Ages (as sometimes it may fall out) and she has a *Cousin* [113] *German* whom she can love, and who is not unworthy of her, it will not be only convenient, but Expedient they should Marry. And it was upon this account that *Zelophehads* Daughters, and the other Heiresses among the Jews were commanded to Marry into the Family of their Fathers; and the next of that Family, it was thought good, should have that priviledg before others. Which Custom (as I said before) it is probable other Nations took up from the Jews.

> *Hic meus Amicus illi genere est Proximus,*
> *Huic Leges cogunt Nubere hanc. Ter. Adelph*[119]

---

[118] "When Ixion tried to make love to Hera [Juno], thus breaking the law of hospitality since he was a guest of her husband, Zeus [Jupiter] formed a cloud into Hera's shape, and Ixion lay with this. He was subsequently punished with eternal torments in Tartarus." Michael Grant and John Hazel, *Gods and Mortals in Classical Mythology* (Springfield, Mass.: G. & C. Merriam Co., 1973), 211.

[119] "This friend of mine is her next relation; the laws compel her to marry him." Terence, *Adelphi*. IV. 5.17. in *A Literal Translation of the Adelphi of Terence*, trans. E. L. Hawkins (London: A. T. Shrimpton & Son, 1891), 36. See note 28.

And thus, Sir, I have considered these Marriages in fewer [114] words then I might have done; but in more, it may be, by farr than I needed to have done. your self, from a right opinion of the thing before, may seem to have a very little, or nothing at all, to do with this Letter, though written to you; and from your great accuracy and Criticallness, I might have fear'd it should come under your Eye. But you know how to excuse as well as how to judge; and *I* was willing it should goe through your Hand to some persons (who *I* think too much want such a thing) that so it might have some authority from you which it cannot have from its *Author*. For though, Sir, [115] *I* have shew'd that such Marriages are not against the *Law of Nature, of God, nor of the Land*, yet, Sir, such an ones Good word as yours, will bequeath a *Strength* to the argument *I* have brought, which perhaps would not be seen without it; and your approbation will make Mens Fancyes submit to truth, when otherwise *I* could have very little Hope from their Reason: a thing which now a dayes, in most men, is conquered by *Humor*, and Overwhelmed by *prejudice*. However, Sir, if you will please to think well of this *Paper*, and will give me that share in your *Love*, which *I* have had hitherto be- [116] yond my Deserts, *I* shall the less matter what others think of it, or me.

Honour'd Sir,

Your, &c.

FINIS

ERRATA.

PAg. 17. l. 9. read *First*. p. 25. l. 16. blot out. *Joseph*. p. 26. l: 4. *assert*. p. 31. l. 4. *and in* Rehobeam. p. 41. l. 1. *and a promise*. p. 42. l. 13. *was* afterwards. p. 45. l. 3. *satis*. p. 46. l. 18. for *patriarcks* read *Nations*. p. 60. l. 1. *grown*. p. 81. l. 1. *one* more. p. 83. l. 6. *is not* inverted. p. 84. l. 1. blot out *he*. p. 96. l. 19. yet *as* in. p. 97. l. 2. *Wife*. p. 100. l. 10. for *forced* read *Freed*.

Biographical Appendix

Ashby, Anne, distant cousin of Lydia DuGard. Her first husband, Edward Ashby, died in 1660, and she married George Bagnall in 1665. The Bagnalls lived in Worcester and provided housing for Lydia from 1670 to 1671. See Letters **19** to **25**.

Ashby, Edward, son of Anne and Edward Ashby. He was an apothecary, living in Worcester, at the time Lydia was living with the Ashbys.

Bagnall, Elizabeth, daughter of Anne and Edward Ashby. She married Nicholas, son of George Bagnall, 25 May 1668, in Worcester, and had one daughter, Bridget, born shortly before Lydia arrived in Worcester. See Letter **20** and Nicholas Bagnall below.

Bagnall, Nicholas, son-in-law of Cousin Anne Ashby as well as the son of her second husband, George Bagnall. He was a brewer in Worcester at the time that Lydia was living with the Ashbys. See Letter **23**. He married Elizabeth Bagnall 25 May 1668. He died 8 November 1670, leaving a daughter, Bridget, and a pregnant wife (HWCRO, Will of Nicholas Bagnall, proved 8 November 1670). The Bagnalls, as well as the Ashbys, were related to the DuGards, for an Alice Bagnall of Worcester was mentioned among the relatives in Lydia's father's will dated 24 November 1662 (William DuGard Will). (See also *Genealogist*, old series [Exeter: William Pollard & Co., 1882] 6:316.)

Barlow, Thomas (1607–1691), friend of Samuel's and supporter of his treatise on cousin german marriages (Queen's College MS 275, fol. 36–39). He received his M.A. from Queen's College (1633), was appointed Provost of Queen's College (1657), served as librarian of Bodleian (1642–1660), was named Lady Margaret Professor of Divinity, and was Bishop of Lincoln (1675). He was able to shift his political loyalties deftly so that he always stayed in favor with those in power. Samuel corresponded with Thomas Barlow about the issues concerning his marriage and borrowed a number of books and manuscripts from him. See Introduction to the Letters, note 3. (DNB, s.v. "Barlow, Thomas"; Wood, 4:333–41; Foster 1:73.)

Bathurst, Ralph (1620–1704), president of Trinity College (1664–1704). He received his B.A. (1638), got his M.A. and became a fellow (1640), was ordained (1644), and earned his M.D. (1654), all from Trinity College, Oxford. He was a divine, a classical scholar, a philosopher; a charter member of the Royal Society; and he oversaw the rebuilding of Trinity College. Bathurst was president of Trinity College the entire time that Samuel was there. Samuel had great respect for him and sought his support. He even showed him one of Lydia's letters, which was an embarrassment to Lydia. See Letters **26, 28, 32.** (Thomas Warton, *The life and literary remains of Ralph Bathurst, MD Dean of Wells and President of Trinity College in Oxford* [London, 1761]; *DNB*, s.v. "Bathurst, Ralph"; *Fasti*, pt. 2:183; Foster, 1:87.)

Bromley, Sir William, lord of the manor of Baginton, Warwickshire, and patron of the living. He matriculated at Hart Hall, Oxford (1632), and studied law at Middle Temple (1634). He was Justice of the Peace and an acquaintance of Thomas DuGard. Because of this connection between Sir William and his father, Samuel was offered the living at Baginton, but he turned it down because it only paid 60 pounds annually. (*Orders Made at Quarter Sessions*, 5:150; *VCH Warwickshire*, ed. L. F. Salzman [1951], 6:23; Foster, 1:187.)

Cotton, Lydia, daughter of Samuel and Lydia; baptized Aug. 20, 1675 (FPR, D4049/1/1). Her mother died in giving birth to her. She was raised by Samuel and his second wife, Elizabeth, in Forton, Staffordshire, and by her own account was treated very well. She married Daniel Cotton of Sandbach, Cheshire, in Tong, Shropshire on 13 May1704 (Shropshire Records and Research Center, Shrewsbury, Tong General Register, 1620–1756 P281/A/1). Lydia was living in Newport, Staffordshire, at the time. Her will is dated 26 February 1705 and is transcribed at the end of the letters in this book (Folger MS X.d. 477/35). See document **35** above. Both she and her newborn son, Dugard Cotton, died 3 March 1705, and they were buried with members of the Cotton family in Holmes Chapel, Cheshire (Earwaker, *History of Sandbach*, 194–95).

Cradock, Hannah, first cousin of Lydia and Samuel, daughter of John and Alice DuGard. She married Edward Cradock, wine cooper, of London, on 17 April 1664 (St. Magnus Martyr Parish Register, Guildhall, MS 28868). In his will William Dugard stipulated that she should be given five pounds (William DuGard Will).

Cross, Abigail, friend of Lydia, wife of Hugh Cross of Barford. Abigail and Hugh had four children, Hugh, baptized 10 August 1662; John, baptized 4

March 1664; Hannah, baptized 2 February 1667; and Elizabeth, baptized 17 November 1670; Elizabeth died just twelve days old on 29 November 1670; Abigail herself died 31 January 1671 of complications from this childbirth (BPR DR48/3). Lydia and Abigail were clearly very good friends, though Abigail was at least ten years older than Lydia. See Letter **24**.

Cudworth, John, college friend of Samuel, son of John Cudworth, vicar of Kinwarton, Warwickshire. He matriculated at Trinity College, Oxford, received his B.A. (1667), his M.A. (1670) and became a Fellow (1672) (*Fasti*, pt. 2:297, 393; Foster, 1:361). Later he completed a B. Divinity (1684) at Cambridge. He was rector of Bradenham, Buckinghamshire, from 1679 to 1681 and then rector of Kiddlington, near Woodstock , Oxfordshire from 1681 to1687. He was Master of Warwick Free School for a short time in 1670, the very position that Samuel's father had held for fifteen years. He visited Barford with Samuel and knew about Lydia and Samuel's marriage plans. See Letters **23, 29, 30, 31**. For the story of the marriage maneuverings of Mary Cudworth, John's sister, see Lawrence Stone, *Uncertain Unions* (Oxford: Oxford University Press, 1992), 78–82.

Dodds, John, friend of Thomas DuGard and vicar of Lighthorn, Warwickshire, a village of about twenty households six miles southeast of Barford.

Dodds, Margaret, wife of John Dodds, vicar of Lighthorn. Lydia talked about her "distemper and worss temper" while taking care of her for several weeks when she was sick and dying in 1672. See Letters **30** and **31**. She died 5 June 1672 (WCRO, Warwick, Lighthorn Parish Register, DR18/1).

DuGard, Anna, cousin of Lydia, born 1646. Anna was the daughter of Thomas and Hannah DuGard and sister of Samuel and Henry. (See entry for Hannah DuGard below.) She lived at the rectory in Barford while Lydia lived there and is referred to frequently in the letters. She married William Fairfax of Barford, 4 July 1676, her father performing the ceremony (BPR, DR48/3). She had two sons and two daughters and was still living in Barford in 1704 when Lydia's daughter, Lydia Cotton, wrote her will. William DuGard, Lydia's father, left her 20 shillings in his will (William DuGard Will).

DuGard, Anne, daughter of Hugh Muston of Tibbols, Kinsbury, Warwickshire. She became Thomas DuGard's third wife sometime in 1670, while Lydia was living in Worcester. She acted as Lydia's mother, supporting her during the last two years of her courtship with Samuel, when the issue of first cousin marriages was at its height. She died 4 October 1683 shortly before her husband, Thomas (BPR, DR48/3).

DuGard, Hannah, daughter of Thomas Hanks of Stow on the Wold, Gloucestershire. She was the first wife of Thomas DuGard and mother of Samuel, Henry and Anna. She died 4 December 1655 and was described by her husband as his "most vertuous and accomplish'd wife" in the Barford Parish Register (BPR, DR48/3). Hannah DuGard talks about her family in letters she wrote to the Wyllys family in Connecticut (*The Wyllys Papers, 1590–1796*, in *Collections of the Connecticut Historical Society*, 21, ed. A. C. Bates [Hartford: Connecticut Historical Society, 1924], 90–91, 106–08).

> I am forst to be short to you at this time by Resone of my presant Condition being I now Lie ine. it hath pleased God to Give me a daughter to my toe sonnes at this time: I have Leene ine somwhat above a fortnight but yet dare not straine my Iyes for present anny furthar but only desier your prayers for this & all the Rest of us. . . .
> Mrs. Hannah Dugard to Mrs. Mary Wyllys (17 May 1646), p. 91.

> My husband is called now into the minnistry to barford 2 miles of Warwick. Resined to him by Mr Brian ye formmer pastor there who himseulfe by ye sennod of devines is sent to be pastor at Covintry. We intreat your prayers for him my husband that God would furnish him for soe great a worke We have not yet Removed our dwelling from Warwick untell we see some hopes of a settled peace – I that was begun to be Called barran God hath givin me 3 Children 2 sones Sammuell & hendary & a daughtter that now suckes whom I haue named Anne aftar my mothers name I pray God make them all something for himsuelf & sarvise. . . .
> Hannah Dugard to Mrs. Mary Wyllys (10 April 1648), p. 107

DuGard, Henry (1645–1671), son of Thomas and Hannah DuGard and brother of Samuel. He was enrolled at St. Paul's School in London between 1663–1664 and may have gotten to know Lydia in London before she moved to Barford (*The Registers of St. Paul's School, 1509–1748*, ed. Michael McDonnell [London: The School: distributed by the Gavin Press, 1977], 244–45). He was named beneficiary in William DuGard's will in the event of Lydia's death before marriage. The will further specified that if Henry did "not take his learning seriously and prove a good scholler" then the bequest was void (William DuGard Will). He matriculated at Trinity College, Oxford, 11 May 1664. Henry was not happy at Trinity College, and there are many references in the letters to his troubles, probably drinking and gambling. He did, however, receive his B.A., 28 January 1668 (Foster, 1:429). He died in Oxford on 27 September 1671 after a long illness and was buried in the church of St. Mary Magdalen, Oxford, as specified in the parish register: "Mr. Henry DuGard, Schollar of Trinitie Colledge, was buried in the Body of the Church the 27th Day of September 1671" (Oxfordshire County Record Office, Oxford, St. Mary Magdalen Parish Register, C2, 1662–1682).

DuGard, John, brother of William and Thomas. He was a citizen of London; he married Alice Wheeler, 18 June 1637 (All Hallows, Honey Lane Parish Register, Guildhall MS 5022).

DuGard, Lydia née Parker, mother of Lydia. She was born in 1610 in London and married John Tyler, goldsmith, of All Hallows, Lombard Street, on 5 March 1640. The marriage was authorized by license from the Bishop of London and took place at St. Nicholas Cole Abbey (St. Nicholas Cole Abbey Parish Register, Guildhall MS 5685). This was her second marriage, for she is named Lydia Dales, widow, in the marriage license; John Tyler died just a year and a half later on 14 September 1641, leaving behind a one-year-old daughter, Elizabeth (Will of John Tyler, PRO PROB 11/187 Quire 99, proved 14 September 1641). Lydia then married William DuGard, 22 March 1642, at All Hallows, Stayning, again by license from the Bishop of London ("Allegations for Marriage Licences Issued by the Bishop of London," extracted by Joseph Chester and edited by G. J. Armytage, Harleian Society 26, 1887, 2:264). Between 1643–1650 she gave birth to five sons and one daughter, Lydia. Only her two daughters survived her. She died at age 51 in London in 1661 (SLPPR, Guildhall MS 7670).

DuGard, Lydia, daughter of William and Lydia DuGard and wife of Samuel. She was baptized in the parish of St. Laurence Pountney in London on 30 September 1650 (SLPPR, Guildhall MS 7670). This Lydia is the writer of the letters; she married Samuel DuGard, 18 April 1672, and was mother to Thomas, Richard and Lydia (WRCO, Warwick, Wasperton Parish Register, MS DR208/1); She died in childbirth 20 August 1675 and was buried in Forton, Staffordshire (FPR, D4049/1/1).

DuGard, Mary, daughter of John Huggeford, of Henwood nr Solihull, Warwickshire. She became Thomas DuGard's second wife, 26 April 1660 (WCRO, Warwick, Solihull Parish Register, DRB64/1); she served as Lydia's mother when Lydia came to Barford to live sometime after 1662 and is referred to frequently in Lydia's letters. She died 4 October 1669, and again, Thomas DuGard described her as his "vertuous and accomplish'd wife" (BPR, DR48/3).

DuGard, Richard, son of William DuGard and Elizabeth Adams. He was born 25 June 1634 in Stamford, Lincolnshire, and in 1644 he entered Merchant Taylors' School, where his father was headmaster (*Merchant Taylors' School Register*, 1:157); he was not living with the family in London when Lydia was born, for he had been admitted sizar at Sidney Sussex College, Cambridge, in 1649 (Venn, 2:72); he matriculated at St. John's, Oxford, 13 November 1650, just six weeks after Lydia was born (Foster incorrectly named him as vicar of Forton. Foster, 1:429). According to Thomas DuGard he died unmarried (*Visitations*, 112).

DuGard, Richard, second son of Samuel and Lydia. He was baptized 29 September 1674 in Forton shortly after Samuel got his position there (FPR, D4049/1/1). Like his father, he matriculated at Trinity College, Oxford, in 1692, got his B.A. in 1695 and his M.A. in 1698 (Foster, 1:429). There is no mention of Richard in the will of Lydia Cotton, his sister, written in 1705. See document **35**. Presumably, he died before then.

DuGard, Samuel (1643?–1697), son of Thomas and Hannah DuGard and husband of Lydia. He was the author of *The Marriages of Cousin Germans Vindicated from the Censures of Unlawfullnesse and Inexpediency* and *Polupaidia, or A Discourse concerning the having many children*. He matriculated at Trinity College, Oxford, 24 May 1661, at age 18; got his B.A. 20 October 1664, became a fellow of Trinity College in October 1667, getting his M.A. on 31 October 1667. After struggling to obtain a position for several years, he became rector of Forton, Staffordshire, in 1673, and stayed there until his death in 1697. He was named a canon of Lichfield in 1697. Samuel married Lydia DuGard on 18 April 1672 by license at the church in Wasperton, and they had three children (Wasperton Parish Register, DR208/1); after Lydia's death he married Elizabeth Kimberly in 1678, and they had seven children; he died on 13 April 1697 and was buried at Forton, Staffordshire (FPR, D4049/1/1). (*DNB*, s.v. "DuGard, Samuel"; Wood, *Athenae*, 4:679; *Fasti*, pt. 2:297, 319. Foster, 1:429.)

DuGard, Thomas (1607–1683), Samuel's father and Lydia's uncle, brother of William DuGard. He was educated at Sidney Sussex College, Cambridge, received his B.A. in 1630, and his M.A. in 1633. He was headmaster of Warwick Grammar School from 1633 to 1647 and rector of Barford from 1647 to 1683. For an analysis of his diary of 1630–40 (BL Add. MS 23,146) and his role in

Parliamentary-Puritan politics, see Anne Hughes, *Politics, Society, and Civil War in Warwickshire, 1620–1660* (Cambridge: Cambridge University Press, 1987), 71–80; and Anne Hughes, "Thomas DuGard and His Circle in the 1630s," *Historical Journal,* 29.4 (1986), 771–93. (Venn, 2:72; Foster, 1:429; *Visitations,* 112–13; *VCH,* ed. William Page [1908], 2:310; HWCRO, Thomas Dugard Will, proved 5 November 1683.)

DuGard, Thomas, son of William DuGard and his first wife, Elizabeth Adams. He was born 29 November 1635 in Stamford, enrolled in Merchant Taylors' School in 1644 (*Merchant Taylors' School Register,* 1:157); he was admitted Sizar of Sidney Sussex College, Cambridge, in 1649 (Venn, 2:72). Both he and his brother Richard left for Cambridge just a few months before Lydia was born. He died unmarried before 1662 (*Visitations,* 112).

DuGard, Thomas, eldest son of Samuel and Lydia DuGard. He was born 1 April 1673 and baptized by his grandfather in the Barford church (BPR, DR48/3); he married Catherine Gower, and they were living in Worcestershire on land inherited from his mother at the time of his father's death in 1697. The note he wrote to his sister, Lydia, regarding division of their property is included in this volume (Folger X.d.477/34). See document **34**. Presumably, he died before 1705, since his sister, Lydia, does not mention him in her will dated 26 February 1705.

DuGard, William, father of Lydia. He was born 9 January 1605 in Bromsgrove, Worcestershire; received his B.A. (1626) and his M.A. (1630) from Sidney Sussex College, Cambridge (Venn, 2:73). His first wife, Elizabeth Adams, died in 1641 and on 22 March 1642 he married Lydia Parker ("Allegations for Marriage Licences Issued by the Bishop of London," extracted by Joseph Chester and edited by G. J. Armytage, Harleian Society 26, 1887, 2:264). He was the father of seventeen children; only his daughter, Lydia, survived him. He was a noted printer in London (Plomer [1907]). He was schoolmaster of Merchant Taylors' School in London from 1644–1649, reinstated 1650–1661; died 3 December 1662 (Will proved 24 December 1662. PRO, PROB 11/309 quire 135). (*DNB,* s.v. "DuGard, William"; 67–68.)

Elliot, Thomas, faithful servant to the Thomas DuGards for many years. He often accompanied Samuel to Oxford and brought horses back to Barford. He married Marian Hawkes, another servant in the household. He died in 1677 (BPR, DR48/3).

Frankland, Rev. Samuel, of Coventry, a friend of Thomas DuGard, headmaster of Coventry Grammar School.

Hawkes, Marian, in service to the Thomas DuGard family. She was given 20 shillings in Thomas DuGard's will and identified as the wife of his long-time faithful servant, Thomas Elliot (HWCRO, Will of Thomas DuGard, proved 5 November 1683). Thomas DuGard recorded in the Barford Parish Registry the marriage of his servants "Thomas Elliot of Sherborn and Marian Hawkes of Fulbrook in the parish of Bishops Hampton" on 4 December 1673 (BPR, DR48/3).

Jekyll, Thomas, college friend of Samuel. He was born in 1646, the son of John Jekyll of St. Stephen's, Walbrook, London; enrolled at Merchant Taylors' School (1652); matriculated at Trinity College (1663), age 16; received his B.A. (1667), his M.A. (1670), his D.D. from Sydney Sussex, Cambridge (1694). He became Vicar of Rowd, Wiltshire (1671), then minister of the New Church in St. Margaret, Westminster, from 1681 to 1698. He set up a school for poor children to be instructed in the doctrine of the established church. He visited Barford with Samuel on several occasions and got to know Lydia quite well. See Letters 9 and 13. He died in 1700 and was buried in the New Church, Westminster. (*Fasti*, pt. 2:297, 319; Foster, 2:806; Venn, 2:466; Wood, *Athenae*, 4:681–2.)

Jemmatt, Samuel, son of the puritan divine, William Jemmatt. He became vicar of St. Nicholas, Warwick, 8 February 1672, and served in this capacity until his death on 3 May 1713. This was one of the positions that Samuel had sought. He got his B.A. (1655) from Corpus Christi and his M.A. (1658) from Magdalen Hall, Oxford (*Fasti*, pt. 2:214, 248; Foster, 2:806). He also served as Master of Lord Leicester's Hospital in Warwick for forty-one years. One of his services was to hold a school in the hospital (*VCH*, ed. William Page [1908], 2:310, and *VCH*, ed. W. B. Stephens [1969], 8:532, 549).

Kimberley, Elizabeth, daughter of William and Elizabeth Kimberley, sister of Jonathan, Samuel and Benjamin Kimberly, related to Lydia and Samuel through their paternal grandmother, Elizabeth Kimberley DuGard. She married Samuel Dugard in 1678 and cared for Samuel and Lydia's three children. She and Samuel had three sons and four daughters, all born in Forton (see note 52 in the Introduction to the Letters). She is mentioned in Lydia Cotton's will as her "dear Honor'd Mother" (see document 35).

Kimberley, Jonathan (1651–1720), son of William Kimberley and cousin of Samuel and Lydia. He matriculated at Pembroke College, Oxford (1667), received his B.A. (1671), his M.A. (1673), and his D.D., by diploma, from Cambridge (1713). He was minister of Trinity Church, Coventry, from 1681 to

1713, chaplain to King Charles II, canon of Lichfield, (1684), and of Westminster (1711), rector of Tatenhill, Staffordshire, from 1713 to 1720. He was father of Samuel, Thomas, and Charles. (Wood, *Athenae*, 4:749; *Fasti*, pt. 2:327, 337.)

Kimberley, Samuel (1649–1723), son of William Kimberley and cousin to Lydia and Samuel. He matriculated at Pembroke College, Oxford (1665), received his B.A. (1668), his M.A. (1671), and his M.D. (1685) (*Fasti*, pt. 2:291, 397).

Kimberley, William, husband of Elizabeth; father of Samuel, Jonathan, Benjamin, Elizabeth and Hannah. He was rector of Redmarley (Worcestershire) until forced to resign in 1661; headmaster of Bromsgrove Grammar School from 1664 to 1670; clerk from 1670 to 1678 in Whitford, near Bromsgrove, Worcestershire, his ancestral home. He died in 1678 just after his daughter, Elizabeth, married Samuel DuGard (Will of William Kimberley, proved 6 November 1678, PRO, PROB 11/quire 358).

Milbourn, Betty, daughter of Mrs. Milbourn of Barford. She was a neighbor and friend of Lydia, about the same age as Lydia.

Mitchell, Elizabeth Tyler, Lydia's half-sister, daughter of Lydia's mother and John Tyler. She was baptized in London 16 September 1641 (All Hallows, Lombard Street Parish Register MS 17613); her mother married William DuGard in 1642 (see Lydia Parker DuGard above). She lived with Lydia and her family in housing provided by Merchant Taylors' School in London until she married John Mitchell, 1 January 1658, and moved to Coventry (SLPPR, Guildhall MS 7670); Lydia went to live with Elizabeth and her husband in Coventry sometime after her father died in 1662. Before 1665 Lydia left Coventry and moved to Barford. Elizabeth and Lydia remained close; Lydia mentioned her frequently in her letters, and after Elizabeth's husband died in 1669, the two of them traveled to Oxford to visit Samuel. See Letter **18**. William DuGard, referring to Elizabeth Mitchell as his "daughter in law," left her 20 shillings in his will (William DuGard Will).

Pestell, William, Warwick carrier serving the DuGard household after 1671.

Pettifer, Jane, sister of Thomas and William DuGard and therefore both Samuel and Lydia's aunt. She was married to John Pettifer of St. Giles, Cripplegate, London. Lydia stayed with her aunt when she visited London. William DuGard willed his sister forty pounds, but with the explicit specification that her husband, John, should not have any benefit of the money (William DuGard Will). John is never mentioned by Lydia.

Pettifer, Jane, daughter of John and Jane Pettifer and, therefore, Lydia and Samuel's first cousin. She married David Atkins of St. Giles without Cripplegate, London, 11 June 1666 (St. Giles Cripplegate Parish Register, Guildhall MS 6419).

Rogers, John, friend of Thomas DuGard and rector of Hampton Lucy in Warwickshire from 1652 to 1683. Hampton Lucy was just four miles south of Barford. He matriculated at Hart Hall (1633), received his B.A. (1636) and his M.A. (1639) (Foster, 3:1274; *Fasti*, pt. 2:383). He served as the Bishop of Worcester's surrogate, appointed to issue marriage licenses for the diocese. He was the official who signed Samuel and Lydia's license on 4 April 1672 (HWCRO, Ref. No. 797, 3A 2035/9 no. 3736). His son, Thomas, became a student at Trinity College, Oxford, in 1676 at age 17 (Foster, 3:1276).

Smith, Mary, Birmingham, sister of Thomas and William DuGard. She is mentioned in Thomas DuGard's will (1683) and also by Hannah DuGard, Samuel's mother, in her letters to Mrs. Mary Wyllys in Connecticut in 1646 and 1648 (see Hannah DuGard above).

Spooner, Margaret, daughter of John Huggeford, sister of Mary Huggeford DuGard. She married William Spooner of Henwood Hall in Solihull. Mary DuGard visited Margaret often during the time of Lydia's letters. Both she and her husband were buried on the same day in 1674 (*Visitations*, 149).

Tayler, Mary, daughter of Thomas DuGard's oldest sister, Margery Orford and her husband Nicholas. She lived in Bromsgrove, Worcestershire.

Twithy, Thomas, an Oxford friend of Samuel. See Letters **27** and **32**. He may be the Thomas Twithy listed by Foster who matriculated at Oriel College, Oxford, in 1670, received his B.A. in 1674 and his M.A. in 1677 (Foster, 4:1525). His father, Thomas Twithy, was a friend of Thomas DuGard from his days in Worcestershire.

Waterhouse, Edward, Lydia's guardian named in her father's will dated 24 November 1662 (William DuGard Will). He was born in 1619. He described himself as "a friend to learning, a servant to religion and a native of London." He was living at Sion College, a center for the clergy of London, when William

DuGard died. He lost a great deal of property in the great fire and wrote *A Short Narrative of the late Dreadful Fire in London* (London, 1667; Wing W1050) appealing for financial assistance in rebuilding Sion College. He took Holy Orders, 7 April 1668. On 27 May 1668, Samuel Pepys described him as

> a fat man whom by face I know as one that used to sit in our church, that after dinner did take me out and walked together, who told me that he had now newly entered himself in to orders, in the decay of the church, and did think it his duty so to do.
> (*The Diary of Samuel Pepys*, ed. Robert Latham and William Matthews, 9:215)

On 31 January 1669, Pepys goes on to say,

> he preaches in devout manner of way, not elegant nor very persuasive, but seems to mean well and that he would preach holily, and was mightily passionate against people that make a scoff of religion (9:432–33).

Lydia was not yet of age when he died 30 May 1670 in Mile End, London, and was buried 2 June 1670 in Greenford, Middlesex (Greenford Parish Register, preserved at Holy Cross Church, Greenford, Middlesex; my thanks to Arthur Johnson, archivist at Holy Cross, for providing this information). (*DNB*, s.v. "Waterhouse, Edward"; Wood, *Athenae*, 2:163.)

Whately, Mary née Kemp, Thomas DuGard's housekeeper from 1655–1658, the years immediately after the death of Hannah DuGard. At that time Samuel was about 12, Henry 10 and Anna 9. Her marriage to Creswith Whately, rector of Tadmarton, Oxfordshire, was solemnized by Thomas DuGard in his church in Barford on 23 September 1658 (BPR, DR48/3). Samuel Whately, son of Creswith and Mary, matriculated at Trinity College (1669), so Samuel DuGard may have had something to do with his coming to Trinity College and would certainly have known him as a college student (Foster, 4:1608). Although Mary died in 1667 Samuel often stopped at the Whately house in Tadmarton on his way to and from Oxford. See Letters 4 and 27.

Willes, John, college friend of Samuel. He was the son of Peter Willes of Limmington in Warwickshire. He matriculated at Trinity College (1663), aged 16; was a Fellow at Trinity College, and received his M.A. (1669); he entered Holy Orders; received his B. Divinity (1680); became rector of Bishops Itchington, Warwickshire and received his D. Divinity (1684). He must have visited

Barford often for Lydia knew him and spoke of him fondly. See Letters 30 and 31. (Wood, *Athenae*, 4:681; *Fasti*, pt. 2:289, 308, 374; Foster, 4:1635.)

Manuscripts Sources

Bodleian Library, Oxford

Samuel DuGard's poem commemorating his uncle, William DuGard, at the time of his death. Bodl., Rawl. Poet. fols. 32–32v, 33–33v

Samuel DuGard to Walter Blandford, Bishop of Worcester, 26 January 1672. Bodl., Tanner MS 44, fol. 282

William DuGard to Samuel DuGard at Trinity College, 8 July 1662 and 16 July 1662. Bodl., Tanner MS 48, fols. 16, 22

Four Sermons by Samuel DuGard. Bodl. Rawl. E69 fols. 17, 28v, 49, 57

British Library, London

D'Ewes Family Correspondence, BL MSS. Harl. 382,69e; 384

Harley Correspondence, BL Add. MS 70233

Thomas DuGard Diary, BL Add. MS 23,146

Cumbria Record Office, Carlisle

Lonsdale Family Correspondence, Lonsdale Collection, D/Lons/L1

Folger Shakespeare Library, Washington D. C.

DuGard Correspondence, Folger MS X.d.477/1–35

Cavendish-Talbot MS, Folger MS X.d. 428/199

Bibliography

Greenford, Middlesex, Holy Cross Parish Church

Greenford Parish Register (owned and preserved by the parish)

Guildhall Library, London

All Hallows, Honey Lane Parish Register, MS 5022

All Hallows, Lombard Street Parish Register , MS 17613

St. Giles Cripplegate Parish Register, MS 6419

St. Laurence Pountney Parish Register, MS 7670

St. Laurence Pountney, Churchwarden's Accounts, MS 7670

St. Magnus Martyr Parish Register, MS 11361

St. Nicholas Cole Abbey Parish Register, MS 5685

St. Olave, Hart Street Parish Register, MS 28868

Hereford and Worcester County Record Office, Worcester

Marriage License issued to Samuel DuGard by John Rogers, authorized by the Bishop of Worcester. HWCRO, Ref. No. 797, 3A 2035/9 no. 3736

Will of Nicholas Bagnall, HWRCO, proved 10 March 1670

Will of Thomas DuGard, HWCRO, proved 5 November 1683

Lichfield Record Office, Lichfield

Samuel DuGard Will and inventory, proved 29 April 1698

The National Archives: Public Record Office (PRO)

Will of John Tyler, 14 September 1641, PROB 11/187 quire 99

Will of William DuGard, 24 December 1662, PROB 11/309, quire 135

Bibliography

Will of William Kimberley, 6 November 1678, PROB 11/quire 358

Oxfordshire County Record Office, Oxford

St. Mary Magdalen Parish Register, 1662–1682, C2

Tadmarton Parish Register 1548–1753, PAR/268/01/R1/1

Queen's College, Oxford

Samuel DuGard to Thomas Barlow, 8 April 1673, MS 275, Barlow Correspondence

Shropshire Records and Research Center, Shrewsbury

Tong General Register, 1620–1756, P281/A/1

Society of Genealogists' Library, London

Boyd's Marriage Index, 1538–1837

Stafford County Record Office, Stafford

Forton All Saints Parish Register, 1558–1760, D4049/1/1

Surrey Record Office, Guildford

Loseley Family Correspondence, Loseley MSS, Correspondence/1083

Warwickshire County Record Office, Warwick

Barford Parish Register, DR 48/3

Lighthorn Parish Register, DR 18/1

Solihull Parish Register, Birmingham DRB 64/1

Wasperton Parish Register, DR 208/1

Acts and Ordinances of the Interregnum, 1642–1660. Edited by C. H. Firth and R. S. Rait. 3 vols. London: Stationery Office, 1911.

"Allegations for Marriage Licences Issued by the Bishop of London." Extracted by Joseph Chester and edited by G. J. Armytage, 2 vols. Harleian Society 25, 26, 1887.

Alumni Cantabrigienses. Edited by John Venn and J. A. Venn. 4 vols. Cambridge: University Press, 1922.

Alumni Oxonienses, 1500–1714. Edited by Joseph Foster. 4 vols. Oxford and London: James Parker & Co., 1891–92.

Ambrose. The Letters of S. Ambrose, Bishop of Milan. Edited by H. Walford in Library of the Fathers of the Catholic Church. Edited by E. B. Pusey. 51 vols. Oxford: James Parker & Co., 1838–85.

Arjava, Antti. Women and Law in Late Antiquity. Oxford: Clarendon Press, 1996.

Athanasius. "Synopsis Scripturae Sacrae." In Patrologiæ Cursus Completus. Edited by J. P. Migne, 282–436. Series Graeca., 161 vols. Paris, 1857–1866.

Augustine, Saint. The City of God. Translated by Philip Levine. 7 vols. Cambridge, Mass.: Harvard University Press, 1957–72.

Bramston, Sir John. The Autobiography of Sir John Bramston. Edited by Lord Braybrooke, Camden Society, o. s. 32. London: John Bowyer Nichols and Sons, 1845.

Batchilier, John. The Virgin's Pattern. London, 1661.

Beier, Lucinda McCray. Sufferers & Healers. London: Routledge & Kegan Paul, 1987.

Bibliography

Beilin, Elaine. *Redeeming Eve*. Princeton: Princeton University Press, 1987.

Beza, Theodore. *New Testament of Our Lord Jesus Christ translated out of the Greeke, by Theod. de Beza with briefe summaries and expositions upon the hard places by the said auctor*. Translated by L. Tomson. London, 1616.

Blakiston, H. E. D. *Trinity College*. London: F. E. Robinson, 1898.

Burton, Robert. *The Anatomie of Melancholy*, 6th ed. Oxford, 1652.

Butler, Charles. *Syngenia, De Propinquitate Matrimonium Impediente*. Oxford, 1625.

Calendar of State Papers, Domestic Series, of the Reign of Charles II, 1663–1664. Edited by M.A.E. Green. London: Longman & Co., 1862.

Care, Henry. *The Female Secretary*. London, 1671.

Chaytor, Miranda. "Household and Kinship: Ryton in the Late 16th and Early 17th Centuries." *History Workshop Journal* 10 (1980): 25–60.

Cicero. *Academica*. Translated by H. Rackham. New York: G. P. Putnam's Sons, 1933.

Crawford, Patricia, and Laura Gowing, eds. *Women's World in Seventeenth-Century England*. London: Routledge, 2000.

Cressy, David. *Birth, Marriage, and Death*. Oxford: Oxford University Press, 1997.

__________. "Kinship and Kin Interaction in Early Modern England." *Past and Present* 113 (1986): 38–69.

__________. *Literacy and Social Order: Reading and Writing in Tudor and Stuart England*. Cambridge: Cambridge University Press, 1980.

DeVaux, Roland. *The Early History of Israel*. Translated by David Smith. London: Darton, Longman, and Todd, 1978.

Dixon, Robert. *The Degrees of Consanguinity and Affinity*. London, 1674.

Bibliography

Draper, F. W. M. *Four Centuries of Merchant Taylors' School, 1561–1961*. London: Oxford University Press, 1962.

DuGard, Samuel. *The Marriages of Cousin Germans Vindicated from the Censures of Unlawfullnesse and Inexpediency*. Oxford, 1673.

__________. *The True Nature of Divine Law*. London, 1687.

__________. *Polupaidia, or A Discourse concerning the having many children*. London, 1695.

DuGard, William. *Græcæ Grammatices Rudimenta*. London, 1654.

__________. *Rhetorices Elementa*. London, 1648.

__________. *Lexicon Græci Testimenti Alphabeticum*. London, 1660.

Earle, Peter. "The Female Labour Market." *Economic History Review* 42 (1989): 328–53.

Earwaker, J. P. *History of Sandbach*. Manchester: E. J. Morten, 1972; first published 1890.

Eccles, Audrey. *Obstetrics and Gynecology in Tudor and Stuart England*. London: Croom Helm, 1982.

Eusebius. *The Ecclesiastical History*. Translated by Kirsopp Lake. 2 vols. London: William Heinemann, 1926–32.

Evelyn, John. *The Diary of John Evelyn*. Edited by E. S. DeBeer. 6 vols. Oxford: Clarendon Press, 1955.

Ezell, Margaret J. M. *The Patriarch's Wife*. Chapel Hill: University of North Carolina Press, 1987.

Fletcher, Anthony. *Gender, Sex, & Subordination in England, 1500–1800*. New Haven: Yale University Press, 1995.

Gardiner, Dorothy. *English Girlhood at School*. London: Oxford University Press, 1929.

Geertz, Clifford. "Deep Play: Notes on a Balinese Cockfight." In his *The Interpretation of Cultures*, 412–459. New York: Basic Books, 1973.

Genealogist, old series. Exeter: William Pollard & Co., 1882. 6:316

Gibson, Edmund. *Codex Juris Ecclesiastici Anglicani*. 2nd ed. 2 vols. Oxford: Clarendon Press, 1761.

Godefroy, Jacques. "Dissertatio de Nuptiis Consobrinarum" (1642). In *J. Gothofredi Opera Juridica Minora*. Leiden, 1733.

__________. "De Incestus Nuptiis." In *Codex Theodosianus*. 6 vols. Leipzig, 1736–45.

Goody, Jack. *The Development of the Family and Marriage in Europe*. Cambridge: Cambridge University Press, 1983.

Gowing, Laura. *Domestic Dangers: Women, Words, and Sex in Early Modern London*. Oxford: Clarendon Press, 1996.

Grant, Michael, and John Hazel. *Gods and Mortals in Classical Mythology*. Springfield, Mass.: G. & C. Merriam Co., 1973.

Gregory, Pope. *A Select Library of Nicene and Post-Nicene Fathers of the Christian Church*. A new [i.e., second] series, edited by H. Wace. 14 vols. Oxford: Parker & Co., 1890–1900. 13 (1898).

Grotius, Hugo. *De Jure Belli Ac Pacis* (1646). Translated by Francis W. Kelsey. 4 vols. Oxford: Clarendon Press, 1913–27.

Grubbs, Judith Evans. *Law and Family in Late Antiquity*. Oxford: Clarendon Press, 1995.

Hales, John. "Concerning the Lawfulness of Marriages betwixt First Cousin, or Cousin-Germans, Septemb. 8. 1630." In *Golden Remains*, 262–272. 2nd ed. London, 1673.

Bibliography

Harley, Brilliana. *Letters of the Lady Brilliana Harley, wife of Sir Robert Harley of Brampton Bryan*. Edited by Thomas Taylor Lewis. Camden Society, o. s. 58, 1854; reprint: New York: AMS Press, 1968.

Hill, John. *The Young Secretary's Guide*. London, 1696.

Houlbrooke, Ralph A. *The English Family, 1450–1700*. London: Longman, 1984.

Hughes, Anne. *Politics, Society, and Civil War in Warwickshire, 1620–1660*. Cambridge: Cambridge University Press, 1987.

__________. "Thomas DuGard and His Circle in the 1630s." *Historical Journal* 29.4 (1986): 771–93.

Hunt, Margaret R. *The Middling Sort: Commerce, Gender, and the Family in England, 1680–1780*. Berkeley: University of California Press, 1996.

Hunter, J. Paul. *Before Novels: The Cultural Contexts of Eighteenth-Century English Fiction*. New York, W. W. Norton, 1990.

Huth, A. H. *The Marriage of Near Kin*. London: J. & A. Churchill, 1875.

Imperatoris Justiniani Institutionum. Edited by J. B. Moyle. 2 vols. Oxford: Clarenden Press, 1883.

Ingram, Martin. *Church Courts, Sex, and Marriage, 1570–1640*. Cambridge: Cambridge University Press, 1987.

__________. "Sex and Marriage in Early Modern England." In *Popular Culture in Seventeenth-Century England*. Edited by Barry Reay. London: Croom Helm, 1985.

Jeaffreson, J. C. *Brides and Bridals*. 2 vols. London: Hurst & Blackett, 1872.

Josephus. *Jewish Antiquities*, Book XVII, Sections 12–22. In *Flavius Josephus, Jewish Antiquities*. Translated by Ralph Marcus. 8 vols. Cambridge, Mass.: Harvard University Press, 1926–1963.

Bibliography

King, Gregory. "Gregory King's Staffordshire Notebook." Edited by Gerald P. Mander. In *Collections for a History of Staffordshire*. William Salt Archeological Society, 3rd series, (1920).

LaMar, Virginia. *Travel and Roads in England*. Washington, D.C.: Folger Library, 1960.

Leigh, Dorothy. *The Mother's Blessing*. London, 1616.

__________ *The Mother's Blessing*. In *Women's Writing in Stuart England*. Edited by Sylvia Brown. 3–87. Stroud, Gloucestershire: Sutton Publishing., 1999.

Macfarlane, Alan. *The Family Life of Ralph Josselin*. London: Cambridge University Press, 1970.

__________. *Marriage and Love in England, 1300–1840*. Oxford: Basil Blackwell, 1986.

Mallet, C. E. *A History of the University of Oxford*. 3 vols. 1924–27. Reprint, New York: Barnes and Noble, Inc., 1968.

Marchant, Ronald A. *The Church under the Law, 1560–1640*. London: Cambridge University Press, 1969.

Merchant Taylors' School Register (1562–1699). Edited by Charles J. Robinson. 2 vols. Lewes: Farncombe & Co., 1882–83.

Miles, Roger B. *Science, Religion, and Belief: The Clerical Virtuosi of the Royal Society of London, 1663–1687*. New York: P. Lang, 1992.

Milton, John. *Pro Populo Anglicano Defensio*. London, 1651.

Moore, Giles. *The Journal of Giles Moore*. Edited by Ruth Bird. Lewes: Sussex Record Society, 1971.

North. *The Lives of the Right Hon. Francis Baron Guilford; The Hon. Sir Dudley North; and the Hon. and Rev. Dr. John North*. Edited by Augustus Jessopp. 3 vols. London: G. Bell and Sons, 1890.

Bibliography

O'Day, Rosemary. *Family and Family Relationships, 1500–1900.* Basingstoke: Macmillan, 1994.

Osborne, Dorothy. *Dorothy Osborne: Letters to Sir William Temple.* Edited by Kenneth Parker. London: Penguin, 1987.

Oxinden Family. *The Oxinden Letters, 1607–1642.* Edited by Dorothy Gardiner. London: Constable & Co., 1933.

Parkes, Joan. *Travel in England in the Seventeenth Century.* London: Humphrey Milford, 1925.

Pepys, Samuel. *The Diary of Samuel Pepys.* Edited by Robert Latham and William Matthews. 11 vols. Berkeley: University of California Press, 1970.

Picard, Liza. *Restoration London.* London: Weidenfeld & Nicolson, 1997.

Plomer, Henry R. *A Dictionary of the Booksellers and Printers Who Were at Work in England, Scotland, and Ireland from 1641–1667.* London: Oxford University Press, 1907.

__________. *A Dictionary of the Printers and Booksellers Who Were at Work in England, Scotland, and Ireland from 1668–1725.* London: Oxford University Press, 1922.

Porter, Roy. *Disease, Medicine, and Society in England, 1550–1860.* Basingstoke: Macmillan Education, 1987.

Porter, Stephen. "University and Society." In *The History of the University of Oxford.* Edited by Nicholas Tyacke, 25–101. Oxford: Oxford University Press, 1997.

Prerogative Court of Canterbury Wills (1661–1670). Edited by J. H. Morrison. London: Morrison, 1935.

Reading, William. *History of Sion College.* London, 1724.

Robertson, Jean. *The Art of Letter Writing: An Essay on the Handbooks Published in England During the Sixteenth and Seventeenth Centuries.* London: University Press of Liverpool, 1943.

Bibliography

Rosenberg, Leona. "Republican Credo: William Dugard, Pedagogue and Political Apostate." In her *Literary, Political, Scientific, Regligious, and Legal Publishing, Printing, & Bookselling in England, 1551–1700: Twelve Studies*. 1:131–159. New York: Franklin, 1965.

Salmasius, Claudius (Saumaise, Claude de). *Defensio Regia Pro Carolo Primo*. London, 1649.

Schofield, Roger. "Did the Mothers Really Die? Three Centuries of Maternal Mortality in 'The World We Have Lost'." In *The World We Have Gained: Histories of Population and Social Structure*. Edited by Lloyd Bonfield, Richard M. Smith, and Keith Wrightson, 231–60. Oxford: Blackwell, 1986.

Schofield, Roger and E. A. Wrigley. "Infant and Child Mortality in England in the Late Tudor and Early Stuart Period." In *Health, Medicine, and Mortality in the Sixteenth Century*. Edited by Charles Webster, 61–95. Cambridge: Cambridge University Press, 1979.

Seldon, John. *John Selden on Jewish Marriage Law: The Uxor Hebraica*. Translated by Jonathan R. Ziskind. New York: E. J. Brill, 1991.

Short-Title Catalogue of Books Printed in England, Scotland, & Ireland, 1475–1640. Edited by A. W. Pollard & G. R. Redgrave. 3 vols. London: The Bibliographical Society, 1991.

Statutes of the Realm, 32 Henry VIII c. 38, 1540; 2, 3 Edward VI c. 23, 1548; 1 Elizabeth c. 1, 1558.

Stone, Lawrence. "Family History in the 1980s: Past Achievements and Future Trends." *Journal of Interdisciplinary History* 12 (1980): 51–87.

__________. *Family, Sex, and Marriage*. New York: Harper & Row, 1977.

__________. *Uncertain Unions*. Oxford: Oxford University Press, 1992.

Tacitus. *The Annals of Tacitus*. Edited by George Holbrooke. London: Macmillan & Co., 1882.

Bibliography

Taylor, Jeremy. *Ductor Dubitantium*. 2nd ed. London, 1671.

Terence. *Adelphi*. In *A Literal Translation of the Adelphi of Terence*. Translated by E. L. Hawkins. London: A. T. Shrimpton & Son, 1891.

__________. *Phormio*. In Terence, *Phormio, The Mother-in-Law, The Brothers*. Translated by John Sargeaunt. Cambridge, Mass.: Harvard University Press, 1912.

Thomas, Keith. "The Meaning of Literacy in Early Modern England." In *The Written Word: Literacy in Transition*. Edited by Gerd Baumann. Oxford: Clarendon Press, 1986.

Tilley, Morris Palmer. *A Dictionary of the Proverbs in the Sixteenth and Seventeenth Centuries*. Ann Arbor: University of Michigan Press, 1950.

Tixall Letters. Edited by Arthur Clifford. 2 vols. London: Longman & Co., 1815.

Turner, John. *A Letter of Resolution to a Friend Concerning the Marriage of Cousin Germans*. London, 1682.

__________. *Two Discourses Introductory to a Disquisition Demonstrating the Unlawfulness of the Marriage of Cousin Germans From Law, Reason, Scripture, and Antiquity*. London, 1682.

Ulpian. *The Commentaries of Gaius and Rules of Ulpian*. Translated by J. T. Abdy and Brian Walker. Cambridge: Cambridge University Press, 1885.

Van den Steen, Cornelius. *The Great Commentary of Cornelius à Lapide*, St. Matthew's Gospel. Translated by Thomas W. Mossman. 8 vols. London: John Hodges, 1876–97.

Vaughan, Sir John. *The Reports and Arguments of that Learned Judge Sir John Vaughan*. London, 1677.

Vermigli, Pietro Martire. *The Common Places of the Most Famous and Divine Doctor Peter Martyr*. Translated by Anthonie Marten. London, 1583.

Verney, Frances Parthenope, ed. *The Memoirs of the Verney Family*. 4 vols. New York: Barnes & Noble, 1970.

Bibliography

Victoria History of the County of Warwick. General editor: L. F. Salzman; vol. 2 edited by William Page; vol. 6 edited by L. F. Salzman; vol. 8 edited by W. B. Stephens; 8 vols. London: Oxford University Press, 1904–69.

Visitations of the County of Warwickshire, 1682–1683. vol. 62. London: Harleian Society, 1911.

Walker, Anthony. *The Holy Life of Mrs. Elizabeth Walker.* London, 1690.

Warton, Thomas. *The life and literary remains of Ralph Bathurst, MD, Dean of Wells and President of Trinity College in Oxford.* London, 1761.

Warwick County Records: Orders Made at Quarter Sessions, Easter 1665 to Epiphany, 1674. vol. 5. Edited by R. C. Ratcliff and H. C. Johnson. Warwick: L. Edgar Stephens, 1939.

Waterhouse, Edward. *A Short Narrative of the late Dreadful Fire in London.* London, 1667.

Watkins, O. D. *Holy Matrimony.* London: Rivington & Co., 1895.

Wing, Donald, *Short-Title Catalogue of Books Printed in England . . . 1641–1700.* Revised and edited by John J. Morrison et al. 3 vols. New York: Modern Language Association of America, 1994.

Wolfram, Sybil. *Laws and Outlaws: Kinship and Marriage in England.* London and Sydney: Croom Helm, 1987.

Wood, Anthony à. *Athenae Oxonienses, An exact history of all the writers and bishops who have had their education in the most ancient and famous University of Oxford, from . . . 1500 to the end of . . . 1690 . . . To which are added, the Fasti or Annals of the said university for the same time.* A new edition, with additions, and a continuation by Philip Bliss, ed. 4 vols. London: F. C. and J. Rivington, 1813–1820.

Woolley, Hannah. *The Gentlewoman's Companion.* London, 1675.

Wrightson, Keith Wrightson. *English Society, 1580–1680.* London: Hutchinson, 1982.

Bibliography

__________. "Estates, Degrees, and Sorts: Changing Perceptions of Society in Tudor and Stuart England." In *Language, History, and Class*. Edited by Penelope J. Corfield, 30–52. Cambridge, Mass.: Basil Blackwell, 1991.

The Wyllys Papers, 1590–1796. In *Collections of the Connecticut Historical Society*, 21. Edited by A. C. Bates. Hartford: Connecticut Historical Society, 1924.

Renaissance English Text Society

International Advisory Council

Peter Beal, Sotheby's, London
Lukas Erne, University of Geneva
M. T. Jones-Davies, University of Paris-Sorbonne
Harold Love, Monash University
Sergio Rossi, University of Milan
Helen Wilcox, University of Groningen

Editorial Committee for *Cousins in Love: The Letters of Lydia DuGard, 1665–1672*, *with a new edition of* The Marriages of Cousin Germans *by Samuel DuGard*
    Arthur F. Kinney, Chair
    A. R. Braunmuller
    Carolyn Kent

The Renaissance English Text Society was established to publish literary texts, chiefly nondramatic, of the period 1475–1660. Dues are $35.00 per annum ($25.00, graduate students; life membership is available at $500.00). Members receive the text published for each year of membership. The Society sponsors panels at such annual meetings as those of the Modern Language Association, the Renaissance Society of America, and the Medieval Congress at Kalamazoo.

General inquiries and proposals for editions should be addressed to the president, Arthur Kinney, Massachusetts Center for Renaissance Studies, PO Box 2300, Amherst, Mass., 01004, USA. Inquiries about membership should be addressed to William Gentrup, Membership Secretary, Arizona Center for Medieval and Renaissance Studies, Arizona State University, Box 872301, Tempe, Ariz., 85287–2301.

Copies of volumes X–XII may be purchased from Associated University Presses, 440 Forsgate Drive, Cranbury, N.J., 08512. Members may order copies of earlier volumes still in print or of later volumes from XIII, at special member prices, from the Treasurer.

FIRST SERIES

VOL. I. *Merie Tales of the Mad Men of Gotam* by A. B., edited by Stanley J. Kahrl, and *The History of Tom Thumbe* by R. I., edited by Curt F. Buhler, 1965. (o.p.)

VOL. II. Thomas Watson's Latin *Amyntas*, edited by Walter F. Staton, Jr., and Abraham Fraunce's translation *The Lamentations of Amyntas*, edited by Franklin M. Dickey, 1967.

Renaissance English Text Society

SECOND SERIES

VOL. III. *The dyaloge called Funus*, A Translation of Erasmus's Colloquy (1534), and *A very pleasaunt & fruitful Diologe called The Epicure*, Gerrard's Translation of Erasmus's Colloquy (1545), edited by Robert R. Allen, 1969.

VOL. IV. *Leicester's Ghost* by Thomas Rogers, edited by Franklin B. Williams, Jr., 1972.

THIRD SERIES

VOLS. V–VI. *A Collection of Emblemes, Ancient and Moderne*, by George Wither, with an introduction by Rosemary Freeman and bibliographical notes by Charles S. Hensley, 1975. (o.p.)

FOURTH SERIES

VOLS. VII–VIII. *Tom a' Lincolne* by R. I., edited by Richard S. M. Hirsch, 1978.

FIFTH SERIES

VOL. IX. *Metrical Visions* by George Cavendish, edited by A. S. G. Edwards, 1980.

SIXTH SERIES

VOL. X. *Two Early Renaissance Bird Poems*, edited by Malcolm Andrew, 1984.

VOL. XI. *Argalus and Parthenia* by Francis Quarles, edited by David Freeman, 1986.

VOL. XII. Cicero's *De Officiis*, trans. Nicholas Grimald, edited by Gerald O'Gorman, 1987.

VOL. XIII. *The Silkewormes and their Flies* by Thomas Moffet (1599), edited with introduction and commentary by Victor Houliston, 1988.

SEVENTH SERIES

VOL. XIV. John Bale, *The Vocacyon of Johan Bale*, edited by Peter Happé and John N. King, 1989.

VOL. XV. *The Nondramatic Works of John Ford*, edited by L. E. Stock, Gilles D. Monsarrat, Judith M. Kennedy, and Dennis Danielson, with the assistance of Marta Straznicky, 1990.

SPECIAL PUBLICATION. *New Ways of Looking at Old Texts: Papers of the Renaissance English Text Society, 1985–1991*, edited by W. Speed Hill, 1993. (Sent gratis to all 1991 members.)

VOL. XVI. *George Herbert, The Temple: A Diplomatic Edition of the Bodleian Manuscript (Tanner 307)*, edited by Mario A. Di Cesare, 1991.

VOL. XVII. Lady Mary Wroth, *The First Part of the Countess of Montgomery's Urania*, edited by Josephine Roberts. 1992.

MRTS

MEDIEVAL AND RENAISSANCE TEXTS AND STUDIES
is the major publishing program of the
Arizona Center for Medieval and Renaissance Studies
at Arizona State University, Tempe, Arizona.

MRTS emphasizes books that are needed —
editions, translations, and major research tools —
but also welcomes monographs and
collections of essays on focused themes.

MRTS aims to publish the highest quality scholarship
in attractive and durable format at modest cost.